THE MAY MOVEMENT

THE MAY MOVEMENT

Revolt and Reform

May 1968—the Student Rebellion and Workers' Strikes— the Birth of a Social Movement

BY ALAIN TOURAINE

Translated by Leonard F. X. Mayhew

RANDOM HOUSE   NEW YORK

For Marisol and Philippe

Contents

    A VIEW FROM CALIFORNIA   3

I   CLASS STRUGGLE AND SOCIAL
        CRISIS   22

II   THE CRISIS OF THE UNIVERSITY   82

III   THE "ENRAGÉS" OF NANTERRE   120

IV   THE BARRICADES   156

V   STUDENTS AND WORKERS   193

VI   THE ANTISOCIETY   242

VII   THE UNIVERSITY IN QUESTION   281

    CONCLUSION: THIS IS ONLY THE
        BEGINNING   344

    INDEX   363

THE MAY
MOVEMENT

A View from California

I once presented some of Alain Touraine's theories and arguments to an undergraduate seminar of some of U.C.L.A.'s most radical students. It was right in the middle of the Cambodia–Kent State crisis. What did a French sociologist have to say to anti-academic, anti-university American students that seemed important enough, right in the throes of their own massive confrontation with the police and a student strike, to get them to meet off campus to study together? Los Angeles is a long way from Paris. Or is it?

What interested these activists in his work was a sound theoretical base that avoids idealistic assumptions. It was the first time they had been offered a unified orientation with which to view the confusion of events and words that make up the student movement.

The analytical literature does not lack for theoretical interpretations. In the *Conflict of Generations* Lewis

Feuer makes an unconvincing attempt to provide a psycho-dynamic explanation of the student movement. The movement is seen as a generational struggle coming from "deep, unconscious sources"; "vague, undefined emotions which seek some issue, some cause, to which to attach themselves." In the San Francisco sociological convention of 1968, Talcott Parsons carried such non-sociology further. Confronted with radical graduate-student, counter-convention "truth squads" who held up placards spelling out "horseshit" at appropriate intervals, Parsons described such activities, and the student movement, as an Oedipal displacement. The attack on the Alma Mater was the unspeakable Oedipal crime accompanied by open aggression on the father-faculty. Seymour Martin Lipset has on numerous occasions taken a psycho-structural orientation which concludes that the movement is "deviant behavior."

From a social-psychological point of view, these explanations are naïve. From a sociological view they are unacceptable. Such approaches ignore utterly the structural determinants of the student movement which is precisely the challenge of sociology. Those American studies of the movement which are not theoretical tend to be empirical social-psychological investigations and surveys that attempt to interpret statistics—what sort of students get involved, what are the correlates of university activism, what are the opinions and attitudes of various groups, etc.

Thus, in American studies of the student movement, as in American sociology in general, there is a breach wide enough to drive a social movement through, unnoticed. Dialectical theoretical analysis is precisely what is so striking in Alain Touraine's work; it is the continuation of a European school of thought that dates back to Hegel and Feuerbach and which is all but totally ignored in the U.S. Those who have offered such a perspective appear more often as social critics (Sweezy, C. Wright Mills), and as social philosophers (Marcuse, Lefebvre), than as sociologists. In effect, the "end of ideology" period in the 1950's served as a theoretical purge; it is only now with the new generation of sociologists that we can expect the entry of the critical spirit into one of academia's most forsaken theoretical deserts.

Alain Touraine's analysis of the student movement is firmly embedded in the European tradition of dialectical analysis of the structural determinants of social movements. Mingled with discussion of the specifics of the May 1968 upheaval in France are major points of analysis of the student movement in general, which are equally applicable to the American situation. What makes this book demanding reading is not only that these analytical insights are dispersed throughout, but that the reader should know something of the theories from which they derive. Touraine's theoretical orientation is more explicit in his later work, *The Post-Industrial Society,* which is published simultaneously with *The May Movement* in English, by Random House.

The May Movement should be read on three levels: as an account of the events of May, 1968, as an analysis of the causes or the meaning and patterns of these events, and as a theoretical orientation from which to fit May, 1968 France into a larger time and space perspective. We will speak here briefly of each of these levels in reverse order, in order to present a few transitional remarks that will aid the American reader to appreciate Touraine's work.

The theoretical orientation that underlies Touraine's analysis is a dialectic of the field in which society is created—classes, conflict, and individuals achieving consciousness. For Touraine, society is largely the creation of the nature of the work in which it is involved. Thus structural and procedural limitations, as well as possibilities for a society, are determined by the nature of its work. The immense instrumental change between the entrepreneurial capitalism of the turn of the century and the corporate capitalism of today thus creates great pressures for accompanying social change. As economic production and innovation has become more dependent on soft-ware than hard-ware, on creativity than on invention, on technology rather than machinery, on cybernetics instead of the market, both the limitations and the possibilities for the "post-industrial" societies have also changed. If the social institutions and organizations have not similarly developed, they will find themselves passed by, outdated, and frequently in crisis. And in fact the political institutions, organizations, and the educational centers of the technologically advanced capitalist world are in a crisis of modernization. They are socially and culturally linked to yesterday and are being subjected to critical analysis and direct attack by those who would change them to fit today's world (technocratic reform pressures) or tomorrow's (student utopian efforts).

As production in a society changes, so do the dialectically opposed groups brought into potential conflict by the nature of the new work. In entrepreneurial capitalism, mass production in the new urban centers brought into conflict the capitalist owners of the means of production and the labor forces who manned the production lines. But Touraine points out that the new technological production in late capitalism does not bring the same two groups into conflict. The basic class polarization of post-industrial society is between technocratic-bureaucracy which organizes production and the experts, professionals and white-collar workers who alone have the necessary skills to make it work. The nature of work in early capitalist society set the stage structurally (created centers of material production) and defined the leading actors (capitalists and labor). The nature of work in corporate capitalist society defines a new structural stage (centers of intellectual creation) and had defined new leading actors (bureaucrats and professionals) .

The conflict in society over the issues raised by the new social-economics will not be fought by the groups and classes of the old society, although their battles still continue and compound the issue. But new groups and classes will face off with one another over new conflicts of interest, and recognizing this we may understand who was at variance in May, 1968. Touraine derives from the complex May events a pattern that explains the cooperation of seemingly diverse groups. What do students have in common with workers in aerospace, radio and television technicians, and managerial circles in industry? All are—or will be in the future—highly trained, white-collar workers who share an opposition to those who direct and exploit their expertise. New social-economics gives us new social conflicts and new opposing groups with new sets of conflicting interests.

With these criteria Touraine distinguished between the highly successful general strike and the student revolt, and looks more deeply into the divisions within labor that lie behind the mask of union solidarity. In France the major industrial union, the CGT, is communist-led and has a deeply entrenched, ideologically oriented, bureaucratic tradition. Yet, everyone agrees the union's officials played a strongly integrative and reformist role in May. This can be explained by Touraine's theories. The change from entrepreneurial to corporate capitalism has made the integration and institutionalization of unionism a mainstay of the social order, although far less so in France than in the United States. Because of this one would not predict radical activity from the heavily bureaucratic unions which have a stake in the corporate democracy of the day. If we look deeper, all is explicable. The specific, and reformist, demands of the unskilled laborers largely supported their bureaucratic chiefs. Unskilled labor, which was center stage in early capitalism, has become increasingly marginal in post-industrial capitalism and more conservative in its interests. Highly skilled and managerial circles, however, supported demands for qualitative change; their managerial and professional skills make them the structural equivalent today of the blue-collar workers of a half century ago. The young workers were by far the most radical both in their demands and their activities; they denounce the reformism of their bureaucratic negotiators. Those in the labor movement who occupied a place in the structure most like the students (the highly skilled and managerial) and those culturally most like the students (the young workers) acted more than just concurrently with the student movement.

This introduction does not allow a full analysis of the theoretical bases of Touraine's analysis. What the reader must do is to attempt to sense the presence of this orientation below the specific analyses he will encounter: What is important is that the analysis is not, as most American efforts, a haphazard explanation of certain events carefully chosen because they coincide with the writer's views. The use of a theory that concentrates on the structural dialectical determinants of social conflict allows an analysis of all of the aspects of the events of May and of the student movement in general. Such an orientation finally considers the student movement as other than an epiphenomenon of displaced psychodynamic imbalances. We see finally the beginning of study of the student movement as a social movement with relevance for us all.

Of the hundreds of books written on the revolution of May, a dozen have already been translated into English. Why one more? Precisely because Touraine's study, unlike the great majority of the others, derives from the specific events certain general points of analysis that are

relevant for the entire Western world. Foremost is his
recognition of the student movement as a revolution
within a revolution; and that the position of the movement is a critique of the technocratic power structure
now consolidating after its own revolution against the
bourgeoisie of entrepreneurial capitalism. The students
themselves are seen as doubly related to these ascending
technocrats: as a modernizing force they promote progressive change, as an anti-society they challenge the direction
of current social change. They are young members of the
technocratic class; but they are also the utopian revolutionaries who wish to destroy the progressively Orwellian
technocratic control. As such they parallel more the
socialists of the mid-nineteenth century than the activities
of the organized labor movement (they are utopian,
populistic, unorganized) ; more the spontaneous Soviet
masses of the early twentieth century than the revolutionary party (they are anti-authoritarian, and anti-
government) .

The analysis of the part-way liberalism of the technocratic class as a function of all ascending classes and as
productive of its own dialectical challenge is of universal interest. Berkeley in 1964 and Nanterre in 1968
were strongholds of liberalism. The movement is sustained and grows on the political repression and police
efforts to subdue it, but it is born under liberal skies.
The contradictions in corporate capitalism and its representative democracies are accentuated in the presence of
liberal parlance and policy. Typically, the students explore the limits of the local liberalism by a minor provocation; their dismay at its superficiality is transferred in
the heat of action to a revolutionary anger.

In viewing the events of May as reflective of the central
conflict of our new society, Touraine sheds light on its
international character. There is no question that one of
the major rallying points of the student movement

throughout Europe is the war in Vietnam. Why should
America's war, albeit inherited, be of such vital concern
to Europeans? The criticism of the social-economics of
the technocratic class offers an insight into the worldwide ramifications of international corporate capitalism:
When these ramifications are made clear (naked aggression in Vietnam, forsaking of internal groups defined as
"marginal," corporate control of democratic machinery,
university complicity in the pseudo-objectivity that attempts to make all this seem unavoidable, etc.), it
follows that some will question the desirability of the
social-economics which lives on such irrationality and
brutality. Students the world over, and increasingly their
elders, have in the last six years learned much about the
role of power, both as constructive, in preempting the
right to define the situation, and as repressive, in falling
back on brutal force to maintain this self-defined "law and
order." The student movement knows well how to use
this double-dialectic of power. In provoking the system
to call out massive police forces, great numbers of individuals are radicalized as they experience or witness
repressive power. They create through their own actions
a new definition of their situation. The student movement
has never been a forceful challenge to technocratic power;
it has served more to expose the ideologically loaded def-
initions and policies in front of which an unchallenged
technocratic capitalism had attempted to construct a
smoke screen of objectivity and neutrality.

The student movement is conceived as a class struggle,
populist uprising and cultural revolt all taken together.
What made May possible, and difficult to analyze, was the
simultaneous outbreak of a crisis of modernization and
a conflict of classes. The student movement, itself participating in both spheres of action, is therefore all the more
difficult to understand. It is in the dissection of the elements involved that the reader can subtract what was

specifically French, and what was international about the movement.

The student movement reveals contradictions and conflicts that are at the heart of the technocratic, corporate domination; as such it is a social movement that indicates a future more than it organizes a tomorrow. The student movement is a reaction to various spheres and degrees of archaism that remains unchanged from bourgeois society; as such it is a populist uprising demanding modernization of various institutional patterns and organizational structures. Finally, the movement is a reaction to the increased range of domination possible in a highly technocratic society, as control of consumption as well as production comes under the auspices of the ruling class; as such it is a cultural revolt that is simultaneously global and personal. As a social movement, the student movement is seen as truly revolutionary though still operating in an absence of a revolutionary issue, as the continued economic prosperity of corporate capitalism makes doubly difficult its demise. As a populist uprising, the student movement is seen as devoid of program, leaders or organization. As a cultural revolt the student movement answers the system's calm but forceful demand to "adapt yourself" with an exuberant shout of "express yourself."

This critical analysis of the movement as a conglomerate reality stresses that the combination of crisis and conflict was both the strength and weakness of the movement. Without the situation of crisis in the archaic and over-centralized French university and government, the movement would have remained small and contained. And yet it is only when the student movement separates itself from such reformist concerns that it will be able to blossom as a pure social movement. Again we witness the power and potential of dialectical analysis in the above example; if we are investigating a given aspect of a social phenomenon, we are led to simultaneously investigate whether there does not also exist a counter-aspect. Touraine presents such an analytical pattern throughout this study: the general strike increased the magnitude of the crisis, but removed the emphasis from the conflict; the labor bureaucracy was reformist and quantity oriented, but there appeared among elements of the rank and file new concerns which are revolutionary in that they are quality oriented. The cultural aspects of the movement gave it a vitality on which it thrived and provided a critique of the Marcusian one-dimensionality of the technocratic culture, yet detracted from the seriousness of the project of a social movement. These are a few examples, the reader will locate many more. What is to be stressed here is the methodological sophistication of a modernized dialectical analysis; it is the basis of this strong effort to understand the student movement, and it must become the basis of sociological investigations in general if they are to realize the challenge of providing society with a truly objective critique.

The analysis of the central importance of the violence at the barricades merits careful attention. As corporate capitalism masks the ideology of its technocratic control behind a mask of objective neutrality, so it masks the violence of its repressive domination behind a mask of liberal goodwill towards all. But the students, first in the civil rights campaign in the South and then at Berkeley, saw behind the disguises the politics of violence upon which corporate capitalism rests. The dissolution of political life in France, and in the United States, leaves a chronic absence of political solutions that reduces these governments, when under challenge, to the use of their police. The violence visited upon those who protest violence in Vietnam and in the ghetto only settles the issue for all the public to see. The identification of corporate capitalism and the various spheres of violence in which it is involved has led to an alignment of issues that recently seemed so diverse. Che Guevara, Huey Newton and Daniel Cohn-Bendit all hold in common a critical analysis that understands the dependency of corporate capitalism on violent repression in their representative spheres. The role of the counter-violence in which they are involved, whether in Bolivia, the ghetto, or on the barricades, is the propagation of this understanding. These leaders have rejected classical Marxist theory; that is what Debré means by the "revolution in the revolution." The education of the masses is no longer accomplished in words, a function of an intellectual avant-garde; it is accomplished with action, and it is a function of a group which dares undertake counteractivity. The students have imported into the West's largest urban centers the guerrilla strategy designed for the East's rural expanses; one expands the movement by demonstrating the feasibility of action and the possibility of success: In the university case, the ensuing repression will shock the liberal masses within which the few radical students are safely shielded, and their surprise at the proximity of violence will quickly provide for the liberals a critical understanding of the role of power in society.

It has been very difficult for many in the United States to understand the anti-liberal aspects of the student movement. Partly this is because "liberal" has been so intricately associated with the advertised image of corporate democracy. We have a liberal democracy, although Vietnam, racism, abject poverty and technocratic centralization are bipartisan policy, and thus not open for political challenge. We have a liberal court system, although student and black activists are never tried by their peers, and receive bail settings and sentences that make it clear that they are being tried as political offenders. We have a liberal press, although it is totally owned and controlled by the corporate giants it dares occassionally criticize, for which it receives ample chastisement. We have liberal universities, although it becomes increasingly difficult for any academic who possesses a critical spirit to find himself a permanent position. And so on.

What has changed is simply that liberalism has been caught with its pants down; everywhere the students turn they see liberalism as a superficial phenomenon buttressed by outright oppression, political repression, and psychological suppression. They reject liberalism in favor of liberation. In so doing they reject argumentation in favor of action, discussion in favor of dialectical exposition, and negotiation in favor of total victory.

The reader will find many other points of analysis that are as relevant to the student activism in the United States as they are to France. Among these are the relationship, present and potential, between students and workers, the crisis and challenge of the modern university, and the discussion of the anti-society. What remains to be presented in the introduction, then, are certain specific aspects of the French university's political and social situation with which the American reader may not be familiar.

That it is difficult to choose where to begin reflects the single most important point: the university's political and social situations are far less distinct than in the United States. The French State is all pervasive; it was, and is, in total control of all planning and discussions affecting the university. On the other hand, the French university is always political; its scandals and crises are political issues of high importance. One can disentangle analytically this institutional complex; but one must never underestimate the extent of centralization in control and decision making even in post-deGaulle France.

Before we speak of the French university it is necessary to make explicit certain areas of great divergency between French and American universities. Too many of the books on May have not bothered to distinguish these two

extremely different types of universities; an omission that
can lead to rather serious misunderstandings. The university in America is absolutely central in the process
of educating both the bourgeois and the technocratic
elite. In France, however, neither elite attends the university; for such high-level education one attends the
"Grandes Ecoles." Pompidou (the State), Sartre (the
anti-State), and Servan-Schreiber (the Technocratic
challenge) did not attend the university, they are products
of these "Great Schools." That an institution is greatly
affected by whether or not it processes a society's entire
elite seems self-evident. Part of the powerlessness of the
French university, and its reaction of withdrawal into
itself by reification of its traditions, rules, and hierarchy,
is a product of its comparative unimportance.

The French university lives a contradictory existence
different from the North American university. On one
hand, the university is rendered utterly rigid by the maintenance of a system of hierarchical academic control and
highly traditionalized and formalized cultural patterns
of professional and interpersonal interaction. On the
other hand, the university is utterly powerless, all decisions
of importance being ministerial in origin. Thus the institutional setting is itself in constant tension, with its
traditionalism ranging from archaic authority structure
to bourgeois cultural patterns. The university is powerless
to modernize itself even if it should so desire. Attempts
are made, as at Nanterre, but such liberalism merely
opens a Pandora's box which it cannot close.

The faculty is on one hand conservative in that it en-
joys the security and status of the 18th century role it
acts out both in its inability to communicate with the
students, and its aloofness from the pressing social problems of the day. On the other hand, the faculty is progressive in that a great many of its members resent the
powerlessness of the university to define its goals or

organization: that is, to take a truly scientific role in its own modernization and in its critique of society. Among its members are those who continue the tradition of French intellectuals; they are in fact an anti-state, enjoying the prestige of a Grandes-Ecoles education and the immunity of a university professorship. Similarly the students are divided into two generally opposed, but occasionally reinforcing groups. On one hand they attack the bourgeois cultural forms of the university; as such they are a reforming, modernizing force. On the other hand, they attack the technocratic conception of the modernized university, and as such they are a revolutionary, rupturing force.

The French university is in a crisis of modernization, yet it finds itself almost totally powerless to alter its rampant archaism. The faculty finds itself split between those who would oppose and those who would support such modernization, and among the latter are those who see university problems as soluble only through political and social change. The students find themselves totally alienated by the apparently irreparable schism between teaching and research, and because the former merely transmits a social and cultural heritage which they find irrelevant, ideologically loaded, and nonsensical. There are those among them who would work within the institutional channels presented to modernize the organizational and cultural patterns of the university; there remain those who see the university as a decoy that plays a major role in obscuring the personal and political repressive violence of corporate capitalism behind a mask of pseudo-objectivity and neutrality.

From this field of oppositions and tensions came May, 1968. The university, caught in scandal, as after the arrests at the Sorbonne, is a political issue of the first magnitude. Even the Rector does not take a decision without checking up to a ministerial level: thus what scandalizes the French university scandalizes the Minister of Education and the Government which appointed him. This aspect of the articulation of the French university with national political life is where the situation of the French university becomes highly divergent from that of the North American university. The field of tensions described above is equally valid in many ways for both France and the United States; it is from these similarities from which comes the convergence of the two student movements. But the American university that experiences student activism is typically a state university administered by a board of non-elected regents. The purpose of the creation of the regental structure of land-grant universities was to divorce the universities from the effects of short term political tides to which they would be subject if administered directly by an elected legislative body. The obverse side of the coin is that the state government is protected by the regents from direct attack. Berkeley became a political issue only after the trial of the arrested students as political offenders. Even then the politicalization of the student movement was largely at the discretion of the politicians; conservative hopefuls assessed correctly the mileage they could make on the public dismay. But in France the politicalization is a direct effect of the student-produced scandal. There is no one for the centralized administration to hide behind; the responsibility to normalize the university setting rests at the ministerial level and is thus a political and never merely an organizational issue.

If North American political life has been reduced to a single dimension by a Marcusian "integration of opposites," French politics in 1968 were definable by a single point: Charles de Gaulle. Making up by far the great majority of government initiative was presidential and ministerial decision. De Gaulle held a respectable balance in the National Assembly, existing comfortably with socialist and communist minorities. In fact, it was precisely the successful integration of the parties of the left into French political life that was to save the Fifth Republic when the chips were down.

Perhaps one of the most striking points of contrast is the presence of an ideological left in France and its total absence in the United States. The concept of a general strike makes no sense in the United States; there has never been one that enveloped more than one city for an extremely brief period. Frenchmen, on the other hand, have seen many and will see more. Unionism in America has never been a radical force, with the brief exception of the I. W. W., labor spent a century knocking at the door of capitalism wanting in. Now integrated to the point of supporting the Vietnam war (it creates jobs, after all), labor bureaucracy and the rank and file have finally achieved what they have strived for so long: an image devoid of any ideological taint.

In contrast, France's labor has never been integrated successfully, and there is still a working class with all of the social and ideological connotations this term implies. The rank and file is left of the vast labor organizations, of which the communist union, the C. G. T., is the largest. The Communist Party itself still polls about 22 percent of all votes in a general election, but it is not what it used to be: today it is highly reformist. In May it stood in sharp contrast to the activist students; both the C. P. and the C. G. T. varied between outwardly attacking the student movement as adventurist and the play of bourgeois children, to calling general strikes and marches in pseudo-sympathy with the youth; a strategic move clearly taken to avoid popular discovery of the gap that existed between labor rank and file on one hand, and their organizations on the other. No political force in French society was so centrally important in supporting the quaking Fifth Republic, and no force suffered so in the

post-revolution elections that were to overwhelmingly
return de Gaulle to power. Touraine's analysis makes
understandable the process by which the labor movement, which was, relatively speaking, rather radical in
France, has become docile and institutionalized. The
society in which it presented a radical challenge was the
bourgeois, entrepreneurial capitalism of the recent past.
Against technocratic corporate capitalism it presents no
threat. Modern capitalism needs a labor force well-
integrated into the mass production and consumption on
which it thrives; it is precisely a relatively well-paid, non-
ideological labor force that can provide the "mass."
Quantity concerns, such as more salary, less hours, etc.
are no threat to a modern capitalism; corporate growth
and increased efficiency-planning can keep well ahead of
the conservative labor demands. The challenge to technocratic capitalism is quality concerns; the pressure is felt
when a social force begins to question the alienating irrational and violent aspects of corporate capitalism.

French society experiences a double dialectic which
must be contrasted to the United States. The latter is experiencing a conflict between the rationalized utopia of
the technocratic modernizers of corporate capitalism on
one hand, and the counter-utopia of the student movement on the other. France, however, is a society in crisis
on two levels. Those who would modernize French
society must constantly battle against those who have a
stake in the continuity of the rigidified institutional and
organizational archaism. The student movement in the
United States indicates a new social conflict; in France
it also underlines a continuing social crisis.

Add to this state of double tension the centralization
and pervasive fragility of the French State, and one can
see the potential explosiveness in France of any social
movement. Political and social institutions in France are
far less capable than in the States of institutionalizing

conflict; serious challenge, particularly if it occurs along both axes of confrontation as in May, finds itself almost instantaneously elevated to a revolutionary pitch, even if there be no revolutionary issue. In the United States the constitution is currently confused by school children with what Moses received directly on the mountain; France has had five republics and would have no particular difficulty adjusting to a sixth. French society, although almost totally resistant to social negotiations, is in fact more open than the United States to ultimate social change.

Whether the new forces that provide a vital utopia in contradistinction to the cement-gray promises of technocratic capitalism can achieve such success is open. Successful technocratic repression of this new social force is a possibility; so, however, is a revolution led by these utopian youth that would change the nature of late capitalist society thoroughly. The outcome is certainly as unclear as the new lines of confrontation have become clear; we have a new ruling class and a new dialectical opposition heralded by the international student movement. In May, 1968, the student movement in France did not attempt to overthrow the state nor provide a physical challenge; it attempted merely to distinguish the power of the new technocratic class from the potential economic rationality and social progress modern society could be experiencing. In this realm the student movement in France, as its companion in the U.S., has been strikingly successful. Ever greater percentages of these ever more youthful societies grow to a social awareness knowing full well that there are alternatives to what recently seemed so objective and neutral. This student movement, and there are those who claim its most radical members are not yet teenagers, cannot be integrated into technocratic organizations because it is not organized. It cannot be negotiated into technocratic politics because it is nonpolitical. It will be dealt with on the level of social forces;

whether the technocratic dominating class can withstand the challenge, or whether this new social movement will in the end topple technocratic corporate capitalism remains to be seen. What is clear, however, is that the gargantuan battle we have seen is only act one. Or, as they said in Paris, *ce n'est qu'un début.*

J. W. FREIBERG

I

Class Struggle and Social Crisis

France is no longer at war: it is modernizing its society,
and, despite rising unemployment, it is becoming rich. In
May 1968, it suffered a severe shock when a movement
launched by a handful of students threw its university
system into confusion, touched off the largest strike in the
country's history, and rocked the foundations of its political regime. It came as such a surprise that both partisans
and opponents of the movement saw it as something unprecedented, an event almost completely alien to the
seemingly settled pattern of recent developments.

This book will dispute such attitudes. The May Movement did not reject industrial society and culture, but
revealed their contradictions and new social conflicts. It
did not stand outside society but at its very center. Its
leaders were neither victims of economic development,
misfits, nor romantics nostalgic for past revolutions.

The movement's deeds, much more than its words, put

an end to the belief that the social order was healthy and free of contradictions and repression inherited from the past. It revealed that in totally new forms, as yet not fully understood, this society, like others, is afflicted with a basic conflict between those who confuse social progress with private power and those who demand democratic control of economic and social change. A new society with new conflicts.

Those who believe that social struggle is exclusively concerned with capitalist property were just as surprised by the movement as those who believe that industrial society means the end of class warfare and ideologies.

Let us begin with a very simple idea: a new type of society is taking shape. Its growth is founded on technical progress, the mobility of the factors of production, and the ability to program, determine the course of, and manage large organizations. Those who direct this growth exercise power not only over workers in factories, but over the apparatus of production and decision-making, the extension of markets, and the integration of workers into large organizations. Growth and power are no longer generated simply by economic activities and relations; society as a whole and every aspect of human life are involved in comprehensive change. The social struggles over this change are also comprehensive. Social struggle and conflict of interest are no longer confined to factories. They appear wherever a society undergoes change and its rulers respond by imposing their own interests.

New class struggles are emerging and being organized in areas which a short time ago were considered outside the sphere of "productive" activities: urban life, the management of needs and resources, education. The formation of elites is contrary to the notion of continuing, or permanent, education; the concern for highway construction conflicts with the desire to participate in urban life; the manipulation of needs stifles the satisfaction of desires;

the obsession with status smothers the personality. The password of the technocrats who run society is adaptation. The May Movement replied, self-expression.

The stake in the struggle is no longer merely profit-making, but control of the power to make decisions, to influence, and to manipulate. This is the conflict that was revealed in May. In France, this programmed society managed by technocrats is as yet neither fully formed nor free of the legacy of earlier societies. The forms of French social organization are profoundly archaic, despite the rapid transformation of economic and cultural life. Styles of management and authority, methods of administration, education in home and school have shown little change; the origins and raison d'être of present practices often lie far back in past history.

Thus, French society is confronted with two types of contradictions. The first is opposition between the technocrats and the worker-consumers and the second is between the technical and cultural realities of modern society and inherited organizational and institutional forms.

French society is in the throes of a conflict and a crisis. The May Movement was both a revelation of the conflict and a reaction to the crisis. Its strength and complexity are due to the fact that it united these two aspects in its action—at least partially during its central phase, the May events combined revolt against institutions that had lost their creative role and were nothing more than cultural and social fortresses of an old order; struggle against political management and authoritarian administration, incapable of organizing and mediating change; and, finally, new social conflicts that were both acted out on the practical level and stated in terms of their own utopian resolution—all of these combined in May.

Caught between two social orders, the May Movement did not fight its adversary directly. It ran up against the

prevailing utopianism of the rulers of society which as-
serted that social problems can be simply solved through
modernization, adaptation, and integration.* As a result,
at the same time that it battled the ruling class, the movement created its own counter-utopia of libertarianism,
anti-authoritarianism, communitarianism, and spontaneity.

Like the socialism of 1848 or the nationalism of the
Third World, this utopia was creative, but was unable to
become a true social movement. For if there was a revolutionary movement, there was no revolution developed.
Though the economy was weak and ailing from unemployment, it was not in a serious crisis; no military or political upheaval threatened society. But the main reason was
that the new forces mobilized in the class struggle were
weak and dispersed.

After May 13, the movement had more opportunities to
speak than to fight. It camped within the walls of the university, in an institution that had practically ceased to
exist.† This accounts for the change of conflict behavior
into crisis behavior; whether it was a question of purely
cultural revolt or a desire for institutional reforms. The

---

* The catchword for all reformers who wanted to adjust the university
to the "needs" of economic life. They accused professors of being locked
into their ivory towers, and of not preparing students for their "active"
professional life.

† Each French university was actually a loose federation of faculties
or schools: medicine, laws and economics, letters (i.e., humanities) and
social sciences, sciences (i.e., natural sciences), pharmacy. Each one is
headed by an elected dean, and managed by the council of the full professors and by the assembly of which full professors, associate-professors,
and sometimes representatives of assistant-professors are members. At
Nanterre the system was slightly more open.

It should be remembered that the Rector, designated by the Government, is not the head of a university but of an academy, that is, of the
whole system of public education (elementary schools, high schools,
technical schools and universities) in a region. The faculty is the only
relevant administrative unit for both professors and students.

utopia degenerated into daydreams or plans for modernization.

Therefore, my analysis of the movement will be critical.
It will attempt to separate the various trends of the movement that were entangled in the events. The May Movement was profoundly creative not in what it expressed
most intensely but in the battle that it lost. The cultural
agitation created by the movement had the least meaning and the least future; it was a reaction to crisis and to
change rather than action against the new forms of power
and domination. Simply on the basis of its words, one
could not understand the importance of its acts, which
announced the appearance of a new power struggle at the
heart of society.

"This is only the beginning." How can one recall these
words without recognizing in the events of May both the
birth of a new social movement and the confusions or deviations of an action whose protagonists, adversaries, and
objectives the movement itself could not clearly define.
The May uprising was more social movement than political action. A century after utopian socialism, at the very
birth of technocratic society, it erupted as an expression
of utopian communism.

This weakness combined with strength, this promise of
the future amid the confusion of the present, was heightened by the special characteristics of the movement's principal agents: the students. To be sure, mere student agitation would not have given the May Movement the
importance lent it by the wave of strikes and factory occupations, and the political uncertainty that followed the
Week of the Barricades; but the fact remains that it was
the students who persistently led and sustained the action.
Because of their backgrounds and their academic experience, they were still very far removed from the oppressive society that their actions revealed. There was a gap
between consciousness and action. By rejecting the bour-

geoisie and appealing to the proletariat, by struggling against technocratic domination and calling for worker management of industry, the movement relived the social struggles of the past, and discovered those of the future. It spoke for the masses, but it was playing the central role in a new social conflict at a time when education, no longer the private preserve of academics, was becoming the concern of French society as a whole and was consequently vulnerable to the coercions of technocratic society.

The student action gave rise to new phenomena. The students had not been, nor could they be, actors in the old struggles invoked by the words they used to mobilize their action. Children of the bourgeoisie, future "professionals" confronting the technostructure, they are between two worlds. To transcend this contradiction, this transitional situation, they resorted to words. In succeeding, they strayed from the social movement that their actions had produced.

The May Movement did not win a victory by defeating its adversary. It did not carry out the revolution. It did not even try to take power. It did destroy the illusion of a society united through growth and prosperity; it replaced the mirage of social rationality and the common good with a picture of society's struggles and contradictions. In the midst of a crisis of social change, it reinvented the class struggle.

A New Class Struggle

The May Movement ushered in a new form of class struggle. More than any other collective action in the last few decades, it exposed and simultaneously formed part of the basic social conflict of our society. This statement is farther from the claims of the participants themselves than it may seem, for it means that we are concerned here with a new kind of social conflict, whose nature and participants are not the same as in the old, strictly capitalist society.

It is not an economic conflict; it does not activate opposition between selfish profiteers and exploited wage-earners. If one considers the participants themselves, the difference is striking: those who counted most in the social struggle were not unskilled workers, recently arrived from the country and only marginally integrated into the mass organizations; nor were they workers in the process of becoming proletarianized. They were students, staff personnel, and intellectuals from the O.R.T.F. (*Office de Radio-diffusion Télévision Française*) or the big firms, especially from the electronics industry. The economy was not in a crisis situation; even if serious unemployment caused young workers to participate in the movement, the outbreak of this revolutionary action cannot be explained by economic malfunctioning of the system of production. French students, like their counterparts in Berlin and Berkeley, clashed with the apparatus of integration, manipulation, and aggression. These words, rather than exploitation, best define the nature of the conflict. It was social, political, and cultural rather than exclusively economic.

The struggle was not against capitalism, but first and foremost against technocracy. This in no way implies that the struggle against capitalism or the "bourgeois" university was not of fundamental importance. The role it played was the same as that played by the struggle against absolutism and the *Ancien Régime* in the early days of the labor movement which explains better than anything else the revolutionary nature of the action, the need to wipe out the past. It does not explain the May Movement's sense of destiny. Its revolutionary prospect was anti-technocratic, while its critique of bourgeois and capitalist society by itself could only have led to modernization or a purely negative rejection of society. I shall return often to the relationships between these two aspects of the movement. First we must isolate the modernity of the present social struggles.

A new type of society has been created by the concentration of economic decision-making power; the increasingly close association between economic and political interests, especially through the mechanisms of planning and concentration; and, above all, the basic fact that economic growth today is determined by the ability to assure technical progress and organize the entire economy.

If the students played a decisive role, not as an intelligentsia but as a social factor, it is primarily because the university's role in this programmed society is no longer the same as it was in liberal society. It can no longer be a conservatory of social and cultural values; by becoming a massive institution it becomes affiliated more and more with the new production apparatus; it trains, especially through the social sciences, persons who will carry out the functions of integration and manipulation without which the social and economic system cannot develop.

I am not saying that the social sciences are actually servants of the Establishment. Such a charge contains more error than truth. I am only saying that the social sciences can be utilized and often debased by big firms and government agencies. This creates a new situation. The process of production is no longer defined only by techniques of exploiting nature. For a long time now, and especially since Frederick Winslow Taylor, techniques of work organization and, more recently, of decision-making have been added. The ever-widening realm of "rationalization" (scientific management) thus reduces the particular domain of the entrepreneur, in Joseph Schumpeter's sense of economic initiative personally undertaken by an individual responsible for its risks and profits.

The central figure in economic society is no longer the

individual capitalist; it is the large corporation which Adolf A. Berle and Gardiner C. Means, in their study of American corporations forty years ago, concluded was a political rather than an economic institution (*The Modern Corporation and Private Property*. New York: Macmillan, 1933).

The technocrat is not a technician. Although a so-called technocratic ideology, born in the United States during the Depression and rooted in the works of Veblen, constantly reappears, it was never very important. In the beginning, it was often tinged with leftism and aimed at transferring the entrepreneurial power of financiers to engineers, who would act in the name of pure technical rationality rather than private interests. It led to a negation of politics and reduced it to a science, as though social choices and values could be entirely controlled by manipulating social elements. It is a naïve idea which naturally leads to greater hostility in regard to popular protest movements than toward the rulers since the latter are more closely linked to technical management.

Technocratic action is quite different and has an altogether different importance. It serves the production apparatus and identifies it with social progress. As capitalist accumulation considered private profit identical with economic growth, so technocratic power confuses strengthening the centers of decision-making and programming with social development. Because the large rationalized organization is now in fact the principal agent of technical progress and social development, technocracy constitutes a ruling class because its accumulation of social resources is, at least partially, at the disposal of organizational integration and power, and creates self-augmenting maladjustments between the "central" and the "peripheral" elements of society.

In the presence of change, technocratic domination leads to increased inequalities; that is why knowledge is

its most important asset. On a certain level, knowledge
alone can be renewed and enable one to profit from
change. Persons without higher education find their
knowledge rapidly outdated and so become victims of
change. In discussing the choice of elites and the groom-
ing of minds according to methods which have the same
end though they differ in the Soviet Union, France, and
the United States, and on the other hand, continuing education, understood in its broadest sense, it is not a question of two concepts of the university, but of contrary
political views.

Both speak in the name of democratization. In the first
view, the word means methodically selecting elites from
all classes of society and isolating them as soon as possible.
In the second, it is a denunciation of the separation of the
elite from the masses.

Technocrats are not a homogeneous group with the
same interests, any more than were nineteenth-century
capitalists. Even less does the existence of a technocratic
class imply that the class holds political power by itself
and that the state is merely its instrument. This is a sche-
matic image no truer today than in the last century.

Technocrats can be allied with those who directed the
first phase of industrialization and were responsible for
the first great accumulation of capital, whether they were
capitalist leaders or Communist industrializers. But technocrats come into conflict with the old ruling classes who
defend their control of society even though they no longer
guide economic growth. As opposed to a bourgeoisie attached to its privileges or a bureaucracy of working-class
origin, technocrats, like every emerging ruling class, are
often liberal, particularly toward a class whose living
conditions they want to improve and modernize, so long
as that class does not take it upon itself to organize action
against social authority.

In France, polemicists like to portray technocrats or capitalists in caricatures which omit the creative economic role they play. This quite natural reaction matches the picture capitalists or technocrats form of popular movements, judging them to be emotional, irrational, and archaic. Need one add that the language of the adversaries in the struggle is not analytical? It is essential here to realize that technocratic power in France is just beginning to take shape, and that as it establishes its power it vigorously identifies its action with the general welfare of society. The May Movement did not set out to defeat its adversary but to unmask it and proclaim an antisociety, so that technocratic power could no longer be confused with the internal requirements of social and economic rationality. It attacked its adversary less in its exercise of power than in its ideology and in the social void with which it protects itself. If it attacked the university, it did so not so much by accusing it of being in the active service of the ruling class as of being the accomplice of the ruling class, insofar as it refuses to analyze and identify it and hides behind the cloak of objectivity its refusal to take cognizance of the facts of technocratic domination.

The movement also carried the struggle into a new area which corresponds to the second aspect of technocratic power and characterizes our programmed society just as strongly as the large-scale industrial, commercial, administrative, military, and educational organizations. As modern methods of production are applied to fields formerly left to craftsmen or small businessmen, the traditional separation of production from consumption becomes increasingly meaningless. Distribution, information, and leisure industries develop. Private life ceases to be ruled by custom or culturally determined responses to basic, general needs; it becomes penetrated by technology and consequently by the interests of the large organizations or groups which hold power.

One of the most persistent themes of the student strife

was the struggle against mass consumption and against the commercialization of human relations, feelings, and sexuality. Some critics pretended to believe that the students and young workers also opposed automobiles and vacations, since they burned cars and attacked the Club Mediterranée. To this charge, why not add that they took a vow of chastity, since they attacked eroticism in advertising! Why not say that it was obviously a case of middle-class youth who were fed up with their own affluence, disdainful of honest people, and hooked by the bait of its first chance to act. The reality is quite different.

What they fought was the manipulation of needs and desires, of leisure and of sexuality by commercial propaganda. This too is a powerful instrument of social integration since, as David Riesman has pointed out, it tends to identify people with social status and consumption becomes not so much the satisfaction of desires as a sign of class affiliation and standard of living. However vigorous this cultural counteroffensive may have been, it would be inaccurate to say that it shifted between the realms of production and consumption. Let us say instead that it spread from one to the other, since economic power is no longer content to exploit the wealth of the soil and the subsoil. As income in excess of subsistence expenditures increases, economic power also manipulates "needs."

Finally, there was a third battlefield on which the view of technocratic society is the most dramatic. The production system, activated more by organizational power than by private profit, creates deeper and deeper contradictions between centers of development and the underdeveloped or "marginal" geographic regions and social categories which are utilized as simple means to strengthen the center that dominates them. This contradiction is most critical on the international scene, where the power of advanced and especially capitalist societies opposes the desire for popular and independent development, inspired both by socialism and nationalism, on the part of an increasing number of peoples struggling against colonial domination.

Whether revolutionary forces exist today only in repressed and underdeveloped countries or whether they can be revived in advanced industrial societies is a question on which the students were often divided. One can well understand that the debate took place, but even more easily that it was not resolved.

German, French, and Italian students feel strong solidarity with the Vietnamese because they are a people fighting the imperialistic domination which is inseparable from the power wielded by the massive organizations of industrial societies. The struggle of revolutionary nations is the strongest condemnation of technocratic domination; because of their common enemy it is united with those who, within advanced capitalist societies, denounce the brutal subjection of certain social groups to the "requirements" of change, to the urban renewal, or to cultural manipulation.

Analyses which can only be cursorily discussed are not what is important here. But it was necessary to point out the various fronts on which it was possible to enter into combat with an enemy still protected by its ideology. Before May, limited intellectual arguments had questioned this or that aspect of the dominant social order. But the May Movement, by its very existence, went beyond the multiplicity of social, national, or international problems and revealed that the system of power and domination was a unified phenomenon.

Against this system of domination, varied in its forms— social integration, cultural manipulation, political aggression—but one in its deepest nature, worldwide social forces of opposition are organizing. They are no more definable in terms inherited from the past than is the system of domination itself. But the May Movement's action contributed to a definition. Since the struggle against technocratic power is not a face-to-face battle and attacks the identification of power with economic rationality and social progress, it cannot begin with a political program and strategy, a clear denunciation of class relations, or a list of concrete demands. The struggle is not explicitly waged in order to control social change, but to assert the rights of "nature" against the power of a social apparatus armed with tools of integration, manipulation, and aggression.

When the conflict is not stifled or incorporated into a tight organizational system, this "nature" can be affirmed for its own sake. Latin American nations have thus struggled in the name of Indo-America against the influence of the United States. In the same way, the notion of youth as a culture unto itself has opposed a culture of pleasure and the individual to the restrictions of adaptation, programming, and investment.

The worker or technician whose competence is increasingly threatened by technical progress can no longer defend only his acquired skills. As a worker, his interests are opposed to those of the large organizations. The youngest and the oldest workers react to the threat of unemployment in declining industries or areas by demanding that society regulate the effects of social change. First they demand guarantees, then, passing from defense to attack, they criticize the so-called economic rationality whose efforts and behavior are often irrational, as far as their own experience is concerned.

The French university system, and above all the faculties of letters, are still far from being dominated by technocratic imperatives. They threaten more than they impose, and the student reaction is closer to that of subject peoples than to that of the technicians of large rationalized organizations. The forms it took are therefore more cultural than social. While the student reaction had difficulty defining the nature of the new social conflict and the vague, relatively distant enemy, it confronted technology with the energy and spontaneity of youth. As a result, the first graffiti of Nanterre (the work of a few situationists * or very small groups in the faculty) expressed a cultural revolt more than a social and political critique. This tendency appeared with even greater intensity during the occupation of the Sorbonne, during which the students, relatively safe from social struggles and confrontations, devoted themselves to cultural expression rather than political action.

It is often said that students cannot form a class because their situation is temporary and because they are not economic performers: they receive no salary, have no jobs to speak of, are not counted among the active population, and in the end represent only a small number of individuals. None of these arguments is satisfactory. A young farmer's behavior is undoubtedly influenced by the fact that he has a good chance of becoming a factory worker or a civil servant a few years later. This does not change, in any basic way, the class situation in which he may find himself. Permanent employment, the termination of a dead-end social condition, can strengthen the solidarity of a group or social category but cannot be mistaken for class consciousness.

The labor movement was set in motion largely by men who were on the borderline of the working class, as close to being artisans as to being workers. More precisely, historical and sociological studies have shown very clearly that the social categories that manifested the strongest class consciousness were not unskilled workers trapped in the proletarian condition, who, for this very reason, as often as not, did not go beyond what has been called "economism," demands concerning wages and working

* A small ideological group, whose influence was important, especially at Strasbourg. They make use of street theater and spontaneous spectacles to criticize society and denounce new forms of alienation.

conditions. Militant class consciousness implies conflict between company profit and the rights of labor, and of professional skill. It is the skilled worker who criticizes the power of the bosses and goes beyond mere economic self-preservation to oppose production to property, progress to profit. It is the same in a programmed society. Class consciousness appears most strongly not among workers on the fringes of, or excluded from, society, but among the technicians in the large modernized organizations. They participate in economic growth and at the same time are able to confront the power of the organizations with the creativity of knowledge and technique.

The student is both inside and outside the world of technique and organization. He participates in modern economic life and confronts the ruling powers with a demand based on his youth and his personal desire for education and expression. A conflict throughout the university concerns the opposition between research and teaching. It is perhaps most strongly felt in the faculties of medicine, where there is a widening gap between the practitioner and the medical researcher whose training relies more and more heavily on the basic scientific disciplines: mathematics, physics, chemistry, and biology. It is the same in the faculties of sciences or letters where the student feels caught up in a system which, through the examination game, is designed to train "elite" researchers or university professors, and rather badly at that.

The Fouchet Plan, worked out by professors from the Faculty of Sciences, has prepared for the separation of the two types of students by creating the *maîtrise* along with the *licence,* thus partially isolating the future researcher from the future teacher.* Most of the students feel exploited by a university system that does not meet

---

* The *licence,* roughly equivalent to a B.A., qualified a recipient for the examinations for high-school teaching. The *maîtrise* is a more advanced degree, oriented toward research.

their needs. This is why pedagogical realities were constantly emphasized by the student movement in May and research was hardly mentioned at all. The silence does not indicate scorn or disdain for research, but violent opposition to a power system that is geared to research requirements and deprives the mass of students of what they feel to be their normal requirements.

As in industry, popular movements in the university combine, more or less effectively, two social groups whose situation and problems are quite different. In one group are skilled workers or young scientists, in the other, unskilled workers or first cycle students (pre-*licence*) most of whom will never reach the *licence*. The candidates for the *maîtrise* (second cycle), students in the third cycle preparing for their Ph.D., along with a certain number of *assistants* (instructors) are in the same situation as the skilled workers at the beginning of the century.* They spoke against the university and those who dominate it, as in the faculties of medicine; *assistants,* or chiefs of clinics, opposed the *grands patrons* † in the name of medical progress and hospital organization.

Their action risked turning into professional self-interest had they not joined forces with the university's unskilled workers, the first cycle students threatened with either unemployment or underemployment. Left to themselves, the latter could only be the laboring masses within a political or insurrectional movement, working with great

---

* Roughly speaking, the correspondence between American and French statuses is as follows:

full professor	*professeur*
associate professor	*maître de conférences*
assistant professor	*maître-assistant*
instructor	*assistant*

† The *grands patrons* are the most influential chair-holders. Their influence was much more important in the medical schools and the law schools and to some extent in the Humanities than in the natural and social sciences.

difficulty toward a critical and revolutionary analysis of the production, organization, and power system. Does this mean that we should speak of a student class? Certainly not, because class is defined only by class relations. The students' class situation is not different from that of the workers in large growth- and change-oriented organizations managed by technocratic elites, who are defined by their decision-making power.

The May Movement indicated rather clearly how the social waters are divided. On one side, at the center of the production system are the executives, supported by an increasing number of bureaucrats exercising authority, those Ralf Dahrendorf calls the service class. Together, they constitute the administrative apparatus of the large public and private organizations. On the other side are both those who can use their technical skills to oppose these organizations' desire for power and integration and those who are most directly subjected to a systematic management and change. Formerly, the area of conflict was between skilled workers and supervisors; today, it is between bureaucrats and experts or, as they sometimes say in industry, between line and staff organization.

Should we still speak of a working class? Yes, if the traditional connotations of the term help to underline the class nature of present social conflicts. It is dangerous to pour new wine into old skins; the important thing is to recognize that we are speaking of a new, as yet unnamed sociological formation. Although not yet fully self-conscious, it has already manifested itself by toppling the traditional distinction between manual and intellectual work.

The fact that most of the workers actively participated in the May–June strikes should not mislead us. Those who were responsible for the social-movement character that these strikes often had were neither skilled workers nor the great organized labor groups such as the miners, the longshoremen, and the railroad workers. The leading role in the May Movement was not played by the working class, but by those whom we can call professionals, whether they were actually practicing a profession or were still apprentices. Most active were those who were most independent of the large organizations for which they work: students, O.R.T.F. reporters,* technicians from research departments, researchers in private or public organizations, teachers, etc. Techno-bureaucrats and professionals are pitted against each other most directly in the new class struggle.

References to class action on the part of students should not be interpreted as proof that the students form a self-contained social category, homogeneous objectively as well as in the opinions and attitudes of its members. We cannot begin by affirming the existence of social categories that would be defined by a certain income level, skill, or education (social participation), or by members with certain common characteristics among which might be group consciousness. We must start from the existence of a system of social relationships made visible by the action and protest of those engaged most actively and directly in conflict and negotiation.

Affirmation of the class nature of the May Movement is not intended to imply the existence of a student class defending its own culture or interests, seeking to better its condition, or strengthening its unity. It is meant to point out that active minorities appeared among the students, exposing by their action certain social problems and contradictions peculiar to a programmed society. Perhaps one day the student movement will be powerful and organized enough to undertake class action directly in the university. At the moment, it is far from that situation. But just as the labor movement made the working

* Radio and TV national office.

class an agent of history, the student movement and other movements are generating new historical conflicts and agents.

Populism

The French university is still far from being a technocratic institution. The movement opposed student subjection to the needs and interests of the large organization or to the system of social integration and cultural manipulation. But what was experienced, especially in the faculties of letters, was the crisis of the traditional university, rather than restraints imposed by the new order.

Like many other European societies, French society is strongly marked by the opposition between technical and economic modernization and social and cultural conservatism. The models and forms of education in home and school are archaic, as are the authority relationships in business and public administration. Their function is not to plan or permit change, but to uphold principles and traditions. The change, already brought about by the material conditions of production, employment, and consumption, is now meeting social and cultural obstacles.

After the war, French society engaged in a powerful and sustained effort first of reconstruction, then of growth. For a long time, the need for self-criticism and self-transformation was avoided as preoccupation with the Cold War and the difficult liquidation of the colonial empire took precedence. The great lines of division in political life were always determined by France's international role, rather than the organization and functioning of domestic society. Political life and thought were dominated by the struggles against American influence, colonial wars, or the Communist Party.

The end of the Algerian War and the transformation of

the Cold War into peaceful coexistence spelled the end of oppositions both fundamental and superficial (in the sense that they had no bearing on the realities of French social life). France, and especially its intellectuals, discovered the reality of prosperity, economic progress, and competition within the Common Market. The 1960s were years of social and ideological calm, scarcely ruffled by the problems of economic reconversion, the disappearance of traditional activities, or transfer of power in certain areas. The old forces of protest lost their influence simply because they were fighting old enemies instead of describing new problems which are now obvious.

The days when we could talk about the end of ideologies, the appeasement of social conflicts, the substitution of strategy for politics and negotiations for conflict are coming to an end. Society, having remained traditional, is again threatened by new economic and cultural realities. The questioning is most brutal in the realm of education. We hear that it is a conflict of generations. As a matter of fact, the rapidity of material and social changes and the sluggish methods of socialization—that is to say, of preparation of the young for social life—make educators—parents or teachers—incapable of being transmitters of social directions or cultural activities.

Secondary schools and universities are flooded by the increasing numbers of young people who are naturally attracted to education in a technical and meritocratic society. Because there has been scant modification of educational functions and methods, young people are immersed in a new society, but cannot participate in it. Youth is swept along in a new world, a world that it usually wants to enter. But it has no way of controlling and making use of that world either professionally, intellectually, or politically. The student and young worker movement would not have been so powerful had it not been based on youth as a productive force necessary to society, conscious of its material and symbolic importance, and at the same time aware of its conflict with an archaic social system that is incapable of renewing itself and proclaims principles it does not put into practice.

In France, this is a problem of special importance. The university system has allowed the number of students to increase at a much faster rate than in other countries, but the system has not been transformed to meet the needs and possibilities of a student population that is larger and less certain of its future than students of the preceding generations. As a result, the students felt that the new society they had entered was incapable of working out its own problems and solutions. They turned on the university and charged that, willingly or not, it was either playing the game of the new rulers or allowing itself to be used. So the relationship between the generations is only a special form of a much more general situation: the breakup of a traditional civilization under the impact of the rise and domination of a more advanced civilization, one that creates aspirations and attitudes which cannot be satisfied by the old forms of social life.

In such cases, certain sociologists speak of "mobilization." A social system in which participation is local rather than general and the elites are protected by social and cultural barriers is outflanked by economic evolution which increases geographic and professional mobility, disorganizes local cultures, institutions, traditions, and urban systems. Such a situation encourages many individuals to become part of the new society. Their energies are directed toward social advancement, and they attempt to make their success acceptable by becoming hyperconformists. But parallel to this acculturation movements develop which range from rejection of the new society and culture to protest not against the new opportunities, but against the new domination. The student movement can be viewed as an example of rejection, protest, or criticism of uncontrolled modernization experienced as domination and exploitation.

This conclusion is related to the criticism based on the notion of counteracculturation already formulated by sociologists of social change. When traditional rural societies are disorganized by a rising urban economy that attracts men and capital and transforms life-styles, the societies harden. Sometimes, as in Brazil at the turn of the century, they even go to war against the new society, or take up messianic movements which are as frequent in Oceania and Africa as they are in Latin America. Such movements are the last defense of a mortally wounded culture. They are also movements of revolt and protest not against a new culture but against a system of domination, especially a colonial system, that removes from all control over social change those most affected by it.

In France, the cultural gap between traditional society and "mobilized" society, which is often defined in terms of mass production and consumption, is not this broad. As a result, the social movements linked to change are more future-oriented. Instead of exalting certain values of the past, they attack the new forms of power and organization.

The modernizer who selfishly identifies the new forms of production, division of labor, and consumption with purely traditional domination by certain economic and political interests, sees such movements as resistance to change and an irrational attachment to traditional ways of life and thinking. Apologists for progress are always quick to charge those who must yield to a society dominated by others with being lazy or uncivilized. Colonizers consider Africans or Latin Americans lazy or unstable. Similarly, the technocrat considers students of the social sciences emotional and irrational. He is not completely wrong because "marginal" members of society do not have the intellectual and political means to clearly distinguish between the possibilities offered by material progress and domination by those who use them for profit.

The student movement was not only an expression of a class conflict. It was a global opposition to a specific civilization and a form of social and political power. The student movement was in a situation similar to that of the beginnings of the labor movement in the nineteenth century or the nationalisms of the contemporary Third World.

In many of its aspects, this movement resembles populism more than class conflict, which is a struggle that develops at the core of a society. Populism—which should not be reduced to simplistic imagery—develops at the moment of entry into a new society. It emerges above all in the name of certain communitarian values and a desire to assure continuity of progress; it rejects exterior agents of progress. It is generally launched by intellectual or political elites who, looking toward the future, mobilize the forces released by the destruction and transformation of the old society. But it is also and above all an anti-elitist, egalitarian, and communitarian movement.

In agrarian Russia, wounded by the penetration of Western capitalism and the development of a commercial economy, populism was not agrarian resistance, but a struggle against the individualism of capitalist profit and the penetration of foreign interests and values. It was a struggle waged in the name of a Russian-style or popular socialism. The same basic inspiration is found in African socialism, that of Nyerere or Nkrumah, and in many Latin American populist movements based on urban populations of rural origin in Colombia, Brazil, or even Argentina—regardless of the differences that separate Gaitán from Getulio and Peron.

It may seem strange to compare the predominantly student movement that broke out in France, a highly industrialized country, to movements brought about largely by the transition from a rural to an industrial economy and, in most cases, by penetration of foreign capital. These social movements should not be expected to show a strict similarity in their components but only a certain analogy in their nature.

In any case, the social classes typical of this new society are still not very organized or clearly defined; their relations are therefore only slightly institutionalized. French students were not considered autonomous agents with political rights, but "passive" citizens in the sense the term had during the July Monarchy.* The militant students' appeal to the people was an attempt to mobilize society against rulers whose foreignness is not national but social, who are like a state apparatus subjecting a society to economic and political domination. We should also add that the contending forces in populist movements represent both the past and the future. On one side, more united than divided, are the old and the new ruling classes; on the other, are both the declining, economically lower social categories and a rising middle class that opposes both the old and the new rulers.

This relatively undifferentiated expression was also present in the May Movement. The attack was not leveled specifically against the new technocrats. It was leveled against the old and the new bourgeoisie, against the mandarins of the past and the new technocratic rationalizers. Young people threatened with unemployment were joined by technicians and managerial employees rejecting the power of the financial bosses of the big firms. The students themselves are both a rising middle-class and a special category hit by the university crisis, especially by the lack of opportunities for study.

---

* The French Revolution, during its first phase, introduced the distinction between active and passive citizen. Only those paying taxes on property received the franchise. This limited democracy was maintained by the Restoration and the July Monarchy. The universal franchise was introduced by the Second Republic.

The May Movement, like most populist movements, launched an appeal that was more emotional than rational. Its appeal to overthrow the supposedly real, mechanistic world was directed to popular energy, to life; and it sounded more like Bergsonian vitalism than the Marxist rationalism the movement claimed as its doctrine.

Class conflict and populism, though clearly different, are united in the present situation, as is true wherever a new society is in the making and the new ruling class, although not yet defined as such, is largely identified with modernization. Disorganization and cultural shock are inseparable from the struggle against new masters. They are combined basic utopianism. A utopia, not a dream. Since the dominant power shows itself only under the mask of modernity, the movement that fights it can assemble its forces only in the guise of a utopian society, free of the contradictions inherent to all development and especially of the concentration of investment and programming power in the hands of ruling groups or systems that subject the whole of society to their influence.

The utopia is mobilization of the personality rather than the working out of strategies. It is detested by parties and organizations; it acts always in ephemeral conjunction with small groups or sects and masses that are barely organized and are dispersed as quickly as they are assembled. As a result, there is great disparity between the leaders' speeches and the true import of their action. They are making history, but not the history they think they are making. They are rousers and inciters rather than leaders or negotiators.

The Explosion

The May Movement was more than the foretaste of a new class struggle and the conquest of a "bourgeois" society by the wave of populism and youth. It was a reaction to a certain way of managing change. Its character was set not only by its own projects but by the obstacles it met— the reaction of those in authority to social problems.

As far as France is concerned, these obstacles are both powerful and ludicrous. The State is centralized and fragile while the university is conservative and disorganized. So the apparent agreement of belligerent language concealed the initially surprising conjunction of two opposing attitudes: on one side, announcement of an antisociety which appealed to spontaneity, fantasy, and pleasure in opposition to all social machinery; on the other, a desire for modernization, participation, and, finally, social integration.

Dadaist disruption was often seen mingling with the social order and with completely reformist attempts to modernize and enlarge professional organizations in the university and in many professions. These two tendencies were not opposed as stable cultural and political positions. They are not movements, but reactions. They are reactions to a crisis and as much a revolt against meaninglessness and obstacles as a push for a new sense of status.

Economic and social evolution has greatly increased the social system's capacity for integration, but effective integration is restricted by the state of society's institutions. The integration has solid material bases, but it has been checked by inadequate institutional adaptation, both in terms of the State and of the economic system.

The student movement at Nanterre might not have touched off a crisis of national importance if there had been less blindness in the adversaries it met, first in the university, then in the State. With regard to professors and department heads, suffice it to say that they were incapable of understanding, discussing, or dealing with the movement. Unaccustomed to making decisions and thinking of innovation rather than how to conserve, were they incapable of facing a totally new and bewildering situation? Though we will modify this judgment slightly later, the fact is that the Faculty of Letters in Paris, which faced the gravest problems, was least capable of understanding and handling them effectively.

But the main thing was the attitude of the State. The ministers—unaccustomed to power or responsibility, more concerned about what their master thought than about national realities—were confused when they discovered the existence of society. They were totally ignorant of the social situation; and since in Cabinet meetings they thought only in international terms, all they could see in the student revolt was the plotting of Maoist groups and the restlessness of middle-class youths letting off steam before settling down, something unpleasant but not really serious. The only response left to the regime by its own *grandeur* was the police.

French employers, whose social thinking is often as archaic as their managerial methods, were satisfied with their primitive authoritarianism; on the whole, trade unionism was a minor nuisance. Employers occasionally worried about the hostility of their staff or the demands of their technicians, but it never occurred to them to try to come to an agreement about real wages, working conditions, and all the problems caused by technical changes, transitions, and unemployment.

The authorities only deviated from their routine to foster economic development. Neither the young technocrats nor the old officials were made to face up to the existence of social problems. Insufficient equipment, horror of criticism, and lack of imagination were the most salient characteristics of the ministries dealing with social problems. Centralism, bureaucratic ritualism, and defense of special interests were reinforced by a regime of enlightened despotism, more concerned with France's international role than with a critical analysis of her society.

In educational matters, M. Pompidou's long administration exhibited a conservatism that was all the more solid because of the illusion of progress created by the accelerated pace of university contruction. The walls of the French State may be Napoleonic, but they enclose contemporaries of Louis-Phillipe, who were just as surprised by the May Movement as the inhabitants of the Tuileries were by the February Revolution.

The rulers were isolated from society by the apparent strength of the State, the growth of production and consumption, and the lofty arrogance of the head of State. Protest movements meant nothing to the ruling systems. In the Ministry of National Education, there was no more concern about the November 1967 strikes at Nanterre than there was in the Ministry of Social Affairs or among employers about the strikes of Rhodiacéta (a textile firm) or SAVIEM (the truck division of Renault). The French were of no interest to their rulers.

Combined as they often are, bourgeois conservatism and the power of the State are usually responsible for the explosive nature of French social movements. In France there are no problems, only scandals and crises. Nothing is more characteristic than the situation of French television. It is well known that whenever something important happens, the French have to listen to outlying radio stations to get more information about it. The inadequacy and distortion of information on French television is notorious. But the only important parliamentary debate concerning television was organized to discuss commercial advertising on the screen. Newsmen concerned about honest, straightforward reporting were not heard; sometimes they were penalized. In this area and others, protest made no impression on the smooth, solid alliance of authoritarianism, bureaucracy, and established interests.

In these conditions, the forces of opposition centered in the sector of social life that was least organized and least institutionalized—independent intellectual circles; bereft of any means of action, opposition deepened into fundamental critism. For lack of objectives, the forces of opposition substituted principles. In France, authoritarianism and conservatism have always created their own antidote: a free, active, innovative intellectual life hardly suitable to the professionalization of knowledge, but very suitable for launching ideologies and campaigns. The intellectuals are the anti-State. Because they have little influence, their thinking is bolder and they express themselves even in the State university system and especially in the faculties of letters where teaching, above all in the social sciences, is certainly not always conformist and technocratic.

This revolt, embittered by political and administrative resistance, was the most visible but not the only reaction to the crisis. It could have been a mask for a thwarted desire for modernization and participation just as well as for a desire to create an anti-society. In the university and in professional circles, themes such as co-management appeared as first steps either toward "student power" in the university, or toward a mode of participation in organization and decisions that would bring about better adaptation to necessary changes and eliminate archaic obstacles. In the first case, the orientation tended toward an unstable mixture of political action and cultural revolt; in the second it tended toward an equally unstable mixture of appeals for spontaneity and for social integration. The university situation, which was simultaneously weak and rigid and imposed only limited restraints on the students, facilitated the development of these multiple and ambiguous appeals to spontaneity. It was the same on the national level, where there was just as much weakening of the social organization as there was social struggle; there was an institutional vacuum in which the proclamation of individual and collective spontaneity resounded with exceptional force.

But to consider this revolt as the main element of the movement would be to consider what was most visible as most important and what was most verbalized as most significant. The revolt was at one and the same time the terrain on which the movement was formed and the backlash of the movement and its confrontation with the social order. While the central forces increased their efforts to engage in political action, they stirred up hopes or refusals that were just as important and equally incapable of furthering the movement of which they were only the fallout. What seemed to be the most direct expression of a revolutionary movement was much more a reaction to a crisis of change. The change was present, it had already begun, it was inevitable; but it was blocked by a political and institutional system that was both rigid and impotent.

If French society had been in a more critical situation, if it had been in the throes of an economic or major international crisis, the social conflicts would have commanded attention as the principal direction of the social movements. At the end of World War I, Dadaism counted for very little compared to the Soviet Revolution and the revolutionary thrusts in Germany, Italy, and even France. Not so in 1968: that is why the effort to transform society was often less visible than were reactions to the crisis and the resistance. This is not meant to imply that the three aspects of the movement that I have attempted to describe are of decreasing importance from first to last but merely to point out that the most spectacular element of the movement—the crisis behavior—was also the least active element historically. It exploded at the moment of disruption whereas only the revelation of new class conflicts could give support to long-term action.

It should also be noted that the cultural and institutional obstacle that provoked the crisis also gave the crisis its political force. Administrative centralization, the role

of the State in French society, made it possible for the May
Movement to go beyond the parodies of revolutionary
action that characterized the movement at the very beginning and at its last moments in Avignon. In combating the
Gaullist regime, the movement escaped the isolation that
threatened, for example, the student uprising at Columbia. It was able to identify its adversary and thus pass from
a cultural revolt to a social and political struggle.

Here we must speak of explosion in two ways. Resistance on the part of the State enabled the movement to ex-
plode rather than remain coiled up in utopia. The inability of the institutions to direct change provoked a crisis
in which the social movement exploded and dissolved into
both simple rejection and simple endeavors of modernization. French society permitted the birth of a social movement more than it favored the formation of organized
action capable of effecting a transformation of the social
order. This is the definition of a revolutionary movement:
the thrust toward a new society and the reaction to a state
of crisis are always mixed, strengthening and compromis-
ing each other at the same time. Such a movement de-
scribes the ultimate future better than it organizes the
immediate future.

Those who wanted to consider only the social order's
interests and its ability to adapt to necessary changes, and
therefore refused to recognize class conflict in French society, were scandalized by a crisis which disorganized
rather than reformed, announcing principles rather
than defining possibilities. They were right to the extent
to which the movement was no more than an explosion.
But when confronted with the challenge and the utopianism of the social movement and its determination to replace the dominant order with a model of social and cultural democracy, their wisdom and prudence quickly led
to counterrevolutionary violence. Moderates became "en-

ragés," while the "enragés" of Nanterre and elsewhere attempted, through disruption, to pave the way for new forms of freedom.

How much is analysis helped by speaking of youth revolt and unrest in the consumer society? A more vigorous image of a revolutionary society is preferable to these vague expressions. In a society in which the system of production is no longer restricted to a particular sector of social life but is an all encompassing influence; where the training of men and the management of organizations largely determine the capacity for technical progress, this movement attacked the entire system of production. The whole spectrum of human activity raised up forms of opposition against the new forms of domination. The opposition was led in the name of the individual and of culture. But the social struggle also revealed a social crisis that involves the transformation of a society whose organization, institutions, and cultural models lag considerably behind its material life and work, and its material and intellectual production.

We will have a clearer picture later on, but this hints at the movement beyond cultural revolution and at how far the critical awareness of social conflicts transcended differences in feelings and behavior that accompanied the effort to combine the student struggle and industrial social struggles. The youth revolt ended up as a digression when the struggle for power entailed direct pressure and replaced self-awareness with awareness of the conflict and the adversary. Carried to the extreme, such an evolution can lead to a confusion inimical to what might be called the culturalist utopia. This danger has always been present in small political groups which are more inclined to denounce their enemy than to create forces capable of fighting. However, it hardly touched a mass movement that was weakly organized, open to spontaneous participation, and closer to revolt than to political strategy.

The cultural revolt had two faces. It was the first phase of still undefined social struggles; it was the direct expression of a struggle that could no longer concentrate all its efforts on labor relations. But the problems of work do not take a back seat to those of leisure; this is absurd. Social power overflowed the large organizations into all aspects of social life. The feeling of exploitation was replaced by the feelings of repression and alienation.

Eventually, this revolution will become more practical: it will wage specific battles. It will be organized, politicized, and based on a more elaborate analysis of the new society. For the moment, it is the force that is destroying, in one blow, the shaky walls of the past and the deceptive calm of the social order.

An intermediate direction finally appeared between the struggle and the social crisis; in 1968, neither France nor its university system was definitely settled in a programmed society. They were still bound by the old capitalism and the old university system. The May Movement fought the past and revealed the future. It promised more than it achieved. It was caught between the bourgeois and the technocratic society; whence the double aspect of each of the elements that I have singled out and which we will now examine in terms of their unity or interdependence.

At the same time that it combats a new social power, the new class struggle affirms a cultural revolt. While these two aspects are undoubtedly connected, they cannot be identified with each other. The populist utopia was the movement of rising masses, but it also held that movement in a state of suspension in an imaginary world. The explosion transformed the cultural revolt into a political struggle against the State; but it was also a crisis reaction, independent of general political perspectives. Since all these trends crossed each other, it is impossible to transcribe the categories of the analysis into moments of description. The cultural revolt was responsible for the movement's greatest strength and its greatest weakness: it enflamed the March 22 Movement and evaporated at the Odéon theater.* The struggle against the State gave power to a movement which was unready to become a political force and acted at the base rather than the summit of society. The catalysts of the cultural revolution, the students, wanted to transform it into a social struggle by allying themselves with the working class; they were incapable of acting alone as the "professional" vanguard of a new suppressed class.

Nothing in the movement was entirely positive or entirely negative. Like the movements during the early days of capitalist industrialization, it discovered new problems before it was in a position to deal with them in political terms. Between the crisis and the conflict, it was torn with contradictions; it transcended them only through the power of its revolt and its utopia.

The May Movement was not motivated by doctrine or by clear goals. It was a force that exploded and bore within itself the contradictions of society. It was not a vision of society, but a historical agent.

Utopian Communism

Was the May Movement composed of several independent meanings linked by a historic event, or was there a certain unity to the movement? My interpretation up to now leads to the second reply. There was no rupture between the various aspects of the movement that I have attempted to sift out and characterize.

As we pass from the first to the third aspect, from the social struggle to the crisis of modernization, we abandon

* The theater was taken over during May and became a permanent forum where some of the most vehement criticisms of the "cultural order" were voiced.

further consideration of the social movement itself and of class relations or contradictions in a theoretical model of society and turn to concrete forms in which a particular, concretely defined and situated national collectivity or institution functions. The first kind of analysis emphasizes the movement's creative initiative, considered to be the inventor or harbinger of a new class struggle. The second looks upon the movement as a reaction to obstacles opposing change. The reaction is not considered to be either a voluntary action or a plan, but a new situation, a new state of the organization and processes of production. This continuity in the transition from one meaning to another is not only present in theoretical considerations; it is present in the development of the facts.

The May Movement arose in the universities, first at Strasbourg, then in a more sustained manner at Nanterre. The students found themselves free of economic restrictions in an institution, the university, that could be considered culturally but not materially repressive. It was characterized more by maladjustment and meaninglessness than by any organized attempt to exploit intellectual manpower. The students' first reaction was one of ridicule and indignation. Moribund culture and archaic education were rejected in the name of youth and life. Thus, the movement began with an affirmation of personality in a world that was more empty than hostile. The crisis of change appeared before the social conflict. During this first phase, the movement was more cultural and university-oriented than social and political.

At Nanterre, in the spring of 1968, the cultural revolt gradually turned into social struggle. Under the partial influence of the Vietnam committees, who were directly responsible for the creation of the March 22 Movement and to some extent for the German students' protest, the May Movement quickly spilled over the limits of the university. There was no practical way to operate on the third

level of the movement before May 13 but as early as April
and the first weeks of May, action directed toward militant
workers and the desire to go beyond university problems
had already developed.

The day after the huge demonstration of May 13 and
the conciliatory measures decided upon by Georges Pompidou, first the "free" Sorbonne, then the Odéon exploded. At the same time, student action became obscured
by the general strike and its resurgence following rejection
of the Grenelle agreements between the labor unions, the
government, and employers by the workers of Renault and
Citroën. But it continued to develop in working-class districts and within companies, thus opening up new aspects
of the movement.

Were not the occupation of the Sorbonne and the formation of free assemblies, the meeting of leftist leaders
and some labor organizers at the Charléty Stadium, and
the June confrontations at Flins, a large Renault plant,
essentially equivalent to the three aspects that I have mentioned: crisis behavior, populist movement, and class
struggle?

The profound unity of the movement was due to the
fact that it was no longer fighting a ruling group defending
private interests but generalized power over social and
cultural life. I mentioned class struggle to emphasize that
the movement revealed and defined the contradictions in
our society, but we should not be too quick to find the
term satisfactory. The struggle was not one of the people
against a particular social group. As the ruling forces
extend their power over society and the system's integrative capacity increases, the class struggle changes not only
its participants but its forms and objectives. The enemy
is no longer a person or a social category, a monarch or a
bourgeoisie. It is the politico-economic power's entire de-
personalized, "rationalized," bureaucratic plan of action.
It is the social order, which has ceased to be a collection

of particular social milieux and groups—families, professions, and life-styles. It is the production apparatus which destroys the barriers of private, local, and professional life. Capitalism had already overthrown the policies that allowed for particularism and local heritage. The sphere of this change has been greatly extended by today's more active and more powerful society.

More profoundly than before, we are what we do and what others do to us, the roles that we play in the social apparatus. Work is no longer activity, production, and profession. It is relationships, communication, and status. Leisure is no longer withdrawal into oneself, one's family, or one's neighborhood group. The culture is controlled and transmitted centrally. This does not mean that contemporary society is by nature totalitarian; this is so only when all means of action are controlled by a central power. The fact that the despotism of old can be totalitarian today is an indication of a transformation found in all types of society: the influence of centers of decision over the members of society is greater and more widespread than before. Even in education, the child was submitted to restrictions and prohibitions; he was placed in a situation of dependence and submission; but the counterpart was the limitation of this social power over him. He spent many hours of his life free of restrictions and manipulation. Today socialization—the spread of society's values and norms—is no longer confined to specialized milieux, to home and school; it is a part of everyday life. It is spread by radio and television, by posters and newspapers, by the audio-visual signals which constantly stimulate and direct.

This technical civilization is not in itself an instrument of domination. But it simultaneously propagates, transmits, depersonalizes, and masks the power of ruling forces that reduce individuals and groups to their place in an integrated hierarchy of production and consumption. If power is not concentrated in a totalitarian State, the feeling of alienation is more diffuse and painful. The more "permissive" society is, the more it shatters the personality. Man is integrated or manipulated without ever meeting an adversary or a master. He is left to himself, deprived of all means of control over his social roles. He is dismantled like a machine, each piece dealt with in a special shop or milieu.

The reaction against this power is not defense of a particular social group that rests on its culture and organization but is simultaneously all-inclusive and highly personal. That is what was meant by "cultural revolution" as the expression was used in May. The starting point for recovery cannot be social groupings. It must be the individual, the subject, who can only rebuild his strength by opposing the forces of integration and manipulation from top to bottom. He attempts to resist a society in which power hides behind the apparent neutrality of technical operations and communications networks, with a responsible plan and a determination to control and take over the instruments of social change, not only in work but in the school, in leisure, and in interpersonal relations.

This counteroffensive is not waged in the name of a heritage or a tradition, but above all in the name of personal and collective rejection. The non-adjustment as well as the challenge and the drive oppose an apparatus which claims to be an obvious reality, a natural necessity, or a reasonable compromise. A social movement is formed only when personal revolt free of the systems of integration and manipulation attacks power, recognizes it, and exposes it. This joining of revolt and attack occurs in different ways in different societies. Let us take only one example.

Revolt and political combat are present both in the United States and in France, but in profoundly different forms and relationships. In the United States, cultural revolt, social criticism, and political struggle are all related; but it is more difficult for them to come together because the State is not as centralized as it is in France. The three aspects of the American movement are represented by rejection of university training, solidarity with the blacks, and the struggle against the war in Vietnam. They mingle constantly; but so far they have been unable to come together in a movement capable of basic action. In France, the social struggle is at the center of the movement; the cultural revolt is almost a by-product of a crisis of change. In the United States, the cultural revolt is at the center of a defensive movement of rejection in contrast to the offensive movement against the centers of power in France. The relative weakness of the economy and the primary role of the State always made the French movement lean toward political, revolutionary, or parliamentary action, rather than toward transformation on the basis of social conditions and authority relationships. So important was the State in Gaullist France that there was a danger of considering only the conditions for taking power and forgetting the strength of the cultural challenge. The class struggle was in danger of being relegated to the role of revolutionary vanguard. The very violence and suddenness of the May Movement should help us to rediscover the unity between class struggle and revolt that exists beyond political action.

To present the cultural revolution as a simple manifestation of socialism attempting to transform the State would be to impoverish the analysis and falsify the reality of the May Movement. The May Movement was not a socialist movement. Like all of the important social movements in highly industrialized societies, it was a communist movement. Its struggle involved the whole fabric of society. The power wielded over society is too pervasive for us to continue separating the words of the slogan: change life and change society.

The more the revolutionary movement concentrated

on societies paralyzed at the threshold of industrialization by archaic power, the more truly political it became, gathering all its strength into a Bolshevik-type society. Today, in post-industrial societies that have entered technical civilization, it can develop only by becoming more and more comprehensive, by narrowing the gap between political struggle and cultural revolution. The movement's unity has been imposed upon it by the gradual disappearance of the distinction between civil society and the State. The complexity and importance of the May Movement were a result of the fact that, through an archaic struggle against the State, the movement discovered the need for a complete indictment of society. The unity and duality of the movement must not be contrasted to each other. Institutional archaism triggered the revolt and allowed it to shake up political society. It could also stifle its revolutionary thrust.

The reexamination of technocratic society is simpler and more unified in theory than it is in social action. The May Movement was creative only in what prevented it from succeeding, its spontaneity. It succeeded in combating institutional opposition, not social authority. Its importance lay in having confronted with the power of cultural revolution the power of the social structure in a situation that combines concentration of the State apparatus and development of the affluent society.

The new ruling class is formed at once by social power and economic modernization. The May Movement was an antisociety and a revolutionary force. The cultural revolution was the very foundation of a class struggle which concentrated not on economic relations, but on the whole of society, because the new social power spread its control everywhere; but it was also the cataclysm of the "bourgeois," privileged, traditionalist world and especially of a university system that has not moved with the times.

Finally, it was the reverse side of an impossible political revolution, of a movement that had to contend with repression and the passive resistance of the forces that had spurred the old social conflicts.

A revolutionary movement touched off a crisis, not a revolution. It swirled around the Sorbonne, camped amid the ruins of the university, and shook the political regime, but by itself it could not become an organized social and political force, capable of fighting the lengthy battles which alone conquer social power. The movement could express more than it could act, challenge more than it could transform. Crisis and conflict, revolt and revolution cannot be separated because what was involved was a premature revolution, an imaginary assumption of power.

If the utopia was so powerful, it was because political struggle was still impossible. The 1848 Movement appeared at the birth of industrial capitalism and not, like trade unionism, at the heart of its development. Similarly, the May Movement exploded at the beginning of the absorption of capitalist society by technocratic society, a development which was only opposed by enemies of the capitalist society who were unable to fight new battles. The movement of ideas and the uprising that exposed capitalist power and invoked the inevitable but still impossible struggle against it has been called utopian socialism. The May Movement should be called utopian communism.

The battle was not fought in the name of social interests, but in the name of anti-power. It was only a beginning. The revolt may have dwarfed revolutionary action, but it was more real and more political than all of the attempts to transform it into a political revolt. The May Movement had no tomorrow; but it will have a future. Its revolutionary action will be pursued only if it destroys what gave strength to the uprising, only if imaginary possession of power is replaced by political organization and strategy. But the cultural revolt opened the door to a direct result that will be its opposite.

The photo in which Jacques Sauvageot, Alain Geismar, and Daniel Cohn-Bendit are side by side was often shown. The unity among them, full of contradictions, was also the movement's. Cohn-Bendit gave birth to the movement, starting with the revolt; Geismar experienced it as an insurrection; Sauvageot dreamed of transforming it into a political force.

Today's utopian communism may become similar to what the labor movement was and no longer is. But now it is just a revolutionary revolt, the expression of a crisis, and the revelation of new conflicts. Its importance lies in what it discloses, not in what it solves.

A Revolutionary Situation?

This concept of the movement, which insists on the contradictions that define utopian communism, differs from the more simple concept that it was nothing but an absolute social break. Was it a revolutionary movement that expressed and exploited a revolutionary situation? Nothing seems to me farther from the truth than this apparently suitable interpretation. The complexity, the shock value, the contradictions of the movement were precisely due to the fact that there existed in France the encounter between a revolutionary movement and a nonrevolutionary situation. The crisis and the conflict were mingled rather than combined.

The conflict and the social movement were on the level of the production and power system; the crisis and the reactions it caused were on the level of the State and its institutions, especially the university. The class conflict was neither experienced by great masses of workers nor directed by a political organization. The most militant elements of the student movement devoted their energies to forging a link between the students and the workers. The nature of this essential unity of social struggles was very clearly defined, especially by the J.C.R. (Jeunesse Communiste Révolutionnaire) , a Trotskyite organization. But the new class struggle could not free itself from the remnants of the old struggle which was becoming institutionalized. Thus the movement was torn between its determination to fight and its limited capacity for revolt. It would be an error to believe that the crisis itself occasioned a revolutionary outcome. Because it was on the level of institutions and ideologies, it was violent and brutal, but always ambiguous. Such crisis behavior does not create revolutionary hope.

Whereas habit leads one to automatically contrast reform and revolution, the antisociety typical of the sit-in in the Sorbonne's great amphitheater was, in fact, only a special kind of modernization. In an article in *Le Monde,* Jean Lacouture contrasted the lower Sorbonne—the continuous meetings in the amphitheaters—with the high Sorbonne, the meetings of various groups in conference rooms to map out university reforms. This contrast was indeed striking. But the meetings in the amphitheaters had no other practical function than to bypass university reforms by a utopian airing of opinions so that reforms could be made without appearing to be reformist. What was clear in the faculties was even more clear in the *lycées* and other cultural institutions. The language used by the professional committees enabled them to run the institutional and cultural blockades and bring about social changes and modernizations which could have been carried out more gradually and with less shock in other societies. Tendencies and transformations whose results will one day soon surprise those who were the most passionate participants appeared throughout the long debates in

the general assemblies. I shall return to that later, but
these remarks should not be considered cynical or disen-
chanted. The general assemblies were not the tool of the
technocrats, but they prepared changes which are part of
modernization more than of revolution. There were undoubtedly non-reformist elements in May–June. But left
to itself, the cultural revolt was more an expression, a
style of personal and collective experience, than a political
and social action because it had no grasp on real situations
and conflicts.

The organization of a society is not simply and totally
determined by the nature of economic and political power.
Whether capitalist or socialist, an advanced industrial
society is defined by its capacity for change, for adaptation
to an environment that is at once unstable and multiform.
This is well known by sociologists both East and West who
for years have emphasized the dysfunctional, paralyzing
nature of the old bureaucratic schema, of pyramidal authority, of special concern for stability and integration.
The student action set the society in motion through
disruption. The champions of the old university system
who placed all their hopes in repression of subversive
activity and in the reestablishment of a traditional, supposedly untouchable university were predictably disappointed. Salvaging the movement was easy for reformers;
it was the only realistic outcome, not of the movement as
a whole, but of the crisis and disruption within it.

The workers' strikes made it possible to recognize the
trade-union section of industry and other reforming measures upheld by the C.F.D.T. which were intended to make
it possible to hasten the disappearance of the old forms of
industrial authority and decision-making.* But the anti-

* C.F.D.T. (Confédération Française et Démocratique du Travail),
formerly C.F.T.C. (Confédération Française des Travailleurs Chrétiens).
The second labor organization in size, after the communist-controlled
C.G.T. (Confédération Générale du Travail). After it dropped all reference

society's utopia could only become a revolution by exceeding its role as the indirect agent of modernization or by letting the social struggle return to the forefront.

This possibility would have become a reality had the university failed to rise above its state of disorganization, and had educational authorities failed to shed their reserve and mistrust and their failure to understand that it was time to innovate, to manage, and to negotiate. New departures are very difficult in the Paris faculties of letters, and there was great uncertainty as to the first steps to propose. Consequently, there was great danger of disorganization, full of schisms and revolts rather than of new social movements. Unless objectives, strategies, negotiations, and, consequently, a certain body of political relationships emerged, spontaneity, and direct democracy would lead to irrational reactions and the manipulation of crowds by small groups or individuals.

These remarks risk overshooting their target: they do not claim that the spontaneous utopia was in itself nonrevolutionary, only that it caused social change to be accompanied by crisis and disruption. The utopia indicated a form of change; it did not determine its orientation. This conclusion leads to another which completes it. The class conflict, another aspect of the May Movement, defined the content but not the form of social change; that is to say, it did not necessarily appear in terms of disruption and violence. Let us return to comparison with the worker movement. It cannot be said that there has been less class conflict in Great Britain than in France, simply because British history has not been riddled with revolutionary disruptions for a hundred years. Revolutions are

_____

to Christian social doctrine, it became a very active reform movement. While the C.G.T. emphasized traditional wage problems, the C.F.D.T. campaigned more actively for the rights of unions, change of the authoritarian aspects of plant organization, the bettering of working conditions and giving the workers influence on economic decisions.

the result of a combination of class conflict with the resistance put up by forms of power and institutions that are archaic or, more generally, incapable of adapting to social change, either because of their rigidity or because of the rapidity and particular nature of the change. It can even be said that a full-fledged class conflict can be at the heart of society and easily lead to negotiations, without implying the need for disruption.

None of the aspects of the movement—class struggle, populist uprising, cultural revolt—was by itself revolutionary. In a revolutionary situation conflict and crisis are combined, and the conflict can only be dealt with by negotiations or by the institutional apparatus. Revolutionary action is the encounter between a social movement and a situation of violence.

If violence played an important role in the May crisis it was because the movement consisted more of invention and formation of class conflict than of full realization. Violence was the means both of introducing new problems and liquidating old ones. This is why it is possible to speak of a revolutionary movement: conflicts could not be institutionalized because of the archaism of the institutions, the total nature of the revolt, and above all, perhaps, because the social action that imposed new problems on the consciousness of the participants themselves and on society as a whole.

The joining of crisis and conflict was far from perfect. The students' revolutionary action originated in the universities, where it was only a cultural revolt, a by-product of the crisis. The utopia was therefore of central importance, because the fusion of crisis and conflict could only be imaginary, a construct of the mind and of the emotions rather than a lived experience.

The "student commune" did not embody the immediate direction of the movement; it was its utopia. It fostered the meeting of orientations which remained opposed, but complementary. Material proof of this was the constant opposition in May between the Sorbonne current and the Nanterre current, even though these expressions give a very imperfect picture. The Sorbonne was simultaneously the center of the antisociety and of university reform. It was therefore the center of the crisis of change and of the disruptive behavior that accompanied it. Nanterre, that is to say, the March 22 Movement—whose mistrust of the Sorbonne world of talk appeared very early and continued to grow—was the principal agent of the social conflict present at the barricades and at Flins. It was committed more strongly to the content than to the form of the social movement and was dominated at once by the desire for social struggle and the spontaneity of the collective action.

Neither of these two collective agents can be simply identified with any of the aspects of the movement that I have attempted to characterize. Neither are they complementary components of a unified collective action. The May Movement was dominated by the union and tension between social struggle and the expression of crisis and rupture. Each of the two components is itself formed of opposing but interdependent elements.

The class struggle, being more imminent than present, was necessarily associated with the emphasis on spontaneity. The "little groups" * that wanted to activate the class struggle in imitation of the traditional working-class, revolutionary parties were outflanked by the collective action. The antisociety also aimed at reform. When it did not, it was condemned to repeating revolutionary phrases over and over, while the reformers, not motivated by a desire for social and cultural disruption, were forced to be

* This term, first used in a derogatory sense by the government to designate various revolutionary organizations, was also used, partly in a joking way, by the street demonstrators to show the incapacity of the government to understand a mass movement.

the agents of a technocratic society; this was clear from the action in the professional schools and even in certain faculties.

The following inference can be drawn from these observations. A revolutionary student action cannot be truly formed until the university, having weathered its crisis, has accepted new forms and has become modernized—then social conflict will be able to enter it instead of fleeing it. The imminent struggles over political freedom in the universities can have no other meaning. Those who think that the question can be solved by organizing a few discussion clubs modeled on Oxford should not be reassured. Like the establishment of the labor movement in industry, the entry of politics into the university will be an instrument of new social struggles. They will be violent or they will develop within a certain institutional framework, depending on the attitude of the university system and its ability to manage conflicts.

Students and Workers

The complexity of the movement is even clearer when we ask if we are dealing with a student movement or with revolutionary militants in the schools whose action was aimed at the working class almost from the very beginning, with the students playing the role of "detonators" and magnifiers. In fact, it is a double question: was the students' role that of an intelligentsia or that of a social base; then, what was the relationship between the student action and the worker action? Each of these problems will be considered in more detail later, but a tentative answer to them will be given now.

At the beginning of the events there was no mass student movement. The weakness of the U.N.E.F. (Union Nationale des Etudiants de France) , especially at Nanterre, and the even greater weakness of the S.N.E.Sup. (Syndicat National de l'Enseignement Supérieur), which was torn between two opposing tendencies, was constantly clear. We spoke about the "little groups" and the "enragés" of Nanterre with good reason. It was the repression and especially the foul play at the Sorbonne on May 3 that provoked the student reaction which rapidly became a mass movement. The participation of non-students in the street demonstrations, which assumed relative importance as early as the Night of the Barricades, May 10–11, became more important during the night of May 24–25. From May 13 on, the wave of strikes became the most important social facts; but after General de Gaulle's speech of May 30, the most important events occurred at Flins and Sochaux (a town in East France where the main plants of Peugeot are located).

University reform can be viewed as a by-product of the movement, accepted and even encouraged by revolutionary militants who were basically not interested in it, but who, because they fear all forms of co-optation and reformism, threw themselves into a common attack, giving priority to the mobilization of workers, the only group whose power could overthrow economic exploitation and political domination. Beginning with the occupation of the Sorbonne, many groups went to the suburb of Billancourt, calling on the workers at the Renault plant to take over the revolution from the weak hands of the students. The students were unwilling to act in the name of their own interests and objectives. They realized that they were young bourgeois; they were willing to be treated as future managers, future agents of capitalist exploitation. They called on the masses to become part of the masses themselves and eliminate the opposition between intellectual and manual work that reproduces in the professional sphere the class domination through which the bourgeoisie exploits manual laborers. Before May 2, the March 22

Movement constantly emphasized the continuity of revolutionary action, from the industrial centers of Caen, Mulhouse, Redon, Lyon, and Besançon up to the Parisian student movement, thus underlining the priority of workers' struggles.

But should we consider this revolutionary rhetoric the historical expression of the May Movement, even though it seems more important, i.e., more creative of historical initiatives, than the discourse of the antisociety that occupied the amphitheater of the Sorbonne?

First of all, the student movement was not a detonator. All during the events, from the Rue Gay-Lussac where the main barricades were built on May 10, to Flins, it was indeed the students who took the initiative. At Cléon (the Renault plant in Normandy) or at Flins as at Thomson, one of the main French electronics companies, or the O.R.T.F., it was the workers closest to the students in age or profession who played the most creative role in the strike movement and plant occupations. Unionists like André Barjonet, Edmond Maire, or Maurice Labi who took advanced positions did not play a leading role and their names did not reach the public with the same force of Sauvageot and Geismar.

On the whole, the workers directed themselves in their strikes. They did not follow the union leaders after the Grenelle agreements, but neither did their movement adopt the revolutionary positions taken by the students. We will go into this later on: the C.G.T. was not outflanked by revolutionary action, but by a movement aimed at what used to be called structural reforms in which the C.F.D.T. attempted to take the active lead. The question is not why the Communists were not revolutionaries, but why they were not even reformists.

The students experienced the action aimed at the working class as action in the service of the proletariat. But the action served better to free the student movement from

its professional and social limitations. It was very easy for
the students to shut themselves up in the universities, to
spread their revolt, and bring about changes in university
life which the technocrats would have supported whole-
heartedly in order to break the resistance of the old liberal
decadent university. In the university, the student does
not meet the class enemy. He only runs up against an impotent administration and aloof professors who, whether
secretly hostile or occasionally sympathetic, are always
powerless and more victims than cause of the university
crisis. Therefore, it was necessary to get out of the university ghetto where the struggle risked enfeeblement and
enclosed itself within a sort of corporatism that would not
upset those in power. The appeal to the working class was
the concrete assertion of a revolutionary movement, a desire for a class struggle on the level of the whole society;
but no massive alliance was achieved.

For the students, the workers represented both a tre-
mendous power and the revolutionary class *par excellence,*
identified with the great socialist struggles and the Russian Revolution. Thus, the students were more inclined
toward an idea of social revolution than toward real workers. This inclination was essential and it had important
results. But it does not mean that we can consider the students detonators who ignited the working masses. The
movement is best explained by the action and situation of
the students.

We must still answer the first question. Even if the students were not a simple avant garde of working-class action, we can say that the student militants touched off conflicts connected with the crisis in society as a whole rather
than with purely student problems. Did the students play
the role of an intelligentsia, similar to that of the students
of 1830 and 1848 or, closer to our time, similar to the
Latin American students of Cordoba and Buenos Aires,
Mexico City, and Rio? We can only reply to this by going

back to our analysis as a whole, i.e., by distinguishing the three principal aspects of the May Movement.

✕   a) The populist aspect of the movement did give the students a role that was not exactly that of an intelligentsia, but rather that of a milieu prepared to express struggles that larger social categories and classes are not yet in a position to undertake. That is the Latin American aspect of the May Movement. It was more in the name of the people than of the working class, it was more against the oligarchies than against capitalist exploitation. In this sense, the students acted in the name of their own middle-class situation, as future managers, technicians, or educators excluded from decision-making systems concentrated in the hands of the upper-middle class and dominant political groups.

b) The intelligentsia theme corresponds best to the third aspect of the student movement, the antisociety utopia. The Parisian intelligentsia mobilized around the Sorbonne and then around the Odéon. Artists, writers, editors of literary magazines, university personnel closer to independent intellectual milieux than to professional scientific milieux were more at ease in a universe of words and ideas than in one of strategy and combat. The flare-up of the student Sorbonne would not have been as lively had it not excited this Left Bank intelligentsia, this society within a society that is unwilling to accept the professionalization of scientific knowledge and is nostalgic for the great historical struggles. But we must say again that this intelligentsia was not a driving force in the May Movement. It did not light or sustain the fire, it was enlightened by it. In sum, the great "intellectuals of the left" played only a modest role, even at the Sorbonne. The most important of them, Jean-Paul Sartre, felt this situation; he confined himself to interviewing Cohn-Bendit for the *Nouvel Observateur* (May 1968) and publicly intervened at the Sorbonne only once.* No important initiative was taken by well-known intellectuals. Most of them mingled with the crowd; some, like Louis Aragon, occasionally engaged in dialogue; but they did not lead the movement. They did not go to the people, they did not harangue the demonstrators. It is surprising that the most visible intellectuals were Nobel Prize laureates for science, who were more reformist than revolutionary and exercised no lasting influence.

c) The student action was most direct in the prospective of the class struggle. The first attacks were launched as early as November 1967 at Nanterre against the Fouchet Plan and against the dangers of selection for entrance in the university.

The "little groups" played an important role at the beginning, but the movement would never have taken shape had the March 22 Movement—which was almost the opposite of the "little groups"—not won a vast audience at Nanterre within a few weeks and created the first embryo of a critical university. The few "enragés" of January were able to mobilize a thousand students in one day in April. In May, there was considerable participation of university and *lycée* students in the assemblies and commissions, and the movement's sphere of influence was quite large. All of these students and sympathizers were far from the extreme politicization of the active militants. They did not distinguish between revolutionary inspiration and professional objectives. The student movement mobilized not only to trigger the struggle of the working class or stir up the people against the ruling oligarchies; it mobilized in its own interests, for the transformation of university organization and the student condition. The attacks against the university, against the content of

* Sartre's interview, in *Le Nouvel Observateur*, May 1968.

teaching and pedagogical methods, against the lack of opportunities and the dangers of selection were content and sharp enough to make the point that university problems today are not only cultural and ideological, but also material, economic, and political. In light of this, the student movement was not made up of an intelligentsia, but of young workers whose problems are close to those of students in technical colleges and apprenticeship schools. They question both the functioning of firms and schools and the essential element of the production system which is more and more based on training and the ability to control and produce technical and economic changes.

This is an important difference from the student movements in less developed countries or in countries where universities are more archaic, as in Spain and Portugal or many Latin American countries. The role of the university in an advanced industrial society is questioned, not only the role of the students in the process of development and liberation of an archaic and controlled society.

In the following chapter, we will see that the greatest turmoil is not in the most modern sectors of higher education. But the important thing is to recognize that the movement is first of all a student movement, formed in the university, mobilizing students above all, nourished not with corporate demands and objectives, but professional, social, and political objectives directly linked to a rapidly expanding higher education that is called to play a new role in a rapidly changing industrial society.

This should justify our decision to consider the May Movement from the point of view of the student action. Some have been tempted to describe a student phase, a worker phase, and a political phase of the May–June crisis and to relate them to the progression of a revolutionary crisis. My analysis is just the reverse: the student movement was indeed the central force of the social movements, but it was manifold. Any other type of analysis would mean refusing to attribute central importance to the social movements in the period under consideration, viewing the May–June events as a crisis of French society or an ensemble of crises of modernization and change. Such an analysis is inspired by conservatism. It refuses to bear in mind that the May Movement questioned the forms of domination and alienation in any advanced capitalist society. All it cares to see in the movement is the rejection of certain curbs to progress and the resistance to changes imposed by the logic of industrial development and its social consequences.

We must avoid the apparent necessity to choose between this interpretation, which serves the rising ruling class, and the reduction of the analysis to the transcription of the ideological discourse of the protagonists themselves. If we fail to relate experience to a complex of social relationships that give it meaning, we forgo all explanation; but if we only see in the collective behavior and social movements adaptation to social change, we impoverish and falsify social reality and succumb once again to ideology. Like the labor movement, nationalism in the Third World, the uprising in Budapest, the Polish October, or the Czech Spring, the May Movement was a collective action in which the profound conflicts of a society, those which best define its modes of functioning and evolution, emerged and organized.

The real importance of the May Movement rests in the unity that was established between the questioning of the fundamental social and cultural institutions in our type of society and a truly political struggle. The May Movement was both impressive and a dead end.

It prolonged and deepened a crisis while reviving such questioning and exposing class conflicts in a society anesthetized by technocratic modernization. We must, once and for all, go beyond enthusiastic support or scandalized rejection. We must criticize the movement—that is to say, we must first recognize its creativity, in order to illuminate not the good or the bad in it, which would be meaningless, but the present explosion and the force of the future that was born in the cultural revolt.

I am not attempting to take a middle position. Recognizing what I believe to be the historical importance of the movement, I am critizing whatever in it is not a force of the future but a reaction to the present crisis. The social movement would not have taken shape without the cultural revolt that was spawned and marked by the crisis. But it only developed by criticizing certain of its forms and going beyond the crisis to engage in conflict.

In Nanterre and at the beginning of May in Paris, the revolt and social struggles were united and the movement emerged. In the amphitheaters of Nanterre, on the Champ-de-Mars, during the first days of the occupied Sorbonne, it was the unifying force of the revolutionary movement that carried the day. Speech was action. Daniel Cohn-Bendit was the architect and the symbol of this rising and flashing phase of the movement. Afterwards, this unity was inevitably broken. The new social struggles were unable to develop; it was only a beginning. At the same time, the student revolt retired within itself—action became atmosphere and excitement replaced mobilization. The labor movement was first of all a questioning of the domination of industrial society by capitalist power; it developed only to the extent that it defended workers and humble folk and attacked the masters of the economy in the name of progress. In the same way, nationalism in the colonized Third World is only effective when, through the struggle against oligarchy and foreign domination, it takes charge of economic development.

Since the social movement of May began as a student movement, it is in the university that this evolution must be achieved. The student movement will develop to the extent that it becomes the defender of knowledge and education and their peculiar requirements and to the extent that it is challenging and at the same time progressive and rational. The summer schools organized by the U.N.E.F.* in the summer of 1968 marked the first stage of this maturation process, this preparation for struggle. But it is to be feared that passive resistance or a spirit of vindictiveness in the university, supported by public opinion and political authorities who want to maintain order at all costs, will considerably limit the field of possible reforms and that the students, considering themselves swindled, will withdraw into brutal opposition. Such a confrontation would lead to chaos.

The student movement cannot make headway in a disorganized or archaic university. In the United States, the movement appeared strongest in prestigious universities: California, Michigan, Columbia. University reform in France will give the student movement the choice of two paths: the movement will either withdraw into a revolt that will increasingly isolate it and make it the spectator of a crisis rather than the agent of social struggles; or it will concentrate on the theory and practice of its struggles and go beyond what was part of its strength but also limited its future: the total revolt against society and culture.

This leads one to think that the future of the student movement will be largely determined by the maturation of conflicts outside of the university, conflicts in the key industries and research departments, and among the technicians and technical personnel who are more naturally sensitive than students to the demands of technical rationality but who are absorbed much more easily by the temptations and demands of professional status.

The May Movement was a thunderbolt announcing the

* Union Nationale des Etudiants de France. The leftist-controlled national student union, though weakened and disorganized in 1968, took a central role in the May Movement.

social struggles of the future. It dispelled the illusion that improvement in production and consumption result in a society in which tensions replace conflicts, quarrels replace disruptions, and negotiations replace revolutions.

The May Movement cannot be understood in reference to French society alone. The national framework is as inadequate for the analysis as it was for the action. Organized or planned development had been going on for twenty years in either a national or a regional framework. Whether in the United States, the Soviet Union, or even Western Europe, it was always within a geographical and political framework, defined by resources and decision-making systems, that the leaders posed their problems and organized their action. Internationalism seemed to have disappeared and to be no more than a tourist theme. But suddenly there erupted in France, a country that is often chauvinistic and xenophobic, a movement that had as one of its strongest features spontaneous internationalism. This theme is even more important because it was lived and not proposed by an ideology. That is why the events in Paris had considerable repercussions in other countries. It was not only because the crisis in France was more general than elsewhere; it was above all because the phrase that the demonstrators emphasized to the residents of the streets that they crossed—"You are all involved"—was indeed addressed to all who felt the restrictions of the economic and political systems.

As long as an analysis remains linked to the functioning of existing social systems, it sticks to defining the special characteristics of the evolution in each country or each region. Of course, today, social change does not take place in France in the same way as it does in Germany or Poland. But, all things considered, it is not in the peculiar situation of the French university, State, or industrial management that we should hope to find the creative raison d'être of the May Movement. It was not an exemplary movement, but its breadth enables us to pose with new force the problems common to societies whose political, economic, and administrative organization is very different from that of France.

Today, it can no longer be said that such a conflict was merely a peculiarity of French society, for beyond the functional problems of a particular society, the conflict exposed the orientation and conflicts of a general type of society. The May Movement was one of the first class conflicts to break out in an advanced capitalist society. Along with the great and more dramatic movements of the socialist countries, it marked the birth of a new period in the social history of industrial societies.

II

❧❧❧❧❧❧❧❧❧❧❧❧

The Crisis of
the University

The May Movement was more than a response to the malfunctioning of the university; various circumstances, especially the intervention of the police, transformed it into a
more general uprising. The student militants were too politicized to react only to their professional situation.
Their agitation was sustained by the war in Vietnam and
by the general problems of revolutionary action in the
world today. (The creation of the J.C.R.* at the Sorbonne
was more an episode in the history of the Communist
Party than the university.)

A Closed Society

The problems of the university can be understood in
two ways. For some, the university is a rigid system,

* Jeunesse Communiste Révolutionaire. A Trotskyite group that
split off from the Communist Youth Organization.

directly controlled by a centralizing administration infatu-
ated with order and principle, crushed under routine, incapable of defining its objectives and making use of its
resources. For others, the university's resistance to an inevitable transformation is only an expression of the role it
plays in the service of the bourgeoisie. It is attached to
bourgeois values, categories, and modes of expression and
changes to the extent that the ruling class itself changes
and modernizes; but it wants to maintain the cultural and
social order that it dominates.

We will begin by considering the first of these interpretations. For many years, the poor output of the university
machine was commonly denounced. The majority of students, at least in the faculties of sciences and letters failed
to obtain their *licence*. Each university year became a
serious crisis, and in Paris at least the crisis grew worse;
the already short university year was taken up by examinations. Through their unions, the members of the teaching profession expressed chronic dissatisfaction and restlessness. The central administration, occupied with many
small problems and individual demands, was seriously
understaffed, with inadequate means of statistical analysis
and programming at its disposal, despite recent improve-
ments.

What is the origin of such a situation—one characterized more by bungling than by exploitation. Above all,
it is the manner of administering the university that
should be blamed. Like the armament industry and State
monopolies, the faculties are subject to direct administrative control, with no decision-making power over their
programs and operations. In the case of the university, the
situation was perhaps more extreme than anywhere else,
since there was no equation between the tasks to be accomplished and the means provided to do so.

For example, one faculty of letters, that of Nanterre,
did not know in July how many students it would have in

October; it had even less knowledge of the number of teaching hours at its disposal even though the *Journal Officiel* (in which the government publishes laws, decrees, and official decisions) specified the instruction to be given and the number of hours to be devoted to each subject in great detail. An extremely simple calculation would make it possible to determine the number of teachers needed for a given number of students and the hours of teaching. But it was absolutely futile to make this calculation since the number of personnel assigned to an establishment were not the results of calculation but of financial bargaining, remote decisions, and deals in which each party attempted to introduce as much mystery and drama as possible in order to reinforce his position at the critical moment. The reasons for such a situation are not so easily grasped. What is the source of this rigidity, this difficulty in adapting to changing conditions?

One explanation comes from the traditional function of the university. Because it is not subject to criteria of profit-making, to the sanctions of the market, because its activity is "unselfish," because it is a cultural museum and at the same time the place where new knowledge is worked out (the practical results of which are difficult to evaluate— above all if they are in the realm of education), the university cannot be managed like a business concern, it cannot adapt easily to a changing environment, and it must necessarily correspond to an "idea" of the university rather than adapt to needs that are difficult to define, given the present state of information. Thus, the university is naturally traditionalist. It hands down the cultural legacy of the past to new generations and forms men in accord with an institutional and cultural model which, since it must have a certain coherence, changes only by leaps and crises.

Such formulae are useful in asking a more precise question. Why is the French university more of a conservatory than a laboratory? We must bear in mind that in France

the university system is only one component in the
system of higher education, a much larger ensemble of
advanced teaching and research institutions. Scientific research is a largely autonomous activity, the mainspring of
which is the C.N.R.S. (Centre National de la Recherche
Scientifique), which is independent of the university but
part of the Ministry of National Education. The C.N.R.S.
was considerably strengthened by the creation of con-
certed programs directed by the Délégation Générale à la
Recherche Scientifique et Technique (General Delegation for Scientific and Technical Research). On the other
hand, there are great establishments of higher education: Collège de France, Ecoles Normales Supérieures,
Muséum National d'Histoire Naturelle, Ecole Pratique
des Hautes Etudes, and others. Finally, the schools are
under the Ministry of National Education, and other civil
or military ministries, and private bodies such as the
Chamber of Commerce of Paris, all of which constitute a
very heterogeneous group with the common purpose of
assuring reliable professional placement.

This description shows that one of the principal responsibilities of the faculties is to receive the great mass
of students. The main part of their teaching program re-
volves around the first years of study, for example, preparation for the *licence*. The reform of medical studies, the
attempt to bring together medical teaching, care, and research into hospital-university centers, will be mentioned
later on. Even though it is slow and difficult, the reform is
evidence of an attempt to regroup one sector of the university. The same tendency appears in a more progressive way in the science faculties. The importance of laboratories and research teams is opposed to the general separation of faculties and research units.

The situation is very different in the law faculties,
which have been able to transform themselves into faculties of law and of economic science, but which ensure only

a small part of the rising economic research linked to the creation of research departments in the Ministry of Finance, to the progress of the I.N.S.E.E. (Institut National de la Statistique et des Etats Economiques), to the work of the Commissariat for the Plan,* the creation of private and public research groups, and, in the educational realm, to the activity of the Ecole des Hautes Etudes and the Collège de France.

The same split between teaching and research exists in the faculties of letters. The most important exception is the union between the Institut d'Etudes Politiques in Paris and the Fondation Nationale des Sciences Politiques. But in the main—and in a spectacular way in the realm of the social sciences—the faculties do not play an important role in research. Even today, sociology, anthropology, and demography have a very small place in the faculties. The C.N.R.S., the Ecole Pratique des Hautes Etudes, the Fondation des Sciences Politiques in the university domain, and the I.N.S.E.E. or the I.N.E.D. (Institut National d'Etudes Démographiques) outside of it have been almost alone in winning recognition for the social sciences in France.

The separation of teaching from research, that is to say, the inability of the university to develop new sectors of research independently, is therefore more pronounced in the sectors that are least sensitive to the demands of the rest of society. The conservatism of the faculties of letters is linked first and foremost to the fact that until very recently they prepared their students almost exclusively for teaching for the university itself. Studies in the humanities have been unable to adapt to the development of research.

* A relatively small organization, made up of high-level experts who propose major economic decisions and organize committees in which representatives of employers, unions, and other interest groups as well as independent experts make recommendations to the government.

This situation is traditional. The history of university activity in France is largely that of the creation of para- or even counter-universities whenever there was a rapid development of a type of knowledge that departed from so-called classical culture. The Collège de France was a Renaissance creation that extended beyond the mainly Latin culture of the Sorbonne and taught Greek and Oriental languages. The Ecole Pratique des Hautes Etudes, created by Victor Duruy, Minister of Education during the Second Empire, was oriented from the beginning toward experimental and philological research and the sixth section of this school, created after the last war, and devoted to economic and social sciences, was, under the inspiration of enlightened historians, the response that the university itself failed to make to the development of the social sciences. The C.N.R.S., for its part, provided the laboratories and research teams for the development of scientific studies to which the university, attached to magisterial courses and an organization based on professorial chairs, found it difficult to adapt.

The inflexibility and traditionalism of certain sectors of the university are not only due to administration methods which, being the same in all the sectors, lead to many absurd results and curb progressive change, but for over a century have not prevented new creations; it is due, much more profoundly, to the opposition between "culture" and technology that is strongly rooted in France and other countries. The university seems to be divided into two parts: one which acts on "nature" or constitutes, thanks to knowledge, models of nature that are linked to a practical activity of society and one which elaborates and preserves society's "consciousness," the spirit of its laws, and the formation of its men through the formation of the teachers. This is the dichotomy that made the introduction of social sciences especially difficult. The specialists in the natural sciences were suspicious of them, and the "literary men" in the humanities, in law, and also in certain branches of medicine successfully opposed an indictment of what they were fond of calling humanism.

Between Bourgeois Culture and the Technocratic Society

Is the rigid and conservative university above all a bourgeois university? Here again, certain facts support this thesis, above all, the social makeup of the university. Before the rapid increase in the number of students, the proportion of those who came from working-class and peasant milieux did not exceed 3 or 4 percent. In a rapid survey taken fifteen years ago at the Faculty of Medicine, we found as many sons of doctors—coming from an active population of about 40,000 people—as sons of workers, peasants, and small-wage earners—coming from an active population of from 12 to 15 million people. Studies by Pierre Bourdieu in particular,* have drawn attention to a situation that has changed notably within the last few years but which has not eliminated the great differences among social categories as far as the opportunity for higher education is concerned. In their class origins and social relations, university professors are even less a part of the lower classes.

But we must resist a too superficial argument. The mechanisms of social selection before the university level are also powerful. The role of the family, of teaching, of a descending organization, or hierarchy—classical, modern, technical—directly transcribe that of the social milieux and help to bring to the university a population that is far

* Pierre Bourdieu and Jean-Claude Passeron, *Les Héritiers* (Paris: Editions de Minuit, 1964) , and, more recently, *La Reproduction* (Paris: Editions de Minuit, 1970) .

from representative of a generation's social composition. Our concern here is the faculties: do they aggravate this social selection? We can believe that they do, at least in certain cases; but if we analyze the determinant of success with greater precision, as Noëlle Bisseret has done, we can adopt her conclusion: "It seems that the elements of the objective situation are determinative, since the rates of success are similar in comparable situations, regardless of the social class to [which one belongs] . . . The success of students from well-to-do classes does not seem to be [necessarily] favored by the cultural advantages that they owe to their family milieu." *

Since the proportion of high school graduates entering the university is exceptionally high in France (more than 90 percent), it cannot be said that the university alone aggravates social selection. Of course, students of working-class origin do approach the university under unfavorable conditions, since many of them must work while studying. Such inequalities are the responsibility of the society, not of the educational system itself.

Since a strong selection has been made before the university level, a bourgeois cultural model is imposed on the students, thus enabling the bourgeoisie to broaden its social bases and cultural defenses. Thus, it is the form of education that must be considered. Pierre Bourdieu and his collaborators touched on essential problems when they said that education is conceived as a gift, not a guide. The emphasis is on the ability to speak, on verbal prowess, on exercises with drilling for competitive examinations, the most elaborate form of which is a four-hour dissertation. From the professor the student learns to behave like a future professor; he is an apprentice learning the rules of the art of exposition and the methods and forms requisite for professional academic success.

* "Le Processus de sélection au début des études universitaires," *Revue française de sociologie,* 1968, p. 197.

The faculties' cultural milieux and the type of training they give hardly produce enthusiasm from the bourgeoisie that they are supposed to serve. The upper middle class sends its children to the university as little as possible and retains private instruction on the secondary level. It prefers the professional schools or even the Institut d'Etudes Politiques (which is less a faculty than a school since admission is not free). The employer class does not hide its suspicion of the faculties, especially the faculties of letters, and for a long time the technocrats and a few academics have been almost the only ones to ask for a profound change in the university.

If the university can be accused of being bourgeois, it is not because it spreads knowledge, ways of thinking, and social attitudes directly favorable or necessary to the defense of the capitalist economy. The link between the university and society is not that direct. It passes through the State which transforms and sometimes reverses it. The State has given the university its uniformity but it also assures teachers of national status, lifelong jobs, and protection against local pressures. It is the State that organizes the recruitment of teaching personnel on all levels, defines programs, the spirit behind them, and methods of controlling knowledge. Finally, the State, in its administration and in its schools, assures career openings for many students, who are thus removed from economic activities.

When a political change brings new social groups under the control of the State, public education takes on new life and organizes the social ascent of children from these groups, simultaneously concerning itself with developing new types and methods of education. After the long decline of the universities of the *Ancien Régime,* the Napoleonic university was first and foremost a rebirth. Just as the University of Berlin—the most important and influential university creation of the twentieth century—was the expression of the Prussian state and its attempt to create a new nation, by freeing itself from the political and social *Ancien Régime,* the French university was always closely linked to the State, weakening during the time of Victor Cousin when the bourgeoisie triumphed and the State no longer conveyed forces of social change, and gaining strength during the time of Louis Liard and Lavisse, more recently at the time of the Liberation. That is why it is now in a weakened position, for the State is more the instrument for the transformation of the ruling classes than an instrument of pressure for new groups on the rise.

In situations of retreat, the university does not place itself directly in the service of the ruling classes. It withdraws and bureaucratizes. The importance given examinations is the best sign of this withdrawal. The examinations even create a lively sense of independence among teachers. Pierre Bourdieu and Jean-Claude Passeron, analyzing the role of examinations, have said quite emphatically that in attaching itself to purely internal criteria for the activity and judgment of students, the university blinds itself and society to the role it plays. The objectivity of examinations also represents a refusal to question the selection made by society itself and the social roots of a mode of knowledge and expression.

The university does not strengthen the bourgeoisie's economic power; but it does strengthen its hold over society. It covers social relations with a solid veneer of ideas. It resists whatever is practical, whatever sheds light on the internal unity and relativity of a type of society, judgment, or taste. It operates more willingly in general ideas than in experience. This concept of culture cannot be separated from society's class structure. The paradox is that while it propounds the eminence and rights of disinterested thought, the university is more loyal to the opposition between servile technique and noble thought characteristic of a class society.

There is much less class content in scientific activity, which is in most direct control of technical progress and therefore of the power of the ruling classes, than in studies that have no practical consequences for society but tend to make sacred the status quo and, above all, the heritage of the past. Classical letters is an example with the clarity of a caricature. While a minority of teachers in this area is engaged in the difficult technical and scientific work that is based on what others call, in a revealing way, para-sciences, such as epigraphy, archeology, or numismatics, the majority clings to studying Greek and Roman civiliza-tions, not as societies or cultures that can be studied with the aid of general methods, but as the origin, perhaps the best of our own civilization. The bulletin of the So-ciété des Professeurs de Langues Anciennes contains more ideology than the tracts of the March 22 Movement. The defense of Latin and its place in French education has nothing to do with scientific interest in this area of studies; it is the defense of a class culture used to combat technical and experimental studies judged to be inferior.

The French university does not attempt—as did for a long time the great English universities or the Ecole Libre des Sciences Politiques, created in imitation of British institutions—to turn out gentlemen but, by giving prefer-ence to transmitted culture over acquired and practiced culture, it remains faithful to the division of a society into two classes, one of which assures the subsistence of the whole, while the other devotes itself to leisure, to general ideas, to the culture that remains when all is forgotten and which thus is only the cultural mark of a superior so-cial milieu.

This cultural conservatism does not contradict the uni-versity's role in social advancement. Up to the time of the massive increase in the number of students and teachers, one of the essential features of the university was the link between secondary and university education, between the *lycée* and the faculty. This link was affirmed and strengthened by the role of the *agrégation*, the competitive examination for recruitment to secondary teaching, which is also the door to university teaching.* Even today, most of the *assistants* and *maîtres-assistants*, not to speak of the professors, in the faculties of letters are *agrégés* who earn considerably more than their colleagues who are not *agrégés* and who embarked on their university career with a doctorate of the third cycle. In their speeches, the Société des Agrégés always emphasizes the social justice of the examinations and the protection they afford against nepotism and local pressures. This is not a false assertion, and there is no doubt about the effort or quality that such an examination demands. But that is not the problem. The *agrégation* forces people and forms of knowledge to correspond to a social codification of knowledge, not to the movement or needs of knowledge itself. The recruitment examinations assure the transmission of culture and their conservative role is even more effective because it is seriously practiced and opens participation, not to the sons of the upper middle class, who are destined to engage in managerial economic and social activities, but to the sons of the lower middle class; and it allows new generations to be trained in a spirit that corresponds to the cultural forms of an unquestionable class society.

This conservative role of the university gives it a certain

* The *agrégation* was created during the nineteenth century, when the *lycées* formed the real center of Napoleon's concept of the university. Today, most university professors obtain the *agrégation* before preparing a state doctorate. The third cycle doctorate, on a lower level than the state doctorate, makes possible recruitment of university professors without the *agrégation*. The Société des Agrégés is a powerful lobby which defends its own professional interests, as well as a (generally) conservative view of the university.

autonomy and even causes it to develop a certain hostility in regard to the ruling class. The faculties of law and
medicine have been the antechambers of liberal professions directly linked to the bourgeoisie. The faculties that
train teachers are often bitterly frustrated by their medio-
cre social position and the opposition to the business middle class. The State, as both the political expression of a
ruling class and the instrument of national integration
and expression of those interests excluded or insufficiently
represented in the parliament accounts for this. An attachment to secularity in education, to Jacobin principles of
national unity as opposed to traditions and private interests, was long at the center of this attitude of limited
opposition.

The image just presented of the university and its place
in society still corresponds in part to today's reality; but if
we only consider this image, we condemn ourselves to not
understanding the raison d'être of the student movement.

The increase in the number of students and the relative
falling-off of classical studies tended to destroy the foundations of the bourgeois university. Not without justification do the most conservative professors complain that the
level of their students is lower. Certain cultural forms,
certain modes of expression are indeed in decline. Students arrive with less and less inherited culture, even when
they come from well-to-do families. What the family
gives them is less important than what they get from mass
communications and their peers. Above all, the role of
the university has been profoundly modified by the economic changes that have taken place in French society
in the last twenty years. The university is not so much
archaic as it is torn by its internal organization, the new
state of society, and new social forces.

The number of students is increasing, and the outlets
available to them are changing at the same time. A rapidly growing percentage of students is called on to work

in closer contact with economic activity; whether they enter large organizations at the middle or upper level, or work in public or private research departments or technical services, they are associated with economic and social decisions. For years, business executives and administrators have been trying to orient law and liberal arts students toward these outlets for which they are unprepared. The university's isolation, its exclusive dependence on a State that both dominates and protects it, is under attack. That is why, instead of leveling their criticism only at the archaism of the traditional university, many students attack the economic and social organizations and the roles they are invited to play in them. Students in the social sciences rebel against the idea of becoming manipulators for large business organizations of the social policy of the State.

Their refusal is strengthened by the contradiction they perceive between an objective, academic education and the tasks to which they feel fated. Whence their resentment of the false consciousness betrayed by academics who are unwilling to understand the social use that is made of the knowledge they transmit. Like any refusal to adapt to a given state of society, this attitude combats the present on the basis of both the past and the future. In opposition to an "empiricism" considered to be the naïve acceptance of a given state of society, accepted as a natural fact instead of being criticized and rehabilitated in its social reality, it invokes both a defense of the philosophical tradition in the social sciences and the desire for a more rigorous, scientific analysis that does not separate concrete knowledge from a critical sociology of knowledge. The attack against the bourgeois university is related then to the submission of education to the influence of the new ruling class and the great combines of production, organization, and management that ensure its power.

The influence that is denounced is neither as complete

nor as direct as some claim. If it were, the technocrats would be less attached to a profound reform of the university. The university does not meet the needs of the large organizations. What should be brought into question even more is the university's inability to resist the pressures of business and of the administration with the critical force of scientific work. If the university gave a stronger position to the social sciences, it could have a liberating influence. But the university does not arm the future manager, technician, or expert with either enough scientific knowledge to oppose the pseudo-rationality of the rulers or a critical training deliberately oriented toward the problems of the contemporary world. It sins more by omission than by commission.

The student movement's struggle against a dominant class or social order is never a face-to-face battle. The university that it attacks is neither in the service of the old bourgeoisie nor in the service of the new; but it fails in both its scientific and social function. Its "abstraction" and "impartiality" irritate the rulers, but even more provoke revolt among those who legitimately expect the university to fulfill its role—which is to analyze the special nature and the limits of all forms of social and cultural life.

What unites the two aspects of the student struggle against the university is the feeling that the university is not free because it is not militant. It should question its own social determinations; but its consistent inability to welcome the newest movements in thought and research make it a subordinate element of the social system. Because it is incapable of looking beyond its own crisis, it can only open itself to external demands instead of maintaining an intellectual and cultural initiative that would allow it to free itself from certain pressures, or at least to take conscious, responsible choices within society. The university sins by default. Its silence satisfies only those academics who call liberty merely the defense of their corporate self-interest.

In contrast to this dependence, the democratization of teaching and the weakening of middle-class control of the university can only result in two distinct but allied operations: first, a strong influence of social values over the socialization of individuals, which alone can lessen the inequality transmitted by family and geographical background; second, almost contrarily, a nonauthoritarian pedagogical relationship. This supposes that the transmission of knowledge or manners of thinking receives less emphasis than training for change and adaptability to new developments. Some educational systems have democratic recruitment programs along with authoritarian teaching methods; others have the opposite.

The French university system has run aground in both areas. The social hierarchy of teaching is very distinct, if only because of the distinctions among the schools and faculties. Pedagogical relationships are authoritarian, less because of the wish of the teachers than because of the weakness of an institution separated from research facilities and condemned to the use of huge lecture halls. Traditionally, the French school wished to be an instrument of social equality while using an authoritarian style of training. Authoritarianism has been weakened rather than replaced by another relationship. Recruitment is not democratic since it reflects or increases social inequalities. The university's crisis is that it is a society of privileges and is incapable of moving ahead either of the two facets of its democratization.

The Retreat

All these criticisms point to a simple theme: the crisis of the university. We must not measure the real univer-

sity against some ideal university—an antisociety in the
service of people and pure science, uninvolved in the actual, existing social order; or a political instrument for
the creation of a new society. Such comparisons are natural for a student movement and add the strength of creative utopianism; but analysis cannot be satisfied by meas-
uring reality against an ideal.

We have said enough about why the university was
dependent. Now we can attempt to understand its inability to combat its dependence and to involve itself in the
existing social organization. If, over the past few years,
the university system had fulfilled any important social
functions, it might have had some capacity for resistance
or dialogue. The ease with which it crumbled in May–
June clearly indicates that it was in crisis, withdrawn
within itself, and disorganized by the changes it was experiencing. How can we define this crisis and this withdrawal?

A university answers certain basic needs of a given
society. It gives professional training to future doctors,
administrators, and teachers; it is a center of scientific and
intellectual creativity; it develops models of knowledge
and thought. It also prepares a certain social elite, a good
number of those who will hold positions of leadership. Its
two basic tasks—intellectual research and social formation
—are both interconnected and at odds with each other.
Universities of different types can be defined according to
the varying relationships between these tasks. A university
will experience a crisis when it is unable to work out or
maintain its specific style of combining these two tasks
and instead turns in on itself and its own operation. In
such a case, it is incapable of fulfilling any social function
beyond purely professional training. Various types of universities fulfill, in one way or another, part or all of these
basic tasks.

a) Liberal universities, in the full sense of the term,

are those which fulfill their social function well enough
so that the governing social and political forces allow
them the independence of movement necessary for their
intellectually productive activity. These universities can
take advantage of this independence in order to allow
their members a certain margin of criticism considered
tolerable by the established order. The great Anglo-Saxon
universities, such as Harvard (the most prestigious of
them) , belong to this type. They are both great centers of
intellectual productivity and centers of freedom, in the
sense of tolerance. This tolerance covers only individual
deviations; it is not at all prepared to accept basic questioning of the system to which the university belongs.
The members of these universities are told: "You are
privileged members of society with fewer obligations than
people involved in the economy. However, you have more
duties which you must spontaneously fulfill; you must
voluntarily respect certain bounds which you transgress
under pain of losing society's confidence and, consequently, the independence allowed you."

b) Other universities experience more or less open
conflict between their social role and their scientific function. The essence of this scientific function may be considered the formation of social elites. As a result, the
university's intellectually innovative role is diminished.
Because society cannot do without scientific creativity,
however, it frequently assigns this role to research institutions whose members are freed from many of the constraints that weigh on university professors, on condition
that they comport themselves as pure scientists or technicians. This is why, in Soviet-type societies, stronger political control is exercised over the university than over the
academy of science, which plays the more important role
in scientific research.

c) Sometimes a university affirms itself primarily as a
force for intellectual productivity. To be able to refuse to

collaborate with the Establishment, it must fight it and put itself at the service of forces and movements of social transformation. This is the situation of the best Latin American universities.

Although we can give only a very summary explanation, we can state that each of these three general situations corresponds to a particular situation in the socially dominant class: in the first case, it matches a dynamic and expanding dominant class; the second fits a dominant class that is stabilized; the third, a dominant class in crisis. In all these cases, however, the university is fulfilling its social function. Even if it is the scene of violent conflicts between its social and intellectual functions, it is not in crisis if its organization and activity correspond to its role in society. Crisis appears when the university, incapable of bearing the tensions necessary to its operation, flees them and defines itself neither in terms of social forces nor of its intellectual creativity, but solely in terms of its own internal principles and needs, its rules and traditions. It then becomes a bureaucracy.

The French university system does not use science to combat power based on heritage and tradition; neither is it a training school for the social elite; and finally, it does not enjoy the ambiguous independence of the very liberal universities. The result is that it is in crisis.

a) The organization set up by the reformers of the end of the nineteenth century was first of all destroyed by the pressure of those who demanded new conceptions and programs. The professors wish to maintain their traditional role by presenting the most recent work in their particular disciplines. They address their students as future researchers. The gap between what the professor expects of the student and what the student expects of the professor grows wider and wider. In some cases, the teachers chose to adapt to their public. At Nanterre, the geography department was the most successful example of such adaptation, under the influence of a department head who gave considerable time to the professional training of the students. This pressure to transform the university into a training school is felt most of all in the provinces. Many students hold posts as teaching *assistants;* they have little time to attend the university, which functions more actively on Thursdays (when there is no elementary or high school) than other days, as a result. Under these conditions, even if the professors are frequently absent, a certain balance is achieved which resembles more a North American "college" than a university. Research is not carried out on a university level. Courses resemble those of a good secondary school, demanding little initiative of the students but giving them serious professional training that corresponds not to the needs of learning but, at least, to the demands of teacher recruitment programs.

The first aspect of the crisis is the reduction of the university's scientific function to professional training. This leads to extreme specialization with the result that current thought and research cannot penetrate this compartmentalized universe. A Greek scholar will have no knowledge of the ethnologist's work; an historian will be almost completely ignorant of modern sociology and economics; the sociologist will know nothing of the methods of biology, not to speak of his ignorance, now made official by the recent reforms, of the history of the societies he studies. Not everyone accepts this professional specialization. Some look outside their university training for the openness of mind and variety of information their faculty refuses them. Literary and political reviews, weekly news magazines, or still better, groups of political or religious inspiration complete the professional training given by the university. This creates a profound division among elements of education which ought to be unified.

b) This concentration on professional training pushes aside the university's role of forming elites. They are less and less formed by the university. The Ecole Nationale d'Administration and the Ecole Polytechnique, not the faculties of law and economics, train those who are in charge of economic management. The Ecole Normale Supérieure has been attached to the University of Paris since 1905 but this connection is quite fictional. The best young physicists have arranged to be exempted from university graduation. A growing number of students at the Ecole Normale in all disciplines consider graduation a necessary drudgery, a rite of passage after which they turn their back on the career it was supposed to open. French teachers, who used to oppose an elite of knowledge to the elite of wealth, respond to the loss of their scientific role by turning inward to defend their professional special interests.

In this way, a bureaucratic system is formed whose norms seek to maintain the system, not to adapt it to the demands of its environment. As these demands change, the norms become more rigorous, exacting, strict—and pointless. The best-known example has to do with the doctoral thesis in letters. Obtaining a professorship is governed, in France as in most countries, by acquiring a doctorate. The doctorate in letters has fulfilled this purpose well; it would be absurd to despise the collection of doctoral theses, among which there are many illustrious works. That is not the problem. The increase in the number of students entails an increase in the number of teachers. The corps of professors has responded to this beneficial development not by expanding but by seeking to maintain its status quo. This creates a deeper and deeper division between professors and *assistants*. It is no accident that the number of State theses defended in the past few years is no higher than it was in 1913. The preservation of this oligarchical body has been implemented by a concentration of power that gives sole responsibility for almost all theses to professors at the Sorbonne. The professors are crushed by this task, but they refuse to give it up. Since the offer of professorial chairs is artificially maintained at a low level while the demand increases rapidly, doctoral candidates are dismayed at the rising price of the thesis. They must work harder and harder while the direction of their theses becomes increasingly superficial, since few professors can truly direct or assist their too numerous candidates.

The proportion of those who abandon the effort is rapidly increasing. Above all, the thesis, the certificate of aptitude for advanced research, absolutely loses this functional role and becomes simply a means of selection. It sterilizes many good minds who are locked, until the middle of their active life, in a situation of apprenticeship and dependence. It is superficial to blame the regulations or the perversity of the judges or the candidates. If the thesis does not answer the most evident needs (the number of accepted theses is lower than the number of professors who retire), the reason is that it is tied to maintaining a "corps." By statically maintaining the category of professorial chairs and limiting access to professorships by personal title, partly for paltry economies and partly to support the famous, the administration has strongly encouraged a process which has gradually transformed men of knowledge into men of power.

c) Thus, a new balance is created: the university insures professional training and defends its own professional autonomy. But such a balance could exist only if teachers and students accepted its limitations. They do. Students (for whom their studies are a means to promotion within the teaching profession in which they are already engaged), and *assistants*, or *maîtres-assistants*, pursuing in their faculty a career often begun in the secondary schools, work diligently and effectively in the faculties on condition that these are of reasonable size and are kept away from the agitation and questioning of the intellectual world, especially in Paris.

We must not underestimate the importance of the university's professional success but we must stress the two quite different types of frustration that it entails. On the one hand, the university fulfills its professional role badly wherever its quarters and environment are notoriously insufficient. If the increase in the number of students has restored life to many provincial faculties, it has swamped the Paris faculties. A lecture course given to fifty or eighty students does not arouse initiative and active participation on their part, but it can transmit some knowledge. Given to an auditorium filled with 500 or 1,000 students, a lecture course is a poor show which can be advantageously replaced by a hurried reading of the mimeographed lectures after Easter. As the faculties become more professionally specialized, they also lose their differentiation. Neither teachers nor students know what is expected of them. The faculties are simultaneously the Ecole Polytechnique, a secondary-school class, and the Université des Annales (a series of lectures, unconnected with the university, attended by the upper middle class). This makes impossible the pedagogical training of future teachers and the clinical training of future physicians. There is no true apprenticeship and hence no communication between teacher and student.

The second and more important frustration is that the university, reduced to this role of passing on professional knowledge, does not create a strong sense of belonging in the best students and teachers. Some professors, like Georges Gusdorf, have reacted against the university's professional specialization by turning backward toward societies in which on-the-job apprenticeship was the essential element of professional training and the university treated only great ideas and lofty culture. This dichotomy directly expresses the opposition between social classes: servile work and noble thought. But many others are less ideological and their attachment to literary discourse is only a reaction against the impotence of the university which has shown itself incapable of elaborating a new "general culture." Here the crisis exhibits its most serious aspects. One speaks vaguely about interdisciplinary works and restores elements of the common tradition. But it is more a matter of a kaleidoscopic juxtaposition than of moving beyond old objects of study for the benefit of new methods of thought. Most often, professors do not adapt to this crisis situation and, in the case of the literary and economic disciplines, seek to safeguard their taste for research outside their faculties. Their university post becomes only a task—one could almost say a benefice in the sense of the *Ancien Régime*—which they carry out more or less conscientiously but to which they do not dedicate the best of themselves.

For his part, the student does not find in the university a living culture, a true apprenticeship, the feeling of participating in the movement of ideas and research. As a result, the university is dominated by an imbalance between what it is supposed to be and what it is, between the efforts of those who are part of it and their experience of it. It is a particularly great imbalance for the beginning students and the young *assistants,* groups which reacted in an especially active way to the breakdown of May. The student is more and more reduced to the absorption, not of knowledge, but of programs or subjects for examination. He has no way to indicate what interests him, to show what he knows, to choose quite diverse and free activities in order to prove himself. All he expects from the university is his diploma, all the more a mockery since it only opens the way to employment with increasing difficulty. The student world becomes a world of silence, formed of conformism or rejection. Teachers caught up in the crisis retreat into a defensive posture.

The S.N.E.Sup., until a recent change in leadership, was different from the independent unions only because it was more insistent in its criticism of the State. The other unions were content with more immediate corporate defense. This was more satisfactory to the higher ranking teachers, tenured professors, and conference supervisors. Union actions were consistently conservative and more nourished by resentment than by a desire for change. They were progressively less able to respond to the discontent of the young teachers, *assistants,* or *maîtres-assistants,* who were formed in new ways and had not passed along the privileged and conformist path of university licensing (*agrégation*), or of the professors and conference masters lately arrived in the faculties after long work in the C.N.R.S. or the large establishments of higher education. The principles that had long nourished the union activity of teachers on all levels—lay control of education and defense of the State against those who hold privileges of money and birth—had long since lost their power. As the material crisis grew, the institution became weaker, increasingly more alien to those who lived in it, accommodated themselves to it, supported it, or called for its transformation.

Many teachers are of two minds concerning their profession: on one hand, they feel bitterness, resentment, or despair because of the crisis; on the other, they have a strong attachment to the forms of professional life, especially to the manner of recruiting teachers by means of the university degree and thesis. They defend these not because they conform with the needs of teaching or research but because of their excellence as mechanisms for selection. Having been deprived of any clear social function, the university no longer defines itself as a group and profession attached to what confers on it its rights and nobil-

ity. The students, outsiders in terms of the teaching profession, become outsiders in terms of the university as well.
It is not a social milieu for them but merely a professional
activity or a student—but not a university—community.

There are then two themes which may seem to be opposed but are actually complementary: the university dependent on the forces governing society and the university
in crisis. Its diminution to the level of a professional school
insures its subjection to the new technocratic power.
While this power works out an over-all conception of society and its organization, the new producers, technicians,
middle-level managers, and experts receive only a piece-
meal training which leaves them dependent. The retreat
of the university community to traditions, principles of
organization, and specific and limited interests leads it to
maintain the cultural forms of an older bourgeois society.
The university lower middle class comes to the aid of the
upper middle class and the State in a way that corresponds
to a by-passed era of social evolution that is under attack
by the new economic and political rulers. The more the
university declares itself independent, disinterested, and
uninvolved in debates and conflicts, the more it insures
the change from the old to the new ruling classes. Its own
crisis is the price it pays. It behaves as if its proclaimed
liberalism disorganized the forces of criticism and opposition, which only makes them turn against the university
itself, since they can neither be led nor fortified by it.

Growth and Impotence

The crisis we have just analyzed is manifested by inability to deal with change—which means that change was
neither forbidden nor blocked. In May, some spoke of the
Malthusianism of the university. Few reproaches are less
well founded, since they are talking to a country which

has brought into its institutions of higher education a much higher proportion of its young people between twenty and twenty-five than its neighbors, Great Britain particularly. If we take into account only full-time students, the rate of school attendance in French higher education is comparable to that of the Soviet Union. Since a high proportion of the sons of the better-off social groups has long received higher education, this increase comes partly from the access of new social groups to higher education and partly from the rapid increase in the number of women students. Every economic transformation and modification of employment causes a movement of social mobility independent of the social regime and of political choices. This common current of social mobility explains why France, Italy, or Great Britain have rates of social mobility comparable to the United States. This contradicts certain widespread images but has been clearly demonstrated by Seymour Martin Lipset and Reinhard Bendix in *Social Mobility in Industrial Society* (1959). Nevertheless, if we press the analysis further, we find important differences among societies. The most notable trait of French society on the whole is that while it has strong upward mobility, it has weak downward mobility. Upper-level families keep their children from moving downward, support them for long periods while they are students, and find a "place" for them by appealing to their connections.

Maintaining or reinforcing social status determines one type of social mobility; gradual upward movement over two or three generations defines another; the formation of new elites from the lower classes is a third type, characteristic of the socialist countries. In France, the increase in the number of university students is due more to the fact that higher studies have become general among the privileged, whose importance has increased, than to a transformation of the social origin of workers and lower level officials accomplished by means of higher studies.

The growth of the university resembles that of the winter sports centers: the numbers of the clientele increase much more quickly than does its democratization. The research of the Centre de Sociologie Européenne expresses this fact more precisely: because the number of children of the prosperous classes who reach higher education has increased more rapidly in recent years than has the number of children from the lower classes who reach it, social inequality in this area has increased rather than decreased. Such facts have led some observers to say that the demand of the U.N.E.F. (Union Nationale des Etudiants de France) for a pre-salary for students would result in an important redistribution of national revenues in favor of the well-off, a veritable reverse welfare program.

The direction of changes is even more important than their volume. While the most pressing needs demand a rapid increase of graduates in the sciences, it is the faculties of letters that develop most rapidly. Even today, we observe a noticeable decrease in the number of candidates for the baccalaureate in the sciences. Both the difficulty and the lack of careful planning of the science programs demonstrate society's inability to recognize the place of science and technology in its culture. We act as if scientists were either geniuses or mechanics inclined toward tinkering and the concrete, while those in the liberal arts, which insure that society will have its critics, are both normal and noble.

Quite simply, the flow of students toward the faculties of letters is the direct consequence of the university organization's failure to adapt to a growing demand. In these faculties, a superficial adaptation on the part of the student, sufficient to get by, is very easy. These studies are reputed to be easy and in general not to require any very specific basic knowledge. Badly prepared and badly oriented students take refuge in them. This flow of students to the literary programs is not in itself abnormal; it becomes so only because the university system maintains strictly limited categories and the students must split themselves into sections which directly correspond to the secondary school curriculum. The importance and pressure of the entrance examinations lead a considerable number of students on dead-end paths. If instead of maintaining the traditional divisions—French, living languages, sociology, history, etc.—we attempted to organize education around major analytical themes—language, personality, development, decision-making groups, planning—we would form students capable of apprehending vast areas of intellectual and professional activity. They would have both more varied outlets and a greater capacity to perform as active citizens.

What is most striking in the recent history of the university system is that French society has no interest in the problems raised by its transformation. The parliamentary debates on these questions have often been terribly poor; the debate on the censure motion of May 1968, did not let this astonishing tradition down. Neither the government nor the opposition was ever able to express itself except in numbers. For the former, the growth was admirable; for the latter, insufficient. They spoke often of money and square feet, almost never of pedagogy or employment, much less of the role of the university system or of the general culture needed in our society. This lack of perception of the changes in the university system is nothing extraordinary. French society has not been conscious of its own changes for twenty years. After the short period of the Liberation, political life dissociated itself from economic evolution and its social consequences. For long years, the majority of workers, whose standard of living was steadily rising, felt a nostalgia for the good prewar years which matched a representation of the facts that was on the whole false. In the same way, as Alain Girard has shown, the demographic renewal has been accompanied by ideas about ideal family size that are totally removed from practice.

While the political opposition was increasingly locked into a defense of the "little people"—to the point that the Communist Party, eager to defend artisans and small merchants against the great monopolies, at the beginning felt some weakness for Poujadism *—economic progress was managed by high-level officials, a few business leaders, and a few politicians. Political life was dominated by the liquidation of the past, the colonial empire, and archaic forms of economic organization. In the midst of these conditions, French society showed itself particularly incapable of implementing new forms of social organization. While economic production was developing, the production of social goods continued to clash with economic or social forces that the political power had no will and the administrative organization had no capacity to overcome. Despite the intentions of Pierre Massé and his collaborators on the Plan, social equipment remained the weak point of French society. Production and individual consumption increased, accompanied by growing inequalities in the distribution of the products of this growth. Collective equipment—dwellings, schools, hospitals—not only increased less quickly but was scarcely modernized at all. The backwardness of the schools is certainly not the most scandalous example.

The centralized State is often accused of being mainly responsible for this incapacity of French society to transform itself and for the crises that result from the bond between a modernized economy and a society that has remained archaic. This accusation is particularly justified in the area of national education, for the simple reason that the field of State intervention is immense and that

* A movement led by Pierre Poujade in the Fifties. A defense of small shopkeepers and craftsmen threatened by economic concentration, Poujadism had some fascist fringes but was rapidly defeated.

this intervention frequently takes the form of direct management. But this is a description rather than an explanation and it is incomplete even as a description.

The French State is strong, centralized, and rigid, but also weak and colonized by private interests. The so-called guardian ministries are really ministries that belong to their clientele. For a long time, the social ministries have been merely defenders of the narrowest corporate interests. The ministries of Health or National Education were not very different in this regard from the Veterans ministry, which is the perfect example of an administration reduced to the role of spokesman for pressure groups in government councils. It would be false to say that the centralization of the Ministry of National Education slowed down reforms demanded by the interested parties. Its role was often the opposite; it favored progress during the slow, difficult bypassing of the social barrier which separated primary and secondary education. Its role in higher education has always been very limited: it administers, it does not organize, still less does it make decisions. From time to time, commissions made up of university representatives and administrators examine certain reform proposals but the former's esprit de corps and the latter's exclusive interests in texts and rules cooperate to keep changes to a minimum. Everything that touches the university system and should be the subject of public debate has always been dealt with in the discreet shadow of bureaucratic and corporate meetings. The only possible result was to strengthen the influence of the powerful and render profound change more and more difficult.

The French State plays two roles. First, with power and *grandeur,* it insures the growth of the capitalist economy, which presupposes growth, coming to take the place of the weakened stimulant of private profit. Second, it permits some integration of social grievances by means of negotiations with representatives of the large social groups. The difference between these two faces of the State is clearly indicated by the differences between the economic and the social administrative agencies in influence, quality, and even in the remuneration of their administrators. While the ruling class is renewing itself, none of the lower classes gets close to power. The working class is practically excluded from politics and the Communist Party is forced simultaneously to reject society and to defend limited social demands within it. The rise in living standards increased society's capacity for integration and hence temporarily weakened the opposition forces that the May Movement, for the first time in a long while, remodeled and revived.

The State has not been a brake on change. It has simultaneously insured growth and held back social transformation, not so much because it was rigid and centralized; but because the new social forces had transformed it. It was occupied only in absorbing old forces and was deprived of the capacity to change society. In terms of the university system, the State restored life to scientific research, created the Ecole Nationale d'Administration, etc., and at the same time let the faculties bury themselves in their crisis. It served the elites well and was concerned only with absorbing the masses.

A Politically Undifferentiated Reformism

In the absence of political debate on the university system, the spirit of reform came both from modernist sectors of the administration and from some sections of the university itself. In the spirit of the plan, some economists asked that the elementary conditions for planning and decision-making be set up in the area of education. Since the scientific groups had to choose and manage increasingly heavy investments, they were aware of the ineffi-

ciency of the university machine. The movement launched
by the Association pour l'Expansion de la Recherche Scientifique, led by André Lichnérowicz and J. Crémieux
Brilhac, was the principal instrument for the modernization effort. The meetings (attended mainly by natural
scientists) at Caen in 1967 and at Amiens in 1968, were
spectacular demonstrations of this criticism of the university system, denouncing its archaism, its inefficiency, its
distrust of rational, scientific analysis of problems of employment, pedagogy, and management.

The May Movement often strongly condemned the
Caen Conference and the movement that occasioned it, all
the more vigorously because the government had shown
sympathy for its efforts. This condemnation must be analyzed, just as the Caen Conference must be placed in its
proper context.

The real question is the role of technocrats in contemporary French society. As a rising dominant class combating the resistance of the old economic and social
powers, with the leftist opposition either disorganized or
in the midst of a difficult adjustment to a social situation
very different from the one that had occasioned the beginnings of the workers' parties and the unions, the technocrats have often been more liberal than authoritarian,
especially when their tasks involved study rather than
management. These modernizers met university people,
generally from the scientific disciplines, who wished to re-
organize the university system. Their practical projects
could rest on a technocratic conception equally as well as
on absolutely opposed social and political attitudes.

At the time of the Caen Conference, the theme of university reform was purely intellectual and professional.
Based neither on a social movement nor a political party,
the reform movement drew its strength from the simple
evidence of the facts. This means that while it could become involved in technocratic moves, the idea of modern-

ization was still politically neutral. The conference brought problems to light and in many cases merely asked that organizational methods acknowledge changes that had already been made or were in the process of being made. The physicists or biologists who asked for the organization of their faculties by department based their requests on changes they had already begun to introduce in the faculty of science. When they asked for the autonomy of the faculties, they could invoke, on the one hand, the necessity for a more flexible and businesslike management of certain investments and, on the other hand, the usefulness of recognizing real differences and disparities among the faculties. Everyone knows that no research program or laboratory can be administered according to the official methods of the administration. The proof of it is the multiplication of non-profit associations set up according to a 1901 law, which the university uses to evade the slow and difficult management of funds in official administrative channels.

This approach, emphasizing practicality rather than theory, was limited in two ways. For one thing, it could act only through persuasion and, given the resistance it met, had very limited effectiveness. In particular, the faculties of letters, whose reform was the most urgent, were hardly represented at Caen and their reaction was most reserved. Secondly, even if the reformers at Caen had had a free hand, they would soon have had to make a choice among a number of objectives that were still somewhat confused at that time when criticism of the university system's archaic structure was the principal concern. Some of their alternatives would have been: adjustment to the needs of society or working out new cultural models; modernization of the university system in view of the state of society or transformation of the university; selection or more active participation in knowledge. These oppositions could only veer farther and farther apart as the chances and progress of reform became more definite. But at the time of the Caen Conference, the problems still lacked political clarification. The proof is that the men who participated in this work or recognized its importance adopted quite diverse attitudes toward the May Movement. To be more precise, at the time the Conference was held, there were two paths open. The one chosen by the Conference organizers consisted in deconcentrating the power of decision-making and returning to the university community the capacity and will to work out responsible polities. The other consisted of reacting against the weakness of the central administration and setting it in order. This course was followed with considerable vigor by the secretary-general of the Ministry of National Education, who had undertaken an analogous task at the Ministry of Labor. In my opinion, the position taken by the reformers at Caen corresponded better to the need for change in the university system than did an effort centered on reordering and strengthening the central administration.

The Caen Conference opened a path which made it possible to avoid the contradictions experienced by the 1959 reform of medical studies which had been introduced by the central authority, occasioning a direct conflict between the administration and the medical profession. Beyond any doubt, the former was basically correct but this advantage was erased by the fact that it imposed administrative methods and professional situations and careers which suffered from all the evils imposed on the whole university system and, indeed, on public service in general. As a result, the administration took on responsibilities it could not really fulfill, being too rigidly bureaucratic to single-handedly bring about change and flexibility. The student movement was right about the facts in its criticism of the Caen Conference, sinie it was revolt and

confrontation, not a spirit of reform, that opened the
way to modernization as well as a more profound questioning of the function of the university system. But many
of the proposals made at Caen were repeated in the May–
June assemblies. Nothing would be more arbitrary than to
imagine that these are two entirely contradictory conceptions of the university system.

The idea of the modern university is as ambiguous as
the idea of the worker aristocracy has always been. Indeed,
this latter group sparked the worker movement but in
isolation it easily falls into corporatism and social integration. It played its central role only in union with the
unskilled and exploited masses who were closer to revolt than to a desire for social modernization. Likewise,
the currents in the university system favorable to the
Caen Conference were able, when the student reform
movement broke out, either to help it deepen into a
movement for social and political transformation, or to
reject union with it and rigidify into technocratic elitism.

At the outset, the Caen Conference and the student
movement struggled against the same university crisis.
But the modernizers were necessarily divided by their
experience of the movement. A modernized university
system strengthens the authority of the new managers of
research and of departments, and this authority can be
put at the service of science and of opposition to social
domination. It can also be exercised in favor of strengthening structures and personal power and can come into
conflict with a movement of mass opposition based on
students and researchers. The alliance or opposition between university modernization and student opposition
became wider or narrower according to variations in the
political situation. Before May, the burden of archaism
and the university crisis was so great that the Caen and
Amiens conferences constituted the first and still politi-

cally neutral phase of a breakdown that became important only when it was prolonged and transformed by student confrontation.

When some university officials sought to head off the crisis by creating conditions favorable for scientific work without a direct social criticism of the university system, some students followed a complementary course that was equally limited and ambiguous. They directly questioned the pedagogical relationship. Nourished on the teachings of social psychology, they appealed to the virtues of non-directive leadership and to the necessity of replacing the auditorium and the lecture—obstacles to communication —with work groups in which student participation was to be as active as possible. In reality, there are two confused currents of thought behind these general plans. The first is a search for participation in work which runs into the same limitations as analogous programs in business and industry; it amounts to making the channels of communication more effective and favoring social integration by avoiding questioning of the social finality of the changes and activities to which one is to adapt. The second current of thought looks for the active destruction of authority, the elimination of the problems that are part of the institution, and the acquisition and transmission of knowledge for the benefit of strengthening primary groups, which could federate with one another but which find their satisfaction only in their own existence. Individuals would be defined by their personal needs and by belonging to the group, not by their work and social situation. In neither case is critical analysis of the institution really even begun.

Thus the university tended to come out of the crisis and confusion by breaking itself apart. On one side, the professors turned away from teaching to dedicate themselves to research. The distinction between the Bachelor's degree and the Master's introduced into the Fouchet Plan by the university representatives indicates this tendency. On the other side, the students retreat into themselves, their milieu, and their primary groups. The relationship between teacher and student is broken; it exists only at the moment of the examination, as a relationship of authority, not of effort. This authority was to be attacked in May and a great number of professors would not even try to defend it.

The university system—especially the faculties of letters —was in a real crisis, possessing only a low-level equilibrium as professional schools only serving teachers. A cultural conservatory, an inefficient, archaic machine, it did not appear capable of transforming itself. As a result, it contributed to maintaining the ethos of the bourgeoisie at the same time as it seemed to offer itself without defense to the reform projects of the modernizing technocrats. The student movement revolted against an institution which did not respond to any expectation, whose meaninglessness could no longer arouse loyalty. But it went farther than this: discovering the great conflicts and hence the profound nature of our society by other means than merely the university experience, it brought the university out of the shadows and revealed the negative role it was playing. The university did not wish to serve the bourgeoisie but, by resisting the student movement, it acted, in violation of its conscience and habits, as a bourgeois university.

III

❦❦❦❦❦❦❦❦❦❦

The "Enragés"
of Nanterre

In 1967, the French university system was not static. While it jealously guarded its organization, methods, and traditions, it was also growing rapidly. As a result, it faced the necessity of changing itself. The faculties of letters were the weakest part of the whole structure. The size of their classes, their attachment to opportunities found almost uniquely in teaching itself, their role in transmitting opinions, ideas, and tastes, all kept them from transforming themselves and changed their growth into crisis. The student movement was in equal disarray; when the university crisis exploded, the U.N.E.F. did not even have a president.

The new student movement was not born at the Sorbonne where it was overwhelmed by the massive size and impotence of the institution, even though the "little groups" were stronger there than at Nanterre. It was born at this new, hastily organized faculty where a tired system found itself weakened rather than revived by a liberal spirit which was more able to restore tolerance than to achieve reform. After the failure of a purely university strike and a series of incidents in early 1968, a movement —later called the March 22 Movement—was formed. Within a few weeks, it acquired wide influence, disorganized the faculty, and either outflanked or absorbed the political sects. Directly influenced by the German S.D.S. (Sozialistischer Deutscher Studentenbund), it was almost its diametric opposite, being nontheoretical and unorganized. It was not up against the strong resistance of an authoritarian organization; indeed, it easily overturned a stupefied and scandalized faculty. When the Nanterre campus was closed for the second time on May 2—the day before the entrance of the police into the Sorbonne inaugurated street fighting—this movement had created and was leading a decisive social force in the week that led up to the Night of the Barricades. What is the explanation of this astonishing success, unforeseen by the majority of professors who, until the final days, remained convinced that the disorder could be ended by getting rid of "ten of these madmen"?

At Nanterre, there was neither combat nor negotiation, just the crumbling of a house that had grown old despite its new walls. The movement did not have to wage long ideological battles or fight against sanctions. Nor was it absorbed in internal struggles. All it did was show that the emperor wore no clothes. The ease of its success might also have been its weakness. Until May 2, it had scarcely gained any influence outside Nanterre. Only the police intervention on May 3 transformed this limited agitation into a mass movement. But when Nanterre was closed and the militants had to move their activity to Paris— which is what they wanted—the movement, whose effectiveness in the following weeks was to move far beyond the influence of the students of the March 22 Movement, was already established. Its three elements—student revolt, struggle against the administrative and political system, revolutionary will to transform society—were already united in practice if not in theory. Sometimes an adversary's resistance unites the forces that fight him. At Nanterre, on the contrary, the emptiness and impotence of the university system insured their integration into a social movement whose capacity for action and mobilization was soon to be revealed. We must analyze this particular situation and see how this social movement was formed, because the passage from a university crisis to the May Movement took place at Nanterre.

Nanterre

Nanterre is the wrong side of Paris. West of the most beautiful neighborhoods and the new residential sections of Saint-Cloud, Neuilly, Rueil, Celle-Saint-Cloud, and Saint-Germain, the city of Nanterre is the image of twentieth-century wretchedness. This is quite different from the scrubbed-up wretchedness of the nineteenth century that the populist poets like to find in the old working-class sections of Paris. This is urban rather than economic misery, disorganized space, a hodge-podge of empty lots, old and new factories, shanty towns, and railroad tracks. The route to the faculty does not cross the center of Nanterre, thus avoiding a relic of the past, the large hospice for the elderly. One must follow a twisting path, skirting the low-rent housing units, some large sporting arenas, the largest shanty town in the west suburbs, and old factories before passing through the construction site of the future subway station to the concrete emptiness of the university area where former military buildings have not yet been completely removed.

Building a faculty of letters in this location is probably

the result of chance. The Ministry of the Army ceded to the Ministry of National Education an aviation materiel depot which was no longer useful. There was an urgent need to construct buildings to house the overflow of students that the Sorbonne could no longer contain. In record time, a new faculty was built on this available land. Indeed, it was not chance that this was the way a new faculty was created. It is to the west of Paris, at the service of the social groups who send the largest contingent of students to the university. Moreover, it is located in a zone that the Paris planners recognize as one of those which must receive the most spectacular promotion in the future. This is where the new industries, the technical research centers, and the laboratories locate and where the middle and higher managers, the new bourgeoisie, live. When Nanterre has been transformed, the passage from the old to the new bourgeoisie will have been completed. Other sections—the Plaine Monçeau, Neuilly, and Saint Germain—are the waystops moving westward the classes which have dominated France for a century.

Today, Nanterre is an urban void, filled with workers of every nationality, native Frenchmen, North African repatriates, Algerians, Portuguese. What relationship would the university population have with its environment? What cultural environment would be created around the professional activity of the university? What would living conditions be like on this relatively small lot, which did not allow for much expansion and was isolated from any real urban center? These questions did not cause any loss of sleep. It was necessary to act quickly, relieve the Sorbonne, and find a place for several thousand students. There was no time to create a campus and a new kind of university life.

Nanterre is created in the image of the university system. The lack of reflection and imagination, the lack of real decision are expressed in the subjection of the stu-

dents, especially those who live in the dormitories, to conditions which have more in common with the area as it
used to be than they do with the Latin Quarter or a university campus. A look at the buildings confirms this first
impression. Neither handsome nor ugly, the buildings
correspond to a clear image of what a faculty should be,
if one accepts an assembly-line conception of educational
organization. They are conceived to insure good spatial organization of production flow. On one side, there is a
vast hall which opens onto workshops in which the masses
of raw material undergo the preliminary processing—here
named lecture courses carried out in auditoriums—and,
on the other side, rooms stacked up on four floors, where
the finishing operations—here named tutored work—are
carried out. At the corners of each rectangular floor, the
offices of the foremen—professors in this case—demonstrate the presence of the bosses. It is true that this factory was put into production under conditions that would
be astonishing for an automobile plant or chemical products factory, since work on the library was only begun in
the spring of 1968. But this unfortunate detail is easily
explained by the fact that the General Direction of French
Libraries is independent of the construction service of the
Ministry of National Education and of the General Direction of Higher Education! At Nanterre, it is not a
matter of living but of producing, or more exactly, of
circulating, of being exposed to a series of acts of teaching.
Production is conceived in the simplest terms. I was im-
precise when I referred to the chemical industry—we
should think instead of the traditional textile plant which
never dedicated much space or resources to research. In
fact, there is no location for research at Nanterre. Efforts
have been made at Orléans-la-Source to obtain an installa-
tion of the C.N.R.S. or of the Bureau of Geological and
Mining Research. Maybe Nanterre is too close to Paris.
Everyone is supposed to be able to go easily to the Latin

Quarter or to the Bibliothèque Nationale. Actually, this requires a two- or three-hour round trip, which makes such excursions practically impossible. Besides, the reading rooms of the large Paris libraries are overcrowded. The Nanterre university area has been conceived as a place where buildings would be raised, not as a place where people live. Good order dictates that one begin with the great buildings, then the roads, then remove the debris, mud, and rank weeds, finally, perhaps, one plants a rose bush.

Just as the large hall that opens onto the faculty's stations is unfinished, its gray walls empty, a shell more than architecture, the land has remained bare and repulsive ever since the opening of the faculty. It was months before one could reach certain buildings other than by crossing a lake of mud; more months before a little grass replaced the gravel in front of the main entrance. People are still in the way in this workshop where it nevertheless would have been easy and inexpensive, but perhaps bureaucratically impossible, to create habitable conditions from the outset. Does this mean that the students and teachers at Nanterre are less well situated than their colleagues at the Sorbonne? Not at all. Both pedestrian and automobile bottlenecks have been avoided. Almost everyone can find a seat and a writing table in the auditoriums and classrooms. The sanitary installations are excellent. Only the university restaurants are overcrowded. Materially and administratively, Nanterre is a great success. Its construction turned all the administrative circuits upside down. Its growth is spectacular. A faculty was created in record time. From 2,000 students the first year, attendance passed to 4,000, then 8,000, to about 15,000 in 1967–68, including the law students; nearly 25,000 were expected for the opening of the 1968–69 school year. The faculty of letters is still growing and an increase is especially being felt in the preparatory year for the Institut des Etudes

Politiques and in the first years of the law school. That
for a few years the faculty, cut in two by the subway construction site, would be unfinished and inconvenient is
neither surprising nor shocking. Both students and teachers were ready to live through this period of creation
which has its inconveniences but its charm as well. The
charm resides in the newness, the possibility of following
the progress of the work, perhaps even taking some part
in the program of completion. But it is irritating at Nanterre to constantly run into an administrative and social
attitude, expressed in the location, construction, and
organization of the faculty, that denies the elementary
conditions of university life. This is a machine for teaching, that is, for preparing examinations, a campus where
a human being is conceived as an aggregate of physiologi-
cal functions—eating, sleeping, walking—but not as a social being and a personality in the process of formation.
Nevertheless, I liked Nanterre from the first day that
I knew it, when I was invited by a psychologist friend to
take part in a thesis jury. In its roughness and distance
from the Latin Quarter, Nanterre symbolized breaking
with the Paris university world. I did not like it for
what it was but for what it was not. By its very existence,
Nanterre was a criticism of the university system. Just
as one can like brutal cities where wealth and misery
clash without being hidden behind a polished exterior,
so Nanterre was the university system as it is, not as it
appears in the piously constructed hagiography: the flood
tide of students, departments to be organized, teachers to
be recruited. Above all, everyone felt that the importance
of Nanterre, as a Paris faculty, was to put an end, by its
very existence, to the Sorbonne's de facto monopoly. Besides, the Sorbonne professors, who would have preferred
Nanterre to be content with teaching the first cycle,
allowing them to get rid of these crushing tasks and to
dedicate themselves to the higher levels of teaching, rap-

idly adopted a very loyal attitude to the new faculty and did not try to bother or dominate it.

Nanterre was a young faculty; the professors were relatively young and, from the outset, the human sciences occupied a more important place than at the Sorbonne. Nanterre was responsive to the will for renewal of some parts of the university community; it possessed no more freedom than any oher institution but, by its very existence, it at least questioned a stifling tradition. Even if there was only a limited opportunity to build something new on this vacant lot, there was at least *some* opportunity. This was enough to raise expectations and hopes. The very isolation could—and in my opinion did—have certain fortunate consequences. Since the students were not absorbed by a Latin Quarter on leaving their classes, at least the resident students were more completely involved in the life of the faculty. Their demands and criticisms were able to be more than purely intellectual or imaginary, and to become a real force for change.

These are the two opposed aspects of Nanterre. It was a new element in university life, capable of attracting in 1967, for example, many excellent professors and capable of awakening hopes in many who actively cared about the university system. On the other hand, it was a stupid creation which isolated the students from every cultural center, built without any account taken of the working and living needs of the first generations of students. This imbalance between expectation and actual experience made Nanterre a weak point in the university system.

The predominant attitude of the teachers and administrators of the faculty was a desire to re-create communication and a social life that was no longer possible at the overloaded and polarized Sorbonne. The hope of living in a more human faculty led several Sorbonne professors to leave the old faculty in order to participate in creating the new one. On the whole, student-teacher relations were more active at Nanterre than at the Sorbonne, especially in the first years when the classes were relatively small and the buildings could contain them without difficulty, at least in terms of the very modest demands made by teachers and students who were used to penury.

Dean Pierre Grappin wished to work very actively to create the new faculty and to inculcate in it a liberal atmosphere. In contrast to the other faculties of letters, Nanterre did not have a council formed only of tenured professors. It was open to conference supervisors and teaching *assistants*. The dean also strove to establish relations, or at least to avoid conflicts, with the social environment. The relatively young council members did not feel obligated to defend tradition and, beyond the usual differences of opinion and attitude, were united in support of the dean, whose energy and goodwill they respected.

Perhaps one ought not to exaggerate the importance of the open and liberal atmosphere of the faculty at the beginning and indeed right up to the outbreak of student agitation. Nonetheless, it was not negligible. The faculty's liberalism was deep enough to tolerate certain actions but too limited to actively question a university situation that impeded independent initiatives. In any case, many of the student militants were aware that Nanterre was a fairly "good deal." At first, the new students missed the Sorbonne and the Latin Quarter; after a year, they were at least also aware of the cleanliness of their surroundings, the more frequent contacts with their teachers, and the dean's efforts to improve living and working conditions at Nanterre.

Dean Grappin's role was important enough for us to try to define the attitude of this man who had the responsibility for the faculty from the beginning. His attitude was not purely individual; it sheds light on the reactions of a number of the members of the university. A native

of the east of France, he did not come from a privileged
social background. He had "risen in the world" through
his studies, as the reformers of the Third Republic had
hoped. He was active in the Résistance and had first-hand
knowledge of great physical danger. A left-wing university
militant, first in the Communist Party and then in the
more militant P.S.U. (Parti Socialiste Unifié), he was at
once socially liberal, culturally authoritarian, and determined to act, not as a theoretician or analyst but as a practitioner and administrator in the modernization of the
university system. This reformer, who tried for a long
time to moderate the misgivings and then the hostility
of a great number of the professors at Nanterre toward
the student demonstrations, in other circumstances could
have been one of the leaders of university reform. He was
the only dean of a faculty of letters to participate in the
Caen Conference. But when the storm broke, his attachment to the professorial fraternity, whose representative
he was, and above all his ambivalence and hostility toward the students whose behavior did not fit anything he
expected and who seemed to him brash, irresponsible,
and too far removed from the hard demands of professional success and social promotion, led him first to vacil-
late to the point of being unable to act and then to retreat more and more into distrust and aloofness.

The failure of this man who in January 1968 was the
target of insults he found all the more incomprehensible
because they linked him, a veteran of the Résistance, with
the swastika, was the failure of university liberalism itself. It would be profoundly unjust to attribute the principal responsibility to him or to portray him as a reactionary, which he never was. A reformer, in favor of the
changes that were possible, but refusing to question an
institutional framework to which he was attached, he encountered revolt and revolutionary violence and was engulfed by them. His liberalism, which had nourished his

reforming intentions before the beginning of the movement, became tainted more and more by hostility and
distrust toward those he considered left-wing fascists. His
moderation and liberalism, as well as his attachment to
order and university traditions, were not at the origin of
the crisis. They contributed to establishing at Nanterre
an atmosphere that was favorable to the development of
the movement but was incapable of recognizing its true
nature.

The University Strike of November 1967

The first demonstration that drew attention to Nanterre was the strike of November 1967. Until then, the
incidents that had taken place there were no different
from incidents in other places. This strike, which has been
overshadowed by the events of spring 1968, was nevertheless important because it typified the efforts and the failure
of a reformist approach. The opening of school in October
1967 was marked by the first application of the Fouchet
reform to all the students except those in the third cycle.
At first, the students' hostility was not directed against
the spirit of the reform, only against some of its practical
consequences. Nevertheless, the violence of this hostility
and the forms it took indicated a state of crisis that went
beyond the themes and objectives of the strike. This explains its nature as both the introduction to and the opposite of the May Movement.

First of all, a certain number of students rebelled against
what seemed to them harassment. They felt that they
were being moved back in the progress of their studies.
In particular, this was the feeling of those who already
had a teaching license and who were scheduled to register
for the second year of the first cycle while keeping the
benefit of the certificate for the following year. Students

who, under the old system, would have completed their license in 1968 found themselves in the first year of the *maîtrise*. As a result, in one year they could not obtain this new title which seemed to them, at least in sociology and psychology, the equivalent of the old license, since it took two years' preparation. This dissatisfaction was not justified from an administrative point of view. It was sufficient to count the required years of study to realize that no student was being put back. But it is pointless to seek the explanation of the November crisis on this level.

It would be more exact to say that the university was holding on only by force of habit and was incapable of being changed. It was to crumble like a house of cards at the slightest breeze. The bureaucratic introduction of change without regard for the reactions of the students hastened the end. During the first stage of the revolt, student reaction was not radical. It did not question the conception and social function of the university but simply opposed the method of change. The students asked to be heard and to take part in the discussion; they called for explanations and adjustments rather than for total transformation. But if these demands were limited and if the sociology student who was the principal spokesman was a moderate, very different from the "little groups" which acquired importance a few months later, the reactions of the faculty and the ministry demonstrated that any questioning of the established order and administrative decisions caused real shock. This strike, aimed at such modest objectives, took place in an atmosphere of great tension. The system within which it took place had no way of institutionalizing conflicts. Liberal reforms sometimes corresponded to good intentions but never to practice.

The November strike presented certain analogies with the later movements: it began in the sociology department and was led by individuals or by small, rather than broadly representative, groups; it aroused defensive reactions on the part of many teachers; it increased the participation of *assistants* and *maîtres-assistants* in the running of the faculty; it occasioned the creation of representative institutions in the faculty; and it obtained no response from the Ministry of National Education.

The role played by students of the social sciences in the student movements is not only true of France but also of the United States, England, Poland, Germany, Mexico, and other nations. It is easy to understand, since it is normal that those who have chosen to study society should be most aware of social problems. The social sciences are what law, history, and political philosophy were in the last century, the principal instruments with which to analyze society. More to the point, while social science students are among the least professionalized, their competence can very easily be used by the social order to insure its integration, defense, and the manipulation of individuals and groups. In France, their professionalization is particularly weak: a sociology degree does not lead to clearly defined employment. For several years, sociological studies were often taken along with other studies. This solution has become increasingly difficult as the teaching hours have increased and the place of "technical" matters —mathematics, statistics, economics, or demography—has become more developed. In the faculties of letters, sociological studies are less easy, at least in the beginning, than the modern language studies that attract so many students. But students who take them are not placed, like the students of classical letters or geography, in a channel that runs straight from secondary school student to secondary school professor.

Sociology students are a little marginal in the university system. A little older than most students, often because they hesitated over their choice of profession, they also are less completely defined by their university activity;

they have many outside social, cultural, or political activities. More aware than others of social problems that are broader than the university itself, they often feel less at ease within the cultural framework of the university.

The same remarks could be made of the sociology teachers. In general, the *assistants* at Nanterre did not come from secondary school teaching, for the simple reason that either teaching or teachers of sociology still does not exist in the secondary schools. The professors were, on the whole, men whose careers and work had developed outside the university. Only one of them had always taught in the faculties of letters, first as assistant and then as professor. The others had spent long periods at the C.N.R.S. or at the Ecole des Hautes Etudes. Almost all were engaged in university level research which they did not, and could not, carry out within the framework of the faculty. Although very different from each other, as the extreme diversity of their positions in May and June shows, they agreed in their very critical judgment of the organization and spirit of the university. Many of the *assistants* felt even more on the margins of the system and closer to the students than to the teachers.

At the beginning of the November strike, at the same time as opposition to the Fouchet Plan was organized especially by the Catholic and Trotskyite students, a representative committee was formed in the sociology department. Its activity and climate remained, until the general crisis in the spring, profoundly different from what one could observe in the analogous committees formed in other departments after the strike. Where the others spoke about liaison committees, in sociology they spoke of the department assembly. The principle was accepted that in everything that concerned direction—not teaching—decisions would be taken by individual count, not according to different groups. This insured the students a strong majority. Moreover, the students insisted on being represented not by permanently elected individuals but by delegates from the working groups who were changed frequently.

The movement that had begun in sociology ran into resistance from certain departments and their student associations, especially the departments of French, geography, and modern languages. The faculty council reacted negatively and attempted to direct grievances to the ministry according to the usual pattern. The dean finally decided to convoke a general assembly of all the teachers—with no power to make decisions—and to invite a small student delegation, which spoke mainly through Philippe Meyer, a sociology student. On the whole, the reactions to his declarations asking for student participation in the deliberations and decisions of the faculty were negative. The dean and the assessor, Pierre Beaujeu, nevertheless endeavored to organize mixed commissions in the departments and to set up a representative consultative commission for the faculty as a whole. This commission played a very limited role because a great number of the student representatives showed at least as much hostility as the majority of the teachers toward new demonstrations by the leftist militants. In terms of its objectives, the strike movement achieved practically nothing, since the ministry showed only very limited interest in examining the grievances. This setback had important consequences.

The November strike can be defined as a mixture of revolt and limited, reformist objectives. Once it had been proven that the path of moderation led only to failure and the creation of a commission without power or will, the spirit of revolt developed by itself and led to more and more violent crises. This strike also indicated the limits of liberalism at Nanterre. It did not provoke repression; it did occasion the initiatives of the dean and led to some effort to institutionalize local conflicts. Judged scandalous by many teachers who talked about the arrogance of the students and did not accept any questioning of their role as directors, it made it clear that the institution's capacity to respond to more profound and more general conflicts would be almost nil. The climate and events at Nanterre in the subsequent period cannot be understood without reference to this first crisis, to the failure of the strike, and to the demonstrated power of opposition, far beyond its limited objectives.

The Scandal

The subsequent period, until the Easter vacation, was dominated not so much by the formation of the March 22 Movement—which was not visible until near the end of this period—as by a radical change in the form of the crisis. It is impossible to speak of a student movement until the great mass demonstrations of the March 22 Movement and, even more important, the Critical University Day on the day following the first closing of the faculty. The expressions that became famous—the "enragés" and the "little groups"—originated in the events of this period, which we can call the period of scandal.

This period is difficult to understand because it can only be interpreted in restrospect as the preparatory phase of the spring movement. Between December and April, three elements, whose combination was to form the central phase of the student movement, came on the scene separately or at least without any organic connection. They were the attack on the university, the appeal to the students, and an over-all social criticism of society. But these elements, which combined to form an authentic social movement—which always involves an individual's defense of himself, struggle against an adversary, and a conception of what is at stake in the conflict—if perceived and experienced in isolation from each other, could only with

difficulty be considered the inauguration of an action that
was to break apart the whole of French society.

a) Within the faculty, the most spectacular actions were
those that indicated a will to break with the university
system. These involved sabotage of the period examinations which was all the more disturbing because this kind
of examination had been established at Nanterre to
counter the cramming and uncertainties of the final examination. Those students in the first cycle who had high
enough grades in two trimester examinations were exempted from the final examination which the others had
to take. In the sociology and psychology departments, the
period examinations were sabotaged or boycotted, which
could only have been a protest against the nature of the
examinations, since in many cases their content could not
have been known. It proclaimed a rejection of the system of studies and examinations.

Before these incidents, small groups had organized a
campaign in the main hall with posters and banners pro-
testing the presence of plainclothes policemen in the faculty and the existence of a "blacklist," a theme which had
great influence for a while in mobilizing the students. It
was never proved that such lists existed or that the administration had asked the teachers not to accept for examinations certain students who had taken part in political
agitation in the faculty.

This agitation would probably not have had much effect
and, in any case, involved only a few people until an incident on January 26 between those carrying the posters
and some officials of the administration. Considering that
an inadmissible disorder had moved into the faculty, they
obtained permission from the dean, who was giving a
lecture at the time, to call the police. The arrival of a few
policemen provoked a brief scuffle and created solidarity
between a good number of the students present and their
comrades who were attacked. There followed a wave of

graffiti and tracts quite openly accusing the dean of being a Nazi. Such incidents, whose political content was far from clear, caused great tension and resulted in almost unanimous defense of the dean on the part of the teachers.

b) The second element that appeared during this period was an over-all political criticism expressed especially by campaigns against the war in Vietnam, which was reinforced by the example of the German S.D.S. At this point, some political groups intervened, although their action was not readily recognized by the faculty as a whole. Militants from the local Vietnam committees broke with the program of the national Vietnam committee. Dissatisfied with public opinion campaigns and more oriented toward direct action (whether or not they were connected with Maoist Communist groups), they undertook actions within the faculty and even more outside it. The destruction of the windows of the American Express office brought them the widest attention, especially because of its consequences at Nanterre itself. This act and the arrests which punished it provoked the actions that created the March 22 Movement. But neither of these two elements mobilized a significant number of students. The actions were the doing of small activist or ideological groups, whose methods were not designed to attract the participation of the students, who did not feel particularly concerned by the demonstrations.

c) This shows the essential importance of the third element, the campaign directed at the students themselves, and especially at the importance of the personal action of Daniel Cohn-Bendit who succeeded in integrating these different elements into a general movement. This student agitation did not have to be created; it already existed, as shown by the incident in March 1967 at the Nanterre student residence, an incident which resembled those that had taken place at other university student residences. This incident was important because it revealed something more than dissatisfaction, a disposition to direct action through extreme means and because it organized students on the spot for objectives that were both general and practical. It was a revolt: residents of the dormitories decided to no longer recognize their regulations. Some boys invaded one of the buildings reserved for girls and spent the night there. The director of the student residences was reduced to impotence. Various political activities were also organized contrary to the regulations.

This revolt has two principal themes, the more visible being sexual freedom. It is difficult to weigh this element in the absence of sufficient information about the internal life of the student residences, but it would be a wrong construction to see it as a desire to create moral scandal. The reality is that relations among the students were just as weak as relations between students and teachers. Most of them lived in isolation, did not know those who roomed next to them, and took part in very few collective activities. This lack of communication showed the weakness or decomposition of any organized student environment and university life. The students' action was certainly an affirmation of sexual freedom and immediately followed a lecture at a student residence on the ideas of the Marxist psychoanalyst Wilhelm Reich. But this defense of a principle cannot be separated from the effort to regain communication and reject isolation by opposing a regulation which was not its real cause but was its most tangible sign.

This leads us to the second theme, the will to determine basic living conditions on the campus. These did not depend on the dean or the director of the student residences but on far-off administrative authorities. The unfolding of the March 1967 incidents is characteristic in this regard. After the overnight occupation of the girls' residence by the boys, the police were called to empty the building but did not enter it. The dean went to the office of the director of the student residences where he was joined by two teachers who had just arrived at the faculty. Along with student representatives, they waited a long time for the ministry to take a position, unable to make a decision or even propose a solution to this minor problem. After a prolonged wait, an answer came from the office of the rector: the students were to show their keys to prove they belonged in the student residence and then could leave freely. The departure of the students took place calmly. The names of at least some of the occupiers were taken, but no effective sanctions were laid down. This incident is revealing. By rejecting this regulation, the students rejected at the same time the whole administrative structure which pretended to be representative but was actually a denial of the most elementary forms of self-determination. This action was at least as much anti-bureaucratic as it was a sexual protest.

This latter element, however, was not absent. It had been proclaimed in 1966 by the situationists of Strasbourg. At Nanterre itself, it was also the occasion of a celebrated incident between Daniel Cohn-Bendit and the Minister of Youth and Sports, M. Missoffe, who had come to dedicate the athletic buildings and especially the very beautiful swimming pool. Cohn-Bendit spoke with the minister and reproached him for not having mentioned sexuality and its problems in his White Paper on youth. At first, M. Missoffe answered calmly. Then, to get rid of this annoying young man, he advised Cohn-Bendit to cool his ardor by diving into the newly opened swimming pool, advice which earned him, it is said, the distinction of being called a fascist by Cohn-Bendit. The incident had a number of consequences: expulsion proceedings were initiated against Cohn-Bendit, who is of German nationality; the sociology department assembly came out in favor

of Cohn-Bendit; the minister intervened in favor of appeasement and even received Cohn-Bendit; a motion
against the taking of sanctions against a student because
he is a foreigner was voted by the representative commission of the faculty. Although the incident was minor,
it gave Cohn-Bendit great notoriety. It also indicates that
the sexuality theme had an importance that went beyond
its specific object.

Feeling himself enclosed in an absurd, if rational, system that he can only interpret as a device of manipulation, the student reacts by asserting what is most foreign
to the world of bureaucracy and management, the affirmation of his "natural" being through his sexuality. Just as
the exploited worker sought to find himself as a physical
force, the student, subjected to social and cultural manipulation, opposes these alienations with the power of Eros.
From the beginning, for the more politicized students,
this reaction was political as well as moral. The moral
themes which concern the conduct of private life do not
demonstrate a rejection of a moral rule and a social
conception of morality as much as the criticism of cultural
manipulation and its political meaning.

French society is much less aware of moral problems
than it is of political and institutional problems. The importance of the social order, the State, tradition, the
Church, and the role of prohibitions rather than persuasion in education have caused the concern for morality
and its defense by society to carry little weight in France.

The French child learns that he is forbidden to do a
great number of things; he is taught more about respect
for rules and appearances than about moral accountabil-
ity. The rigor of the rules and the rigidity of the institutions are accompanied by a liberty in terms of inclina-
tions and a confidence in "nature" that one does not find
in societies where the child is asked not only to accept but
to approve and will the rules, and where moralism spreads

from private into public life. For these reasons, the student revolt was not a moral revolt, even when it attacked commercialized consumption. It did not feel moved to reject urban, industrial civilization and either accepted the hippy withdrawal with difficulty or transformed it rapidly into political criticism. This is why the incidents at the student residences and the swimming pool contributed to the creation of a climate of social revolt quite removed from the need for "escaping the crowd" that those who judged the student movement from beginning to end by means of summary formulas like to see in it.

There is a great difference between the acts of revolt and provocation at the beginning of the year and the action of the movement in April. At the beginning of the year, the three themes I have just distinguished were not unified in a political action movement. They were mixed together in a general attitude of revolt. The important word was *repression;* it was a matter of fighting every form of repression: administrative, political, intellectual, sexual. All constraints and authority were seen as opposed to what can only be understood as total liberty. This is an affirmation more moral than political, opposing Man to society and its alienations, which evokes Feuerbach more than Marx.

How did the student action change from isolated acts of revolt against repression to a political and social movement?

Cohn-Bendit and the Formation of the Movement

Primarily through the personal activity of Daniel Cohn-Bendit, the three issues we have discussed—rejection of the organization and structure of the university system; protest against the Vietnam War, that scandalous sign of the genocidal aggression of a society that claims to be creative of prosperity and equality; and an appeal to the student situation—were gradually unified within the movement. This man was the principal spokesman of the student movement. It is essential to see him at Nanterre during the weeks when he was the undisputed leader of the movement. In this limited arena, he acted in the same spirit and manner as he did later during the more dramatic days from May 3 to 13.

Daniel Cohn-Bendit, a third-year sociology student, was first of all a man of words. During his sociology courses, beginning in 1966, he spoke up constantly, discussing, commenting, criticizing. He rejected neither instruction nor study but could only participate aloud. He was excited and violent, animated with a kind of holy anger against phoniness, lies, and silence. An orator and spellbinder, he was also capable, an instant after a great conflict, of calmly discussing the meaning of a situation or action. Above all, he was able to arouse people, often provoking fear, reserve, and hesitation but almost always sympathy as well. He was the torrent that overwhelmed the "little groups" so comfortably closed up in their doctrine and strategy. With outbursts of laughter, he sounded the notes that brought down the august and tottering walls of the university and the social order. He was a man of revolt, not of alliances and strategy. Perhaps because he did not have the responsibility for any group, he provided the essential element of critical action within the movement. His role was to break down the structures. He accomplished it almost by "playing" in the faculty, with more embittered passion each time he came into conflict with the structures of the "left." He had to restore words and deeds to the people, denounce the trickery, schemes, revolutionary words, and conformist action of the Young Communists and their party and rediscover worker agitation behind the union organizations.

If one believes that the May crisis could have brought

about a new grand alliance of leftist forces and a new
Popular Front which would have moved further than its
predecessor because of the widespread strikes, then Cohn-
Bendit was a divider. If, on the other hand, one thinks
that the workers' organizations were irretrievably involved in a process of social integration and that May was
the beginning of new breaks and new movements, then
the activity of Cohn-Bendit, which could not enjoy immediate success, has a great future. As he wished, he broke
or at least cracked the masonry that blocked the well-
springs of revolution. On May 13, at the Champ-de-Mars
and before then at Nanterre, he renewed the activities of
the revolutionary groups, inciting them to discussion by
banishing slogans and rejecting party terms in order to
rediscover the words *comradeship, spontaneity,* and *movement.* A total stranger to demagogy and party spirit, he
turned rejection and scandal into instruments to form a
creative movement with violence and reflection. His role
was brief, since he was expelled on May 21; I do not believe that it was finished. He was a man of the uprising,
not of organization; he was not a manager but a leader.
   His activity was never more important than between
March 22 and April 2. March 22 was a day of rape and
scandal. When the arrest of the local Vietnam committee
militants, including an alumnus of Nanterre, was announced, a meeting that had begun in an auditorium
ended in the invasion of the administration building by
students who moved into the council room on the top
floor. Until very late that night, eating sandwiches and
drinking beer on the grand oval table, these students,
liberated from the phantom of the university, discussed
policy and, following the example of the Berlin students,
began to prepare the first activities of a critical university.
From this moment on, the faculty was in a state of crisis
from which it escaped only by disappearing into the
silence of summer. While incidents proliferated, the real

explosion was in words and all forms of political activity.

When a Critical University Day was announced for March 29, the faculty council decided to close Nanterre on that day. The discussions were held calmly on the grass around the buildings. The U.E.C. did not participate; the U.J.C.M.L.* remained silent. On March 30, the council, after long discussion, decided to adopt several liberal measures and to make an auditorium available to political groups that requested it. But on Tuesday, April 2, all activity at the faculty was disrupted by a Critical University Day that opened with a meeting attended by a thousand students at which Wolff, one of the leaders of the German S.D.S., spoke.

The dean had left it up to the department directors whether or not to put lecture halls at the disposal of the work groups formed by the students. Those in charge of philosophy, psychology, and sociology agreed to do so and about ten groups met, using most of the rooms on the sociology floor. All the themes which were to be taken up again beginning May 13 at the Sorbonne—the university, culture, the war in Vietnam, student-worker relations— were present. April 2 was important because from then on it was impossible to speak of "little groups" and a handful of "enragés" who had often been considered the only participants and leaders of the agitation. What some had been calling the huge mass of serious students amounted to 500 people at a meeting, entrance to which was regulated by young men wearing *fleurs de lys* in their lapels. Beginning on April 2, the movement was a reality; its audience grew rapidly; the hostility among the student associations grew even less audible and scarcely counted for anything.

A few weeks earlier, the most active militants and Cohn-

* Union of Communist Students; Union of Young Marxist-Leninist Communists (Maoists).

Bendit himself had insisted on the passivity of the great majority of the students and their servility and had proclaimed their role as agitating minorities. Those who signed the tract "Pourquoi des Sociologues?" condemned or refused to admit that there was any such thing as a student problem. For them, the students did not represent a significant group. But the very militancy of the minority allowed them to forget their isolation until the vast majority of the university, and not only a few dozen sociology students, was part of the movement.

The evolution of the students' spirit would merit a sociological study and would demonstrate the limitations of a too naïve conception of public opinion. It is certain—a limited investigation proves it—that at the beginning of the year a majority of the students judged the faculty favorably. It is also certain that the student associations which condemned the "enragés" so violently and for so long, represented the opinion of the majority of the students. These opinions were not modified by propaganda or material pressures. The consciousness of collective problems gradually imposed itself and absorbed opinions which were always marked by a practical viewpoint: "things being what they are. . . ." The movement did not grow organically out of dissatisfaction with a general condition, but revealed its contradictions and politicized the population through its words and deeds.

In April, the movement took possession of the faculty; not to attack instruction but to exist outside it rather than to destroy it. During this whole period, the courses themselves were hardly disturbed. A few incidents occurred but no tutored work meeting or sociology course was stopped. Once a group of students forcibly invaded the dean's office to get him to sign a statement but they did not respond to his refusal with any physical violence. The movement preferred to ignore the habitual activities of the faculty and was absorbed in the affirmation of it-

self and in its development. The walls, especially the immense walls of the great hall that runs the entire length
of the faculty, were covered with graffiti, photographic
montages, and wall posters in the Chinese style, covered
with tightly written text, which were removed every night
and reappeared new every morning. These mobilized attention, reflection, and participation.

The Decomposition of the Faculty

The reactions at the faculty to these activities have only
local interest. Nothing leads us to believe that they would
have been very different anywhere else. The most noteworthy fact is the weakening of the policy of moderate
liberalism followed until then by those in charge of the
faculty. More and more, the council was divided into two
camps of unequal importance while a certain number of
moderates retreated into silence. If only a few desired repression and an appeal to the police and the courts, a
very large group of professors adhered to the so-called
Declaration of the Eighteen which threatened a teachers'
strike unless the students conformed to the rules and limits set by the council on March 30 concerning political
activities in the faculty. In very lively discussions, this
group was opposed by another very small group that
stood behind an open statement on the student movement
that had been edited by three professors, one each from
the French, philosophy, and sociology departments.

But the newest element was the intervention for the
first time of the *assistants* and "teaching" *assistants* acting
collectively. An important number of them, particularly
in the French department which had been considered
"calm," split with the council and stood with the opposition. On April 23, *assistants* in psychology and sociology
committed themselves even more clearly to the students'

side. These groups, which represented the great majority of the teachers, had remained in the shadow until then. At the time of the November strike, they had seemed to take the side of the institution against the students but without intervening on their own. In April, a strong minority of the *assistants* and *maîtres-assistants* took an attitude that became more and more explicit. This showed the weakening of the traditional relationships of authority and presaged the participation of a notable number of *assistants* and *maîtres-assistants* in the May Movement. This period ended on May 2 with a new closing of the faculty, motivated by the fear that on Friday, May 3, violent incidents might pit movement militants against Occident groups (small extreme right-wing organizations) called, according to rumor, to Nanterre from Paris and other French cities.

This decision probably influenced the one taken the next day at the Sorbonne. In reality, it only recognized a de facto situation. On one side, the teachers in the faculty who were opposed to the movement were more and more determined to put an end to a situation they judged intolerable. On the other side, the student movement overflowed from Nanterre and called for demonstrations in Paris. A crisis had begun: it could not be resolved nor could it take place within an isolated, suburban faculty. Neither the closing of Nanterre on May 2 nor its reopening, decided on May 9, had any determining influence over the events of the week of May 3–10. The Nanterre phase of the movement was finished, but not the role of its militants, particularly those in the March 22 Movement.

A Student Revolt?

The issues and forms of the student action at Nanterre were similar to those at Berlin, Berkeley, and Rome.

Beyond the profound resemblances, however, there were also notable differences among the movements, due to the diverse situations in which the student movement developed. To point them out will help us better define the particular characteristics of the Nanterre movement.

In Italy and Germany, university authoritarianism and its concrete expression in the personal power of the chair-holding professor are much more accentuated than in the United States, where departments and institutes are strongly organized. This is also true in comparison with France where, while the departments are certainly weak and are really only sections, there are no powerful chiefs—in the faculties of letters at least—since instruction is separated from research and decisions are made by the professors as a group. Consequently, in Italy and Germany, the strictly university struggle against still-powerful organizational forms inherited from the last century has the greatest importance. In Italy, the archaic nature of the university system, which stands as a screen between the students and society, is the dominant issue. In Germany, Berlin particularly, the rigidity of the hierarchy and the personal power of the professors manifest the historic role of abstract reason and the State in the formation of the German nation. As a result, student opposition is concentrated on philosophical analysis and political action more elaborately than anywhere else. In both these countries, the violence of the university conflict isolates the student movement, although in Italy it has found some support in the Communist Party.

In the United States and France, the movement is more directly turned outward. In the United States, it did not really begin in the universities but in the South when students participated in the civil rights movement in which some of them died. The problem of racism and the Vietnam War are so important that the first serious incidents bore directly on the freedom of political expression and on freedom of "advocacy," that is, the freedom to organize demonstrations directed toward objectives that went beyond the campus. For a French parallel, we might imagine the Nanterre students demanding the right to prepare on campus for a demonstration against *Le Figaro* or the American embassy. In France, the call to political action outside the university is effective to the degree that the Communist Party and the C.G.T. seem to carry on a living revolutionary tradition. To this first difference between the United States and France—the existence of a revolutionary element in the labor movement—there is added a second. If there were attempts at Berkeley to suppress the Free Speech Movement, there was also negotiation, largely because the university senate, at least at first, supported the student grievances against the pressure of the state regents. In France, it was less a matter of conflict than of the decomposition of a decision-making system that had long been paralyzed.

Hence, in France, more so than in Germany, Italy, and the United States, the student movement quickly moved out of—or was expelled from—the university faculty. The university system was neither solidly conservative enough to repress the movement nor sufficiently ready to bargain in order to contain it and allow it to develop within itself. While at Berkeley and Berlin strictly university agitation lasted for years and the Italian universities were paralyzed for a long time, the crisis at Nanterre lasted scarcely two months, and everything concurred to throw the movement into the streets: its rejection by the university and the government as well as its own desire to move toward the working class. In France, massive action within the university system came after the most violent moment of the crisis rather than before it. In contrast to Germany, where the "critical university" led to the "extra-parliamentary opposition," the French movement might well develop in the opposite direction and discover, after the torment of May, a more specific university of intellectual opposition, attacking the faculties which either did not know how or were unable to profoundly transform themselves in June and the months that followed.

Let us, nevertheless, not exaggerate these differences between the national movements. The Nanterre movement was not simply political action on the part of small groups concerned with doctrine and strategy. The weakness and disorganization of a university which had accepted change without knowing how to change itself enough to direct it, created a situation that favored a conflict which finally destroyed the university system. Factually, it was a revolt. The students did not act in the name of any party or political force organized on a national level and seeking to seize power. But the revolt did not set such a goal nor did the student militants wish to act in this way.

Though at Nanterre in April there was a brief attempt to set up a critical university, this aim was neither central nor isolated. Even though the small situationist group concentrated principally on the student situation and the commercialization of mass culture, the spring revolt was less a questioning of the culture than a political criticism of society. The attacks were only secondarily aimed against teaching. The movement developed more out of the university than against it; the attacks against it focused more on what was called its subjection to the middle class and the State than on its practices and quality. The most spectacular confrontation did not pit revolting students against conservative professors but against a Communist Deputy, a specialist in university affairs who also passed as being in favor of new initiatives within his party. Politics above all.

From the outset at Nanterre, the social force that was established defined itself by the struggle against power, an approach that was reinforced by the extreme inability of the faculty to recognize the gravity of the university crisis and the seriousness of the student movement. The majority of the professors quickly sided with the positions of the dean and considered as dangerous deviationists those few among them who affirmed that the student opposition could not be repressed and that the criticism of the university was well founded and inevitable. (There is scarcely any need to add that during the period we have considered the Ministry of National Education accorded little importance to incidents they considered unpleasant but minor and for all of which they blamed the "Chinese.") What was new in this revolt is that it gave priority to acts of disruption over intellectual criticism or political strategy. In practice, this meant that it was a direct action movement that did not work through a U.N.E.F.—weaker at Nanterre than nationally—and did not base itself, as the student movement at the Sorbonne had done a few years earlier, on analyses carefully worked out by intellectual groups.

The movement at Nanterre was entirely unbalanced; it had no organization, no doctrine, and no program. It was condemned either to exhaust itself where it was or to throw itself into more and more general activity. It was not a movement that had grown up in the midst of doctrinal and political struggles. Its action was not defined by direct opposition to a clearly defined social enemy, since the faculties of letters are not yet a powerful arm in the service of technocracy. The revolt was provoked by these faculties' attachment to old-fashioned cultural models and their present decomposition as much as by the scarcely begun subjection of some of their graduates to the control of the giant organizations. One must avoid excessive parallelism with the activity of the revolutionary socialist parties of the beginning of the century. Must we then move toward an inverse interpretation and say that the Nanterre movement, and the entire May Movement as well, was the expression of a crisis of change and particularly of the decomposition of the university system? This interpretation explains certain behavior and even a general tone which marked the movement. A good many of the incidents at the beginning of the year were revolts against meaninglessness, scandal responding to absurdity; expression often outran analysis and action.

But for this very reason the January demonstrators remained isolated in the faculty. Their influence was spread further not by their own proposals and deeds but by the administration's calling in the police. Not all the agitators became political activists. Their role was not very visible during the central period of the movement and reappeared only at the end when a kind of cultural conflict succeeded the real social struggle. The movement was framed within social and cultural demonstrations but it was formed against them as well as through them. It existed only because it fought in a practical way against the order it opposed instead of simply disengaging itself from it by a negative rejection which would have been more emotional than political. Its essential accomplishment was not the disorganized outburst of a rejection of culture and society, which would have accentuated the distance between the tendencies whose opposition I have described, it was just the opposite: their integration, their transformation into a movement capable of very diverse actions, ideas, feelings, and ambitions.

The emptiness, disorganization, and meaninglessness of the university were important precisely because they wiped out the particularities and limitations of the student experience. The Nanterre militants did not have to fight against the university which had no policy, took no initiatives, and did not even try to deal with the conflict in its midst. No screen blocked the sight of the passage from the old middle-class culture to the new role that the university was getting ready to passively assume in the "techno-structure" being formed. The student was not held back in "professional foolishness." He found himself in the midst of a crisis, with no protection against the rhetoric of the middle class, even on the left, or the grip of the new masters of society.

A composite of rejection of the past, struggle against the future, and revolt against present decomposition, the movement was led into total opposition. It no longer discussed or argued; it rejected dialogue. This was both crisis behavior and the point of departure for utopian activity, a total commitment to an entirely new model of society which becomes a political force through violent action.

The students moved from crisis to action because they felt threatened; at first, by the surveillance of the police and the alleged blacklists but, more importantly and in a more massive manner, as the university, overwhelmed by numbers, tried to get rid of a great number of students. Examinations no longer judged work; they selected and eliminated students. The threat of this selective process, associated with the Fouchet Plan, was the most constant theme of the agitation of these months. Not without reason, for the current in the university that favored it rapidly gained ground as the large faculties felt themselves increasingly submerged by the increase in the number of students. The realization on the part of many that opportunities were lacking led them to imagine that the government had decided to resolve this problem by brutally reducing the number of students. Many rumors circulated; irrational in terms of their precise content, they were justified if one considered that the government might well have been capable of barring entrance to the faculties, since it seemed incapable of redefining them and enlarging their functions. The convening of a ministerial commission, which never got beyond the stage of preliminary work and in which opinions were very diverse, along with the personal decision of the president of the Republic to introduce selective measures, strengthened the fears of the students toward the end of the period under consideration.

It is not sufficient to speak of crisis; the weakness and contradictions of the university organization were threats as well. The crisis of a system may explain the breakdown of individuals, their contradictions, their inability to organize and assume their social existence; it does not explain how a social movement is organized or how discontent is transformed into revolutionary opposition. If the crisis in the institutions had been less profound, the attack on the social order could have taken other forms and its tone or methods would have been different. But its fundamental themes, freed of the confusion of global struggle, would only be accused more strongly of this confusion. These themes were debated and articulated after May 3. Because the university system was in crisis at a time that society was developing and being transformed, the student movement, from its formation at Nanterre through scandal and provocation, exposed conflicts and prepared for struggles that concerned the whole of society.

Never could the term *movement* have been better used. This revolt was the deed of individuals who were not rebels but revolutionaries. The difference between the two attitudes is that rebels reject the established order and revolutionaries appeal to forces capable of destroying it and replacing it with another. That, at that date, this appeal was quite vague, that it determined attitudes rather than forms of organization is extremely important but must not obscure the essential consideration. Perhaps because the "enragés" of Nanterre did not run up against real repression in the faculty and because their movement remained limited and did not spread into the other faculties and universities, they did not settle into a student struggle but quickly assumed a general political orientation.

The coalition of the small political groups—Trotskyite, pro-Chinese, or anarchist—with the March 22 Movement, which lacked organization, insisted on spontaneity, was basically indifferent to purely university problems, and wanted to bring about the rebirth of the workers' struggle that had been swallowed up in political and union structures, ended by creating at Nanterre what has been called a detonator of more general social conflicts. This expression rightly recalls that the movement was not strictly a student movement. This particularly explains why a body of professors, who at first favored a liberal policy at the faculty, were rapidly bypassed and a majority of them were pushed toward a defensive and increasingly "disciplinary" attitude, ritualistic and repressive.

After May 13, the main activities of the March 22 Movement did not focus on Nanterre. Indeed, since May 2 the student agitation that was led by this movement constantly bypassed, in its inspiration and objectives, the framework of the university.

IV

❧❧❧❧❧❧❧❧❧❧❧❧❧❧

The Barricades

The movement that started at Nanterre in spring 1968, after the failure of the university strike of November 1967, was not defined by objectives specifically concerned with the university; it developed outside the U.N.E.F. Using spectacular tactics, it proclaimed a basic break with the university institution and the society of which it is part and which it serves. It carried within it the seeds of revolt rather than just a reform effort. But it would not have won such a large hearing in the faculty within a few weeks and could not have spread in such an extraordinary manner after May 3 had it not also directly concerned the students.

This elementary observation shows how far the movement was from the program of the "little groups" at Nanterre and other places. Distrust of the students was a fundamental attitude of these groups, as they defined their principles and programs and behaved like micropolitical parties or subversive intellectual groups. The situationists at Strasbourg, through the Schneider-Vayr Piova group, were not content to show the emptiness of the U.N.E.F. by seizing control of a local chapter. In a brochure, "De la misère en milieu étudiant," basically authored by Mustapha Khayati in 1966, they had attacked the students themselves as prisoners of a decadent bourgeois culture, bearers of ideology rather than consciousness, and incapable of historical action. The tone of the militants of the C.L.E.R.—Comité de liaison des Etudiants Révolutionnaires—which was to become the F.E.R. (Fédération des Etudiants Révolutionnaires) —was entirely different. They affirmed that the working class was the sole revolutionary force and reduced their university program to a struggle against the Fouchet Plan and selectivity and hence a defense of employment.

The March 22 Movement was also convinced that students must act within the labor movement, which in turn had to be freed of its bureaucratic shackles. After May 13, it essentially dedicated its activity to efforts directed toward working-class sections and industry. It remained, however, a student movement. Its social criticism originated in opposition to the condition of students and the organization of the university. It was neither a sect nor a cell but an open movement that accepted as members all who actively took part in its practical actions. Its lack of concern with orthodoxy minimized the internal quarrels that hinder the development of dogmatic groups. It addressed itself openly to the students with a practical daily program. It created a climate, entered into discussion with everyone who was interested, and multiplied its initiatives.

The kind of action inaugurated at Nanterre provoked the repression of May 3. It also explains the spontaneous response of students who were not connected with any particular political or intellectual group. More and more

massively, these students gave power to the movement
that was to climax on the Night of the Barricades, May
10–11, before precipitating an even broader social and
political crisis. Just as at Nanterre the preparatory phase
of the movement had succeeded in uniting programs or
intentions of revolutionary action to a student revolt
which was both immediate and global, so also during the
week that was the central moment of the strictly student
movement, two forces joined and reinforced each other:
the struggle against governmental and police repression
and self-affirmation, the creation of collective consciousness and action. While the launching of the strikes and
the consequent intervention of the political and union
organizations after May 13 gave the social crisis much
greater breadth and strengthened the militant students'
resolve to join the workers' struggle, this also introduced
a break in the movement as well as a transformation of
the student movement itself which was led to act on several
levels at once.

At first sight, the week of May 3 to May 11 seems dominated by the descent into the streets of a movement that
had until then been essentially confined to Nanterre. Student agitation seems to have been transformed into a
riot or perhaps an insurrection, as if the student movement met repression and counterattacked by taking the
offensive against the State, the master of the university. I
believe this view to be superficial and even false. The
student action during these days was not the beginning
of an insurrection. The essential fact is not the attack
against a regime but the formation of a social movement,
the active joining in the struggle against repression of
diverse and often divergent elements. The internal history of the movement is more important than the history
of its relations with other political and social forces. This
is true to the degree that during those days nothing
counted but the students' action and their conflicts with

the police. Parliament carried on its discussion amid general indifference; the political parties and unions were prudent and moderate in their attacks against the "little groups" without making any direct intervention; the government's only important role came from its weakness and contradictions. The barricades of the night of May 10–11 were a clear sign that the action had turned toward the creation of a movement rather than toward insurrection. They marked off a closed field within which were created group-consciousness and the consciousness of involvement in a common action. Barricades are not an offensive weapon, nor are they preparation for an attempt to seize power. The movement which was established behind them was not a political movement attacking institutions; but it was more than a revolt.

It was unable to all at once organize around itself the whole of a political struggle whose terms and forces had existed before it and now resisted the introduction of a new generation of social struggles. The best action possible within the situation of the new student movement was the integration of a social revolt with a properly political intention, that is, one directed against political and social power, the regime. At the same time, the movement necessarily moved beyond this limit of the possible; it was revolutionary, which indicates its nature and historical future. But what is beyond the possible, while it may not be any less important, is not as capable of creating and directing an historical situation as what corresponds to a movement's possibilities at a given moment. This was not the beginning of a revolution but the birth of a revolutionary movement.

After May 13, the action at the Sorbonne—a mixture of a cultural revolt and transformation of the university, street demonstrations, and campaigns directed at industry—will remain joined by many bonds but will no longer have a real unity. During the week of May 3–10, the unity of the movement, which was not ideological or doctrinal but practical and on the level of concrete action, was recognized by all and was experienced as such by the participants. We must analyze the evolution that carried the students' action to the point of its maximum possibility, which was well within the intentions and motivations of the militants but far beyond their expectations or anybody's predictions.

In the course of these days, a new element appeared: the students' action, having been expelled from the faculties of letters, took to the streets. It ran up against what one calls the forces of law and order and drew in, not the chosen directors of the university, but the political power itself. We must especially consider this conflict between the student revolt and the system of political decision-making. One can speak here of riots—although the term merits criticism—rather than revolutionary crisis. A social force conflicted with legal power and order. The whole of society was stupefied and hesitated to take sides.

The Split

At the outset, there was repression which began with the entrance of the police into the Sorbonne. This event had much greater importance than the closing of Nanterre or the announcement of the coming appearance of eight Nanterre students before the disciplinary council.

A few hundred militant students, the majority of the "activists" (with the exception of the U.J.C.M.L. [Union des Jeunesses Communistes Marxistes-Léninistes]) , gathered in the courtyard of the Sorbonne. This was a further development of the action at Nanterre which had been chased from that distant suburb by the closing of the faculty. As had happened there, a countermove by the extreme right-wing Occident (which had some support in the law school) was reported and some extreme right-wing groups demonstrated on the Boulevard Saint-Michel. In the face of the agitation in the Sorbonne courtyard, Roche, the rector of the Académie de Paris, a member of the university, professor at the Collège de France, and also an authority named by the government, may have thought that he would not be able under these conditions to close the Sorbonne as simply as Nanterre had been closed. Fearing that the students who had gathered would take over the premises, he decided, with the agreement of the dean of the faculty of letters, to have the place cleared by the police. Having confirmed this order, the police proceeded with the evacuation and, without much violence, led the assembled students out into police vans. It is not important to know whether or not those in charge of this operation saw it as an unexpected opportunity, once and for all, to get rid of all the agitators, who had imprudently gathered inside this marvelous trap. What is important is that the entrance of the police into the symbolic center of the French university system and the exit onto the Rue de la Sorbonne of the militant students who had been handed over to the police were immediately seen as a use of force, a blow against the university, and brutal repression. Violent clashes broke out immediately and spread rapidly. Opposition turned into combat. There was great surprise on both sides but the sentencings *en flagrant délit* on Sunday under very unusual circumstances, the expectation of the students' appearance before the disciplinary council, and, above all, the stationing of the police in the Latin Quarter around the Sorbonne and its surroundings, provoked the anger and revolt of a great mass of the students and indeed of the whole student body. And meanwhile, the resolution of leading groups or individuals showed itself as they did not hesitate to attack the police barriers. The extension of the movement was first of all a reaction of defense:

"Free Our Comrades" and "Liberate the Sorbonne." In a few hours the students were transformed from a heterogeneous, diverse, and disoriented mass into an individual. Not, of course, that all the Parisian students came into the streets but when did the labor movement ever gather all the workers?

That is the first and most extraordinary fact. The U.N.E.F. and the S.N.E.Sup. entered the movement but it was the movement that moved them forward; the established organizations, without which action would assuredly have been very difficult, did not launch the movement. This spontaneity did not fuse all the groups—the "little groups," the March 22 Movement, the U.N.E.F. militants, and the great number of students with whom young workers and unemployed young people quickly mingled—but it did unite them in the active expression of revolt, indignation, and resentment and in the push toward social transformation.

The movement was neither conscious nor organized. The street action was not like moving a piece in the political chess game. It overturned the pieces and the game by the violence with which it responded to violence. For the first time in a long while, demonstrators did not flee before the police after they had chanted slogans and waved banners. Groups of young men attacked the police barriers. The offensive came from the people and the police, all kinds of police—it is not important to differentiate among them—were reduced to behaving not as "forces of order" but as occupation troops, surrounded by hostility, covered with insults, attacked with stones, defied by compact columns which quickly learned to protect themselves with helmets, handkerchiefs, goggles, and garbage-can covers against the police clubs and tear gas grenades. The confrontation of Friday the third, Monday afternoon the sixth, and the night of Tuesday to Wednesday the eighth were marked by extreme violence; there were hundreds

of wounded even though the police had not fired their
guns. Opinion in the Latin Quarter and in the whole
country favored the students. The occupation of the Sorbonne, the arrests and condemnations were viewed as
scandals. Perhaps because they did not make good people
fearful, the students had the psychological as well as the
tactical initiative and could mobilize for themselves hostility to the police, defiance of the State, and the confused
desire to escape the silence and pretenses of society. In the
streets of the Latin Quarter as at Nanterre, violence
created a split and this split mobilized people. Without
the casualties of Friday and Monday, the mass marches,
the first of which crossed Paris from the Latin Quarter to
the Arc de Triomphe on Tuesday the seventh, would
not have been possible.

An Insurrection?

Was this the violence of an insurrection? If the response
must be negative, it is not only because at this date the
movement remained limited, a students' or young people's movement whose political objectives remained vague
and which did not attack the centers of power or arms
depots, the courts or the prisons, but more because the
movement depended on the police reaction and occupation to nourish it rather than to draw it into offensive
action.

If it is not exact to speak of purely defensive action, at
least the effect of the demonstrations was much more a
matter of involving people, mobilizing them, and leading
them to participate than of beating an adversary. The
columns of demonstrators, whether they were crossing
Paris or attacking the barriers of the C.R.S. (Compagnies
Républicaines de Securité) —a section of the police created
after the revolutionary strike of 1947—were a proclama-

tion rather than a combat maneuver. Especially during
the first days, they affirmed their existence by marching.
They appealed to the public to participate, to become
active. They discovered and affirmed themselves as a mass
movement by taking over the streets and attacking the police. How different from the cohorts of May 1 or other
so-called popular demonstrations, when the slogans have
been worked out, decided upon, and passed on in advance
and the notables march at the head like the immediate
family in a funeral procession! There was extraordinary
inventiveness in terms of words and gestures. Thousands
of hands with all ten fingers spread chanted with one voice,
"Ten Enragés"; a group that filled the Boulevard Arago,
the Boulevard Saint-Michel, or the Champs-Elysées thun-
dered: "We Are a 'Little Group.' " Demonstrators snake-
danced in the Japanese fashion and addressed the public: "Your Children Are Concerned, You Are All Concerned."

This student revolt was also an appeal to the people.
The signs of revolutionary action quickly appeared:
clenched fists, singing the "Internationale," the words to
which had been quickly relearned, and the red flag everywhere, pulled from the national flag by tearing off the
other colors. The continuity of revolutionary action was
spontaneously affirmed and realized. As the days passed,
the unity of the students and workers in support of socialism was more and more strongly proclaimed. The
earlier opposition of the political sects, which distrusted
the whole student movement as well as any action for
university reform, was bypassed. Revolt against the Fouchet Plan, against the occupation and closing of the Sorbonne, against the imprisonment or detention of demonstrators was joined to an attack on a society and regime.
At that moment, the attack was perhaps even more directed at a regime and a political order for the immediate adversary was the police: "C.R.S. = S.S.," cried the

demonstrators marching in front of the police with their arms raised in the Nazi salute. This was also the theme of one of the posters (later published by the workshop of the Ecole des Beaux Arts) which were to cover the walls of the faculties and the Latin Quarter. Let us not, however, set up an opposition between a political struggle and a social struggle, between opposition to Gaullism and opposition to capitalism. The movement formed and transformed itself out of its immediate action, out of events and visible objectives perceived by all, out of a demonstration or a fist fight. The most immediate struggle nourished the most general revolt.

During that week, violence was rarely excessive or the expression of an inability to act in a practical way or to attain objectives. Each incident raised the consciousness of struggle to a higher level, until the Night of the Barricades. It was different later, after May 24 and at the beginning of June. But from May 3–10, violence created the movement; it revealed the conflict and explained the state of things. It carried the word, engendered reflection, and made decisions. It was experienced as the response to a violent situation camouflaged behind absurdity, injustice, and the good conscience of the established order, all manifested by the actions of the police.

The Decay of University Power

These demonstrations and clashes caught the government and, even more so, the university unaware, even though it was the rector of the university, Roche, who had precipitated the crisis by calling the police to clear the Sorbonne. The university authorities kept silent or limited themselves to ridiculous disciplinary repression which, the students felt, showed bad faith and contributed to the police repression.

Eight Nanterre students had been summoned to appear
on Monday morning, the sixth, before the university
council sitting as a disciplinary committee. On that day, it
was to hear the accused and prepare a decision which
would be given on the tenth. The students had the right
to be assisted by defenders, either attorneys or members
of the university. They decided to be represented by
four Nanterre professors who had offered to defend them.
Only one student, a member of the F.E.R., refused the
hearing and read a statement rejecting his judges before
he withdrew. The others were questioned and made their
statements in a Sorbonne that was isolated, while students
massed before the main entrance. Some professors from
the science department succeeded in gaining entrance to
the office of the rector and by their presence supported
the attitude of their colleagues at Nanterre. The whole
affair was a distressing symbol of a university system too
exhausted to feel its agony. Three days after Friday's confrontation, in an empty Sorbonne controlled by the police,
dignitaries of the university—more than one of whom
must have found it painful to be there—discussed the
disciplinary failures of Cohn-Bendit and his comrades who
were accused of having held meetings without permission
and of having disturbed the peace. The affair was so
badly managed that, at the suggestion of the dean of
Nanterre, it was soon forgotten. The rector did not wish
to be at the center of a new scandal. This was the one and
only action taken by the University of Paris. It becomes
easy to understand why transformation of the university
could not be discussed within the framework of the institution itself. It was going to take a louder noise to rouse
the deaf.

The Ministry of National Education had shown only
limited interest in the events at Nanterre. It did not
take them seriously and failed to inform itself adequately,
both because it was overwhelmed by its own impotence

and because its confidence that the institution was too weighty to be overturned isolated it from what was happening. It had almost no knowledge of the events. The only matter that occupied its attention was the great quarrel between the minister, Alain Peyrefitte, and the secretary-general and between this latter official and the bureau. Having been ordered by the president of the Republic to prepare measures for selectivity and sensing this to be dangerous ground, it moved forward with great reluctance, preparing to ask Parliament to recognize that the baccalaureat should no longer automatically open the door to the university. It planned no concrete measures before the beginning of the 1969 school year. The minister thought he had plenty of time and busied himself dissipating the atmosphere of distrust that had been introduced by his predecessor between the minister and the teaching profession. He wished to give priority to pedagogical reforms and interested himself in the Amiens Conference as he had in the earlier conference at Caen. He wanted to wait, to move step by step, to go along with adjustments rather than introduce radical changes into an enterprise with such unpredictable reactions. He had not wanted to take responsibility for the closing of Nanterre a few weeks earlier nor had he wanted to appear as the originator of the call to the police to empty the Sorbonne. He was all the more unwilling to take major initiatives because he had never held unshared authority even in his own domain. The Elysée Palace (residence of the president) and Rue de Matignon (residence of the prime minister) governed the Ministry of National Education as much as its own offices on Rue de Grenelle. The president of the Republic had such horror of disorder that one could not move very far in a discussion that had been precipitated by the action of the "enragés." The prime minister had too much attachment to the traditional university and too little esteem for the social sciences to be disposed to move in the direction demanded by the psychology and sociology students of Nanterre.

After the massive demonstration of Tuesday, the seventh, which remained calm through the whole evening, everyone felt that a new offensive phase was being prepared, because the movement that had that day accepted the fruits of Monday's battle could not, without exhausting itself, endlessly move around Paris as if it accepted the police occupation of the Sorbonne. While the National Assembly was meeting that Wednesday in the presence of the Minister of National Education, some members of the university took different initiatives in their own name. Several Nobel Prize laureates, led especially by Jacques Monod and Alfred Kastler, asked the Minister of National Education for a gesture of appeasement. A Nanterre professor made contact with some members of the Cabinet and suggested that the minister announce his decision to reopen the faculties as a first step toward a relaxation of hostilities. As the demonstration planned for the end of the day was gathering at the Halle-aux-Vins, where the new Science Faculty had been built, a certain relaxation was evident. These university figures and those who shared their feelings had no wish to act as mediators. On the contrary, they were among the few professors who had openly taken the side of the student movement; but they wanted the university institution out of the hands of the police. The reopening of the faculties and the liberation of the prisoners would make the university face its responsibilities. The pause that they won did not last long and did not change the conditions of the struggle. Some militant students proclaimed their intention to enter the Sorbonne at any cost, a proposal that the government was all too pleased to take seriously. The Night of the Barricades was to demonstrate, a few hours later, that this was not, however, the intention or objective of the student movement.

When the decision to reopen Nanterre did not cause a major incident, the minister still decided not to reopen the Sorbonne for fear that courses could not be renewed in a normal manner. This was indeed predictable, for the situation was far from normal. Obviously only the most direct pressure was possible. By midday Friday, everyone knew that the evening would not be calm. The government knew it too, and had the bridges guarded by sizable contingents of police.

When the Prince Dreams

The vacillation of the government during those days—and this would be most obvious during the Night of the Barricades—cannot be explained simply by the fact that the prime minister was away on a visit to Iran and Afghanistan. Any politician of the old school would have felt the ground trembling. But these ministers, informed or not, authoritarian or liberal, were not representatives of the country; they were the prince's clerks. According to their varying abilities, they did their jobs and worked toward fostering growth and modernization. They distrusted the former leaders and had been seduced by the new ones. And they didn't really believe that there could be huge and open social conflict in a society where there was great material progress and in a country that conceived itself as playing a decisive role on the world scene. They had the same peace of mind as the bourgeoisie of Louis-Philippe's reign who did not foresee the revolt of the workers because they identified themselves with the new society and thought they were progressive since they were fighting the Ancien Régime and the clergy. They were sure of their strength because they had, they thought, bridged the old and the new ruling classes.

But above all, the ministers were too dependent on the

prince to be able to undertake any real political action.
It took a precise threat, the recognition of a serious political risk for this regime, to appeal to a political man, a
man who knows both how to listen and when to speak,
how to exercise imagination and how to negotiate. For
the court cannot live completely sheltered from the noises
of the city and the countryside. For several years, it has
been the role of one of the most able men of the Fourth
Republic, Edgar Faure, to fill in the gaps and negotiate
with the country. The ministries of Social Affairs and
National Education, on the contrary, both antiquated
administrations, highly regulated and covered with the
cold remains of old social conflicts, tended to concentrate
all decisions within the Cabinet, depending directly on
the ministers. The grasp of social reality was reduced to
stormy but steadily maintained conversations with important members of the professions and the unions.

The impotence of the government climaxed at the high
point of the crisis. On Friday, May 10, the student reaction to the refusal to reopen the Sorbonne, to the maintenance of police forces in the Latin Quarter, and the con-
finement of the arrested demonstrators was so clearly
expected that the government prepared itself for some
attempts at conversation. Through the intermediary of
Sarda, attorney for the U.N.E.F., and P.-M. de la Gorce,
both left-wing Gaullists, discreet overtures were made to
the leaders of the student organizations, Jacques Sauvageot
for the U.N.E.F., and Alain Geismar for the S.N.E.Sup.
Conversations through representatives or through Radio-
Luxembourg went on intermittently from midafter-
noon to the end of the evening. Nuanced formulas, in
which a word or the tone of a phrase was sometimes modified, were used in a manner that might have suited a
meeting of the United Nations or a labor negotiation with
groups already broken into the slow and complex strategy
of conflicts that have already been largely institutionalized.

These efforts were a mockery after a week of demonstrations, fights, riots, when addressed to a movement that was both multiple and spontaneous and to leaders who were not at the head of structured groups, maneuvering in the calm of their offices and conference rooms, but were engaged in the preparation of a massive demonstration and were later to be at its heart, standing on a bench on Rue Gay-Lussac in front of the Radio-Luxembourg car. The next day, M. Pompidou, disembarking from his airplane after the battle, did not hesitate to speak publicly on radio and television and did not back away from extremely frank formulas, which demonstrated particularly the subjection of the court system to the executive power. On Friday, no ministerial voice made itself heard and this silence was all the more strongly resented because the conversation between Alain Geismar and the vice-rector, Chalin—broadcast by Radio-Luxembourg and heard by the demonstrators over transistors the people living along the streets put in their windows—announced that a quick response was expected from a minister to the three points demanded by the leaders of the demonstration: opening of the faculties, removal of the police, and amnesty. For over an hour, this response was awaited but never came.

The same silence and impotence greeted several final efforts that were made in the course of the night. In particular, this was the case with the mission of exploration and discussion, rather than negotiation, undertaken at the initiative of a professor by a group of professors and students, among whom were Daniel Cohn-Bendit, a professor from the Paris Faculty of Science, another from the Sorbonne, and another from Nanterre. Before observing the action of the students and understanding the meaning of the Night of the Barricades, we must pause one last time over the behavior of those who were separated and protected from the students by the helmets, clubs, and grenades of the police. This delegation entered the Sorbonne before midnight to see Rector Roche. Sad, silent, hardly really present, he at first refused his visitors' request to leave the Sorbonne and inform himself directly about the situation in the Latin Quarter. He then repeated the themes that had already been discussed for several hours. When the delegation made him understand the urgency of a clear and public act, he retired to a neighboring room with the vice-rector and the secretary-general of the university to telephone his minister who then spoke to one of the professors, who impressed on him particularly the necessity of arranging for removal of the police. The minister, who along with the Minister of the Interior, Christian Fouchet, and the interim prime minister, Louis Joxe, represented the government at this movement, answered only by repeating the impossibility of capitulating in the face of a riot. Before returning behind the barricades on the Rue Gay-Lussac, the visitors asked the rector for his resignation as a gesture indicating that the university authorities refused to associate themselves with the attack on the students. When he refused, they left. As they crossed the first barricade at the entrance to Rue Gay-Lussac, the first tear gas grenades were falling; it was 2:12 A.M. The government had been too far outstripped by the events, too isolated, and without support in public opinion to be able to undertake a strong policy. It found itself suddenly facing a situation from which there was no way out. Disorders which had been judged minor suddenly became a conspiracy against public order and the foundations of the regime and society. It never gave a political reaction; it never showed itself except through the police. Neither of the two leaders of the political system made his voice heard; no minister dared to speak, discuss, or negotiate; the rector remained silent even though the vice-rector had tried to take some initiative, particularly on Tuesday night.

The directions given to the demonstration which

started from Place Denfert-Rochereau were not governed by any knowledge of the situation in the Latin Quarter, which was nevertheless very simple to obtain. The blockaded bridges indicated that the government's essential consideration was to keep the demonstrators from reaching the Right Bank and approaching Avenue Kléber, the site of the Vietnamese peace conference to which the president of the Republic attached the greatest importance, since it witnessed his personal influence in world affairs, or threatening the Elysée Palace or the Ministry of Justice, headquarters of the interim premier, or the Hôtel de Ville, which evoked memories of the Commune. That day—as well as the next day in M. Pompidou's capitulation speech—the student movement was not taken seriously. Let it agitate on the Boulevard Saint-Michel, even give it the Sorbonne; the Latin Quarter is used to such incidents and society cannot be threatened by students.

The Night of the Barricades, May 10–11

The Night of the Barricades was neither a riot nor an insurrection. Why then were there barricades?

The demonstration—which had moved around the Latin Quarter along the Boulevard Arago, Rue Monge, and the Boulevard Saint-Germain, becoming angry as it neared the C.R.S. barring the streets leading up the hill—went back up the Boulevard Saint-Michel and came out on Place Edmond-Rostand in front of the Luxembourg Gardens facing Rue Soufflot, which was blocked. It was a moment of confusion. Moderate elements, the Communists in particular, wanted to carry out a labor union-type march; others, like the F.E.R., whose sympathy with the workers made them mistrust purely student objectives, rejected the temptation of direct action and an attack on the Sorbonne. At the same time, small groups began to pull up paving stones, proclaiming both their unwillingness to be led around Paris by the government and its police, and their determination to attack the Sorbonne and to provoke the most violent disruption as the only means to mobilize the revolutionary forces.

If they had been followed, it would have been insurrection, all the weaker because nothing indicated that the proletariat was ready to come from East Paris and the suburbs in order to create a new Commune. It was the explosion of a still badly integrated and unorganized social force, the movement of students and other youth elements. The best representative of this movement, its spontaneity and its power of involvement, Daniel Cohn-Bendit, armed with a bullhorn, called out orders or rather incitements to action that were completely opposed, the apparent naïveté of which demonstrates novelty and imagination. Having put an end to the pressure for aggressive action by calling out, "We will not enter this whore of a Sorbonne so long as our comrades have not been freed," which had been suggested to him by a philosophy professor who found himself near him at that moment, he then called out: "Don't stay crowded together here; occupy the Latin Quarter from Rue Gay-Lussac to Rue Mouffetard. Form groups of twenty, fifty, or a hundred for discussion and action." The important thing for him was not violence but formation of determination for collective and responsible action. He wished to break down the passivity and unconsciousness that can cover mass demonstrations as well as violent and limited acts. It was a matter of transforming the revolt against the student situation into revolutionary consciousness that would raise itself into political action and become capable of drawing together all the revolutionary forces of society.

These group discussions could not be calm conversations. The work of tearing up paving stones continued;

the police were a few yards away; it was necessary to defend oneself and be able to retaliate. The barricades were
defensive armor, not offensive weapons. They were the
enclosure built around a society in the process of formation, in which students and young workers were beginning
to unite and which was becoming conscious of itself by its
physical separation from the territory occupied by the
police. This was the ultimate realization of a critical university: the creation opposite the Sorbonne, which belonged to the police, of a Latin Quarter that belonged to
the students and the people. On certain barricades under
construction, there was a strong offensive spirit, especially
on Rue Le Goff where there were many young workers.
Only the influence of Cohn-Bendit avoided an attack on
the C.R.S. barriers facing the barricades. In other places,
it was a small camp constructed without strategic planning, simply a work of lived political thinking, that enclosed the demonstrators and put them at the mercy of an
encirclement. The barricades enclosed only a few thousand demonstrators but it was a people's society confronting the police, who were the only real evidence of the
dominant order whose leaders were hiding behind them.

The popular character of the society behind the barricades was reinforced by the attitude of the inhabitants of
the section, especially on the Rue Gay-Lussac, who aided
the demonstrators, kept them informed, later threw them
water to fight the tear gas, and sheltered the refugees. It
was reinforced also by the radio, for the demonstrators
felt the presence beside them of millions of listeners in
Paris and the whole country, who were overwhelmed
and, for the most part, favorable. (The Radio-Luxembourg reporters, especially, gave the events in the Latin
Quarter unprecedented coverage.)

That small groups invented urban guerrilla tactics in
the field, climbing onto roofs, spreading barbed wire,
pouring out the gasoline from automobiles that were over-

turned or used in the barricades, is certain; street fighting is learned more rapidly that way than by studying
official or revolutionary strategy courses. There was no
plot, no secret leaders—simply a refusal to leave the
Latin Quarter to the police and a determination to exist
as a group and a movement. The barricades were the
response to a social order reduced to the massive, mute
power of its police. They can mean the uprising of a group
that has lost its power and throws itself into violence to
save its self-rule and escape its impotence, as was the case
in Algiers. They can also be the revolutionary act of a
social movement which has not encountered any particular adversary and cannot define any precise objective
but which runs up against the brick wall of the established
order, the real union between the forces of domination
and the institutional system. The barricade is the weapon
of those who cannot make themselves heard because they
are not recognized, because they do not fully recognize
themselves, because they embody grievance and revolt.

If the Night of the Barricades had been an insurrection, Saturday morning would have dawned on a catas-
trophe, the victory of the police and repression. But it was
a night of victory, since it caused a government retreat,
launched the general strike of May 13 and the factory
occupations that followed it, led to the student occupation of the Sorbonne and the other faculties—in short,
made society enter an unprecedented social and political
crisis. The old university, cowering in silence, sheltered
by the C.R.S., died because the students constructed
their barricades facing it. All the hierarchies, all the forms
of authority were broken by what was both a rejection
and an affirmation. The Night of the Barricades could
have been a burst of violence in which the student movement would have been dissolved but, on the contrary,
violence was carried to the barricades from the police

side. After the attack was launched by the policemen in black or khaki, the violence—not the actual fighting but the brutality of those who are pure force—broke out, not only in the streets, courtyards, and apartments but even more scandalously in the police stations, the police vans, and the Centre Beaujon, where most demonstrators were imprisoned, which was to become, especially on the second Night of the Barricades (May 24–25), the headquarters of cruelty. The government reacted to the students' action only through the police: in the end, the individual policeman, more so than the police department, rediscovered the habits of the "rat hunts"—without, however, going as far as in the good old days of the Algerian war and October 1961 when Algerians were massacred—and responded with racist and xenophobic brutality, lewd, savage, and uncontrolled.

Liberal or tolerant members of the university had in the end acted only by subjecting students to a disciplinary tribunal. Likewise, on a different level of violence, liberal ministers and a prefect of police, who undoubtedly strove to limit the brutality, acted in fact only through the clubbings and cold-blooded savage violence in the police stations. Even before the strike movement caused a few days of strictly political crisis in which the student movement could not directly take part, the Night of the Barricades was the culmination of a social crisis, of the decomposition of a social order ornamented with *grandeur,* principles, and institutions but reduced to the most sordidly violent response to the outburst of opposition and revolt which accused and revealed, beyond all appearances, its repressive nature. The police violence was not only a moral and juridical scandal. At the heart of a society settled in self-satisfaction and good conscience, it revealed the established order's inability to organize, since it was reduced to repression.

Birth of a Movement

After the Night of the Barricades and the May 13 strike which was a response to it, the social and political crisis assumed far broader dimensions than the university system's problems and the student movement. For many of the most active student militants, for example, the March 22 Movement and the U.J.C.M.L., the labor strikes, displacing the union bureaucracies and certain pressures toward self-management, assumed much more importance than the events of the specifically student-oriented week of May 3–10. This feeling was justified because, as has been said many times, the student movement was not primarily an effort to reform the university but a basic indictment of society and its culture.

If the May Movement was not simply a response to the crisis in the university, neither was it the action of an intelligentsia acting as an avant garde of a new worker movement. It was specifically a student movement only to the degree that it was not an authentic social movement and to the degree that it demonstrated the archaic and maladjusted nature of an educational system in crisis. It was also an uprising of the young who are both attracted and marginalized by social change. Finally, it was instrumental in creating a new class conflict in which the elite workers are no longer the principal protagonists but are replaced by technicians and experts—whether we call them by these names, or whether they are workers in certain industries or students—as the leaders of a class that opposes the brokers of technocratic power. These three meanings were joined during the week that led to the barricades. After that, they separated from each other because the student movement could not transform itself into a complete class struggle. The violence, the activity in the worker movement, the cultural revolt, and the

transformation of the university often continued to con-
verge and were often expressed at the same meetings and
by the same individuals but they were, nevertheless,
distinct.

The Night of the Barricades was not the most advanced
point of the May crisis but it was the high point of the
creative unity of the movement. It was a unity grown out
of revolt and a break with society rather than the kind of
unity developed from practical politics, revolutionary or
reformist. All the richness and complexity of the movement after May 11 can be understood as a combination
of efforts to pursue this unity beyond what had been
possible in that given historical situation. The May Movement was able to pose problems but could not resolve
them by initiating specifically political, organized action.
It stood at the juncture of two societies which have in
common certain forms of economic management but
which are profoundly different, not only in terms of economic power but also in terms of historic situation, since
the weight of twenty years stagnation is still felt after
twenty years of growth.

Getting rid of the leftovers of the past and at the same
time struggling against new powers and new constraints
may produce either a revolutionary movement or merely
a brief, violent crisis. The first outcome is more probable
if an economic and political crisis is precipitated and if
an ideological and political movement is able to take the
initiative away from an archaic political power. Essentially, this was not the situation in France. Gaullist power
was not that of the old bourgeoisie; it was built on what
can be called monopoly capitalism, organization capitalism, or technocracy. Despite sizable unemployment, the
French economy was not in crisis in 1968 and, despite
its fragility, it was coming close to the full realization of
the industrial Common Market under conditions which
were not catastrophic. If many students and young work-

ers faced serious employment problems, these were due at
least in part to the fact that they were badly trained. On
the whole, French society was not engaged in any on-
going economic, political, or military crisis. Those who
rebelled in May demonstrated their rejection of a particular social way of life rather than their inability to subsist materially in society. There was more revolutionary
will than revolutionary situation. As a result, the movement was more capable of opposing society than of over-
coming it, of imagining new forms than of transforming
it; it was also more capable of expressing itself than of
organizing. Therefore, the Week of the Barricades was
both the moment when the new power of opposition
affirmed itself most forcefully and the starting point of
less immediate actions which were richer in programs and
political plans but which could not enjoy such obvious
success.

We must go back to the events themselves, which we
have already rapidly described, in order to understand
what happened during that week. The Night of the Barricades was more than the culmination of a week of confrontations, more than material defeat for the students
which provoked such a public outrage that it turned into
a victory by the government's capitulation. The image of a
gradual approach toward violence explains nothing. The
Night of the Barricades directly occasioned the general
strike of May 13 and the later occupation of the university faculties and factories, whereas one week before there
had been only a university crisis and some street clashes.
Such a change signifies that in a few days a social force, a
social movement, had been born: a group was defending
its interests, fighting against an adversary, wrestling with
the direction of society. This had repercussions in other
social groups and in places far away. These three elements
may have been mixed in the ideas and rhetoric of the
preceding weeks but they were not combined in practice.

In the course of the week, we find them separated into clearly distinct tendencies and moments.

In the first place, the self-defense of the students and the crisis in the university system maintained a kind of independence from each other. The S.N.E.Sup. entered the movement as a force concerned with the university and Alain Geismar became a central figure in the movement only gradually. Constantly, but especially on Tuesday, May 8, overtures from the Minister of National Education met a favorable response there. The professional educational associations and the majority of the teachers who took part in the student movement did not wish to limit it to the university but wanted the movement to be allowed to return to the faculties so that it could impose changes on them. Whatever judgment one may make of this tendency, it existed and was strong enough to prove that the self-defense of the students was not entirely based on a purely insurrectionary movement. That it did not carry the day is partly due to other opposing tendencies in the movement and especially to the impotence of the minister, whom the Elysée Palace forbade to promise amnesty and who did not dare to reopen the Sorbonne.

In the second place, there was the struggle with the adversary, the police, backed by the government and the regime. The police action of May 3 and the street fighting that followed brought about the participation of many who did not feel directly involved in the struggle over the university. Militant determination was combined with a sense of solidarity with comrades who had been wounded or arrested. This tendency did not characterize any particular group as much as it was a collective reaction—a crowd reaction, if one wishes—that was able to lead from street fight to riot to insurrection. Violence responded to violence and also affirmed itself by its very power to create a rupture in society. On May 10 and 24, tearing up of paving stones was primarily the work of this movement of violence, this spirit of combat. This element, however, can no more be identified with the whole of the student movement than the preceding one, to which it was opposed but with which it was combined.

Then, in the third place, there was the appeal to the working class, the student movement's growth beyond strictly university problems and the use of revolutionary symbols. This component grew continuously stronger in the course of the week and prepared the way for the extension of the movement, the general strike, and the workers' occupation of the factories. But it also maintained a certain autonomy. The political groups most oriented toward the working class—the Communist students, the young Marxist-Leninists or Trotskyites of the F.E.R.—did not play a central role in the student demonstrations and, significantly, did not take part in the Night of the Barricades. Autonomous or even opposed to each other as they may have been, these elements of the movement were united—not fused, for their differences reappeared after May 13—in the course of the week strongly enough that on the morning of May 11 everyone definitely sensed the existence of a movement. How did this union, this integration of diverse, complementary, or opposed elements come about? It was due partly to an action internal to the movement and partly to the general situation.

The action within the movement was, to be more precise, the work of the March 22 Movement, the J.C.R., and the leaders of the student associations. Of the three groups, the first was the most important. The week belonged to Daniel Cohn-Bendit and his comrades because they had already achieved, as we have seen, the fusion of these three elements within their Nanterre movement. They were revolutionaries oriented toward the working class, who still recognized the leading role of the students and were not locked into political or organizational bureaucracies. Organized for immediate, violent, and aggressive actions, they were not the extremists of the movement but rather its central unifying force. The J.C.R., which was more highly organized, also played an important role by refusing to follow the F.E.R. in considering student problems secondary to the worker problems. Finally, the student leaders played a unifying role. Alain Geismar had reached the presidency of the S.N.E.Sup. by overturning the majority faction and breaking with the policy of defense of special, corporate interests. He kept its defense of the university from setting itself limited objectives. The position of Jacques Sauvageot was similar. The U.N.E.F. scarcely existed any longer and could not be influenced to limit itself to objectives concerned with the university. By politicizing its activity, it was able to come back to life and emerge from the decline into which governmental persecutions and its own internal dissensions had plunged it.

But despite the importance of these unifying forces, they would not have succeeded, had the government not powerfully aided them. On the evening of May 8, there was talk of demobilization. Speaking of May 9, several militant leaders have themselves said, "If the government had pulled back, we would have pulled back too." But despite the promise to reopen the Sorbonne, it remained closed; the arrested demonstrators remained imprisoned. The "university" effort of Tuesday was forgotten thirty-six hours later. The most violent tendency within the movement was never very important in itself; there were not many students who were prepared to start the kind of confrontation that would lead to insurrection. But the government unified the movement by its very weakness; the police were important. Students who saw only the massive barriers of the C.R.S. attributed to the government a strength and unity it did not have. If it had spoken, it could have caused hesitation and division but its silence looked like a firm position. The surrounded and occupied Latin Quarter and the locked-up Sorbonne concentrated the students' anger and aspirations. Neither a policy of firmness accompanied by explanations nor a real effort to negotiate would have allowed the movement to take on such strength. The absence of policy, which reduced the government to the police, drew the students, through the dialectic of violence responding to violence, into a kind of impasse.

But an impasse for whom? For the student movement, if it had been only the agitation of small groups or a schoolboy disorder. On the contrary, the impasse, which took the form of the barricades, accomplished the fusion of vigorous elements united in the struggle against the police. Since the police and the State forbade the Sorbonne to the students, this concrete situation imposed unity on the student movement: the occupation of the Sorbonne provoked the student defense; the power of the police aroused violence in return; the involvement of the State caused it to be indicted.

But a complete and lasting unity could not be formed in the streets. After May 13, participation in the workers' struggle, violent street actions, and the transformation of the university became once more what they had been: activities united by many bonds but at the same time increasingly independent of each other. By June 10, there was a great difference between what happened at Flins; between the Renault workers' and the students' confrontations with the police; between what happened in the streets of Paris when the third wave of barricades was raised and what was being argued and expressed at the Sorbonne and the law faculty. No political organization, no political structure, no ideological and strategic program came along to unite into a coherent and centralized movement what had been molded by street battles. But the movement continued to maintain united strength through the diversity of its activities.

The essential point of our analysis in the second half of

this book can be summed up in these terms. The three areas in which the May Movement acted were: transformation of the university system, cultural revolt, and the workers' struggles. Each of these brings into play one of the three elements that constitute a social movement: group defense, attack on an adversary, and the redefinition of the social situation. After May 13, the history of the movement is one of tensions in each of these areas between the isolation of specific actions and the consequent breakup of the movement, and the involvement of the total social movement in each of its areas of application. On one side, there were university reformism, cultural subversion, and the move toward the people, elements opposed to each other but being, in common, dispersed elements of a movement that has broken up. On the other side, at the same time, there were the desire for self-management, the introduction of opposition into the university, and the joining of students and workers, all distinct but connected forms of the action of one single social movement that defines and establishes itself through these complementary actions. The unity formed on the barricades was not maintained in the form of a political organization but did continue to exist as social practice, despite conflicts and partial divisions.

For those who wish to write the history of a crisis of French society, the Week of the Barricades is only a beginning, a step on the ladder that will lead to May 29–30, when the future of the regime seemed suspended, when everything came undone, when the departure of General de Gaulle was expected and desired even in the ranks of his most committed partisans. But if one chooses to center the analysis not on French society but on the social movement formed within it—transcending the level of French society both by its social impetus and by fitting into an international tendency—the Week of the Barricades must be considered the central moment of the movement. Dur-

ing those days, a social movement was formed whose implications, crises, and victories were spelled out in the
following weeks. Despite the immediate pressure of action,
or rather because of it, the fundamental problems of the
new movement were argued out in meetings, gatherings
of militants, and tracts. That week did not overturn the
world; it was not the political achievement of decades of
revolutionary analysis and practice. But it created, beyond
protests, revolts, and sects, a new social movement that will
perhaps be dismembered, disorganized, or repressed but
which will mark, directly or indirectly, the social history of
the years to come.

The Barricades of Anger

Before successively treating the three areas of the May
Movement's activity—the worker struggles, the cultural
revolt, and transformation of the university—we must
pause over the street demonstrations of May and June
which led to the second and third Nights of the Barricades
and to confrontations that were sometimes even more
violent than those of May 11, without the same importance. As the principal problem became the task of joining
the spectacular but limited student movement to a more
massive but more controlled worker struggle, the meaning
of the street demonstrations changed. For a time, they retained their power to inspire and fuse the young workers
—students, laborers or employees, and unemployed persons—but they also served to point up other more influential events and they manifested a violence in the midst of
which a revolt, which could not articulate its own political
meaning, was liberated.

After several relatively limited demonstrations, a demonstration on May 24 led to what has been named the
second Night of the Barricades. It was a day of riots quite

different from May 10–11, primarily because of its social composition. The most important gathering took place when the students converged on the Gare de Lyon toward the end of the afternoon. The march sponsored by the C.G.T., which involved fewer people and was less dynamic, passed relatively unnoticed. (When part of this union march crossed the student demonstration near the Gare de Lyon, some of its participants, especially young workers, joined the students.) The demonstration of May 24 was more an affair of young people than of just students. There was no distinction between students and young workers, both groups about equally represented and equally mixed in the scuffles and struggle against the police violence.

The more general character of this demonstration occasioned a change of location of the action, a change that was accentuated even more in the later demonstrations. Since there were barricades at the entrance to the Rue de Lyon and the adjacent streets, an immense turn, initiated by Geismar and Sauvageot, carried thousands of demonstrators to the Place de la République, where there was fighting; to the Stock Exchange, where a fire was lit; and to the Place de l'Opéra and the principal boulevards before the call to the Latin Quarter was heard again and the most violent fights broke out on the Boulevard Saint-Michel and its neighboring streets. The form of the conflicts also changed: fires were lit and the barricades, no longer only protected camps, became more spectacular. On the Boulevard Saint-Michel, which is difficult to block and to defend, barricades were built, reinforced with trees that had been cut down. The police tactics also changed: the war of strategic positions became a war of movement. After an intense preparation with tear gas grenades, the C.R.S. charged on the run and a giant bulldozer, borrowed from the army, destroyed the scarcely built barricades. The repression also became much harsher; during that very night the Beaujon Center witnessed the most systematic and brutal violence. In the middle of the night, the student Sorbonne became a place of refuge and an aid station where the wounded and escapees from the fighting on Boulevard Saint-Michel and the Latin Quarter crowded in.

It was a night of rioting rather than revolt, during which the police were often outmaneuvered by a more mobile adversary which held a great portion of the center and east of Paris for a number of hours. At this date, public opinion was certainly much less favorable to the demonstrations than two weeks earlier. These demonstrations were better organized. On the Rue de Lyon, in the beginning of the evening, the March 22 Movement formed a strongly equipped battlefront to defend themselves against the police clubs and gas. Alain Geismar was the central figure of that day. Less directly bound to the student revolt than Cohn-Bendit, since he was both a teacher and a leader of the S.N.E.Sup., more "insurrectionary" and less attached than he to the expression of revolt, he was the leader of the great days during which the fusion of students and workers was forged in conflict with the police. During that night, the movement came closest to becoming an insurrection. It had taken for its objective the Hôtel de Ville to celebrate the hundredth anniversary of the Paris Commune. When the demonstrators arrived at the principal boulevards and the Place de l'Opéra, some groups wanted to press further, to attack the Elysée Palace and occupy the whole center of Paris. I believe it was the J.C.R. that influenced the demonstrators to turn back to the Latin Quarter, thus choosing to strengthen the fusion of students and young workers within the framework of the struggle launched by the students and to turn its back on insurrection.

The night of May 24–25 was the most violent moment of the May Movement and also a turning point in its evolution. It possessed the same power to inspire as on the first Night of the Barricades when the labor struggles were in their first phase. The negotiations at Rue de Grenelle began only on May 25 and on June 2 the rejection of the agreements by the large plants and the strikers renewed the movement. The night of May 24–25 was a cause of unrest and splintering as much as it mobilized and united. (Two days later the U.N.E.F. organized the meeting in the Charléty Stadium which we will discuss later.) As a political demonstration with no clear viewpoint, it had no immediate importance. Essentially, it was an effort to keep the movement from wasting its energy in useless violence. The movement no longer had to affirm its existence; it did have to transform itself, one way or another, into a political force and into a struggle focused in places of work.

The Minister of the Interior, whose lack of comprehension of the students and university personnel was exemplary, declared that the demonstrations after the Night of the Barricades were the work of the underworld, hoodlums, and delinquents. On the contrary, what is striking is the almost complete absence of looting and violations of common law all through this period. As for the young people who already had a bone to pick with the law, his accusation was never denied; indeed it was welcomed by the students who saw them as victims of society rather than criminals. This attitude sometimes assumed naïve forms, as in the affair of the Katangais * at the Sorbonne, but it testified to a conception of social pathology to which the sociologist can feel closer than he can to the ideas of the police or the idea that guided the Ministry of National Education for so long.

In refusing to act as guardians of the social order, the

* A group of delinquents who elected themselves security guards in the Sorbonne during the last days of the occupation. They took their name from the group of foreign mercenaries hired by the Katanga government during its secession.

students felt themselves in solidarity not only with the
workers and the unemployed, but also with the victims of
social disorganization. Every revolutionary movement
bears within itself an antisociety, hidden by the official
society, made up of the exploited, dominated, and alienated men who have been crushed by this society. The participation of non-student elements does not cast any doubt
on the usefulness of the demonstrations at a given moment. This participation, denounced by the courts and
the police, was actually a plus for the movement. My judgment is quite different from that of the courts: the street
demonstrations allowed the movement to become conscious of itself and hence reinforced it. After May 13, progress could only result from actions directed toward more
practical objectives, participation in the worker movement, or active criticism of the university institution.
After May 25, no street demonstration had any decisive
importance. They were reactions, aggravated by a sense of
impotence, especially at the time of the incidents at Flins.
The demonstration that gathered on June 11 at the Gare
de l'Est rapidly became violent. The police made many
arrests even before it began. After crossing Paris, it returned to the Latin Quarter where the clashes were very
violent. That was the third Night of the Barricades. There
were more barricades than on May 11 or 25 but the fighting was also more mobile. It was a night of anger and
desperate rebellion, a night of retreat rather than conquest. The demonstrations continued even after the closing of the university faculties, becoming increasingly
sporadic and marginal to the principal events of June and
July.

Rioting was not confined to Paris. In many large cities,
Lyon, Bordeaux, and Toulouse among others, events similar to those of May 24 took place, often with great violence. Emerging from the universities, the movement
broke into full view and clashed first of all with the "forces

of order" as the institutional expression of social power. This was a very transitory stage in the history of the movement and one which the most active militants never considered an end in itself, not because they were opposed to violence but because at no time was the student movement interested in a specifically political solution, as its relations with the political parties and unions show. It was never really a question of overthrowing Gaullism in order to replace it with a leftist government, a new Popular Front negotiated at the summit. This profound hostility toward political structures, even in terms of opposition to the regime, explains why, if there were riots, there was no insurrection. It also defines the difference between the demonstrations of the Week of the Barricades and those in late May and June. Only the former created revolt and mobilized forces that were then applied to basic activity in the action committees, factories, and businesses, and in the university faculties. Early in the evening of May 24, the demonstrators listened to de Gaulle's speech and his decision to organize a referendum. The speech was greeted with indifference more than anger. Nobody wanted to wage a struggle against de Gaulle. The struggle had to be against the society whose reality and contradictions were covered over by the Gaullist phenomenon and its reduction of the problems of society to problems of the State.

The May Movement could not be a directly political movement since it did not conceive itself in terms of political institutions and forces. The demonstrators were indifferent to the Parliament and contemptuous of its debate on the censure motion in the National Assembly. They were not concerned about obtaining a political solution to a crisis.

The student street demonstrations were never aimed at overthrowing the State. The C.G.T. demonstration on May 29 was the first to speak in a specifically political manner. If the demonstrations of May 3–11 were characterized by political pressure and the birth of the movement, those of May 25, June 12, and the other days were only a desperate search for immediate action. Such action had no more creative power once the movement was involved in the factories, working-class sections, university faculties, and the professions. Just as rhetoric was often separated from action at the Sorbonne or the Odéon, so in late May and June demonstrating in the streets was more and more separated from practical measures. The joining of energies had already been replaced by social struggle.

V

Students and Workers

From the outset, the student movement was disposed toward the working class. Its attack was more directly aimed against capitalism and Gaullist power than at the university system. The Night of the Barricades made possible the general strike of May 13 and its consequences. It would be erroneous to conceive an opposition between the student movement and the worker movement, as if they had only accidentally coincided through indignation against police repression. At the same time, it must be admitted that the working class did not rush into revolutionary action. Some groups participated actively in the movement: young laborers and workers in the advanced technical industries and research. But the mass of the working class either did not seek or avoided contact with the revolutionaries. Is the explanation of this fact necessarily either resistance or betrayal on the part of the most powerful union organizations? This is not a satisfactory explanation. Betrayal by the leaders does not explain the absence of a powerful revolutionary movement among the workers during May and June.

The May Movement called for revolutionary action and consequently appealed to the working class which had been the principal agent of such action in capitalist countries. But the movement's struggle revealed new kinds of conflicts in a new society. Certain categories of industrial workers are as much involved in them as the students. But today the working class as such is no longer the protagonist *par excellence* of historical evolution. There is a profound difference between the revolutionary action of the worker movement, which fought against capitalist property, and the May Movement, which was concentrated in certain university faculties and industries and marked the beginning of social struggles against a new type of economic organization and power: technocracy. When the new conflicts came to light, the older ones had already largely lost their capacity to arouse revolutionary action. There were several reasons. The older struggles had been institutionalized and the leftist parties had a good chance of electoral success in the near future. The main reason was that the working class, the manual laborers in the large companies —the "producers"—no longer historically constituted the agent of revolutionary action in our society, except in the "party subjectivism" of the Communist organizers.

Under other circumstances, the movement could have led to the victory of an insurrection or at least to an attempt to seize power. Once this outcome had been excluded—and almost nobody believed it was ever really a possibility—the May Movement seemed foreign to the efforts of the Communist Party or the Fédération pour Proposer un Gouvernement de Front Populaire, just as the 1848–1849 social movement had nothing in common with the political efforts of the leftist but middle class Ledru-Rollin. The May Movement never had political expression. It could never be more than a minority, even when it drew millions of workers into the strike. While this success allowed a new social class to define itself in action, it also created the illusion of a unity of conflicts and struggles that did not exist.

The May Movement invented new revolutionary perspectives, not in terms of imagination or theory but by its practice and its will. That it was always attached to the notion that these were the direct prolongation of the proletarian movements and revolutions does not discourage us from following an analytic approach that takes more exact account of what happened. The gap that developed between the revolutionary forces made up of workers and students and the political and labor union organizations is not to be imputed to one group or another, to Cohn-Bendit and Geismar or to Georges Séguy and Waldeck-Rochet, both in the Communist Party. It manifested a generational change in class conflicts. The continuity of revolutionary inspiration must not be allowed to hide the presence of new leaders, operations, and conflicts. Even though the new movement picked up earlier themes and appealed to the participants in earlier struggles, it was only able to grow by fighting tradition, conceptions, and forms of action that no longer corresponded to the present social situation. The movement's ideas were necessarily less innovative than its practice. Therefore, instead of merely reviewing its declarations or taking time to examine the quarrels, it is best for us first to consider the situation of the working class and its actions during recent years.

Evolution of the Working Class

In order to defend the idea that new class conflicts manifested themselves during May and June, an explanation must be sought in the transformation of the condition of the working class and also in the new practices introduced into the struggle in industry. As the March 22 Movement repeatedly insisted, one must refrain from making everything begin from March or May 1968 and remember that new types of conflicts broke out, albeit sporadically, well before spring 1968 in industry if not in the university.

For the past ten years, worker activity within industry can be detected only with difficulty. This statement may seem surprising; is not the labor union movement by definition situated within industry and directed against its capitalist management? This commonplace definition is deceptive. On the level of worker causes and the actions undertaken to sustain them, union activity under the Fourth Republic was clearly dominated by a defense of wages aggravated because of almost constant inflation and by political action that moved from the great insurrectionary strikes of 1947–1948 to the strikes launched to oppose American policy in Korea and "Ridgway the Plague." The great strikes of the summer of 1953 were both economic and political.* This terminology, which is totally inadequate today, recalls an action that was very similar to that of the C.G.T.U. in the Twenties. Opposition to the capitalist regime led to a total rejection of structural reform and to exclusive concentration on defense of wages at the same time as the labor force was mobilized for political objectives toward which only the action of the party could direct it, since they transcended the limited and spontaneous interest in worker problems of the masses.

This union of wage defense and political opposition was

* The strikes of 1947 and 1948, first launched in the coal mines, came after the exclusion of the Communist ministers from the government and after the Marshall Plan.

The Communist Party organized a major demonstration against General Ridgway during the Korean War.

The general strike of 1953 was initiated by post office employees during the summer and resulted in a political crisis.

applied particularly well in the public sector, the only strong position of French unionism, weak in private industry and even in the large companies but powerful in the nationalized sector, reaching the highest rate of union membership among teachers and postal employees. The C.G.T. never utilized the company industry committees created at the Liberation as bases for worker control over certain aspects of industry. On the contrary, a constant effort was made to block these committees from acting independently of the union. That the union was not recognized within industry is not simply the result of ownership authoritarianism. The leadership of the C.G.T. did not campaign for such recognition because it was afraid of anything that could appear to incorporate the union into industry. On a more general level, like the Communist Party, the C.G.T. style of unionism—the only really important one among the workers—defended all the "little people," wage earners or not, against monopolistic concentration. It waged a violent campaign against the C.E.C.A. and the Common Market, forecasting the collapse of wages and social advantages, when they were higher in France than in Germany and Italy, and predicting that free trade could only bring about equalization on a lower level.

Oriented in this way, union activity produced no great, over-all movements. There was a multiplicity of actions in defense of wages and numerous work stoppages on the occasion of even international political events. The climate was not set by an effort to agitate in order to increase the number of workers participating in union activity. Instead, there was a series of actions for which certain categories of workers were mobilized in order to unmask or repulse the enemy and combat the forces of reform. This military language can be appropriate in a period of revolutionary upheaval and offensives but expresses a weak degree of participation on the part of the concerned "masses." Militants, more at home in the bureaucracy than in the workshop, organized retorts, responses, and counter-attacks. It was still the France of coal, vineyards, and the civil service, in which the workers were used to depending on the State for increases and guarantees because the industrial enterprises were weak and themselves dependent on the State. In addition, they were internally governed by limited authoritarianism sometimes completed by a paternalism that had no concept of negotiation or worker claims.

If this picture is oversimplified, so be it. The fact remains that during the ten years between the split among the unions and the end of the Fourth Republic, trade unionism was neither an independent element of French social and political life nor a social force vitalized by its own internal transformations. We have set this description within the chronological framework of the Fourth Republic primarily for convenience; however, this has been largely true during more recent years also. The decline of certain sectors of industry, like the coal and iron mines and metallurgical enterprises, has in certain cases accentuated the defensive tendencies of the labor unions, limiting them to quantitative demands. Nevertheless, it is not artificial to place the break in 1958. Because the accession to power of the Gaullist regime weakened the role of Parliament and the political parties, it provoked the development of organizations which partially substituted themselves for the parliamentary parties. This was the role of the clubs and also of the unions, especially the C.F.T.C. (Confédération Française des Travailleurs Chrétiens), which became the C.F.D.T. after 1964. This organization, which had long been dominated by a social Christianity that was more traditional than reformist, had begun a little earlier to transform itself, thanks to veterans of the J.O.C. (Jeunesse Ouvrière Chrétienne), and to move among the workers instead of being confined to the large stores and offices. Some of these leaders, particularly Gilbert Declercq, a union leader in Nantes—which is no accident, as we shall see from the events of May–June 1968 —proposed new offensives like democratic planning, later called the counterplan. These tendencies were sometimes criticized as too participationist and ran into trouble because of a policy on profits which, according to union criticism, really amounted to wage controls. During the subsequent years, this led to increasingly vigorous activity within industry that was oriented toward qualitative, rather than merely quantitative, demands and concretely attacked power, management, and the organization of work.

This trend was joined by the leaders of the C.G.T. and especially by the militants within the large companies, who found themselves increasingly separated from the leaders of the local and regional unions, who remained organization men. The strikes against Peugeot at Sochaux —again we come to one of the most active centers of the 1968 worker movement—waged in a company that was adopting modern production methods and hardening its work schedules and internal organization, were a new kind of strike led by young militants who singled out the production schedules to indict the whole management of the industry. This new kind of union activity followed the even broader program adopted by the Italian metal workers' union, the communist-dominated C.G.I.L. under the inspiration of Bruno Trentin and Vittorio Foa in particular. These men established a close connection between industrial demands and general political and economic objectives, which until then had been separated. By analyzing modern capitalism, they rediscovered the central importance of problems connected with industrial management and the consequent necessity that labor action carry the combat onto this terrain instead of remaining either short of or beyond it. Not only did this new kind of union activity concentrate on the large industrial concerns and stop giving in to the Poujadist defense of all the "little people," but it penetrated the new skilled categories: technicians, technical agents, and staff. The first union struggle that attracted attention to this renewal of labor unionism was led at Neyrpic and its subsidiary Sogreah by personnel among whom technicians and staff members were a very important group.

More than anyone else, Serge Mallet (in *La Nouvelle classe ouvrière* [Paris: Editions du Seuil, 1959]) observed what he called the new working class, deliberately giving the expression an opposite meaning to the one given it at the same period by other observers. They were speaking only about the incorporation of the workers, especially young workers, into the consumer society and a lower middle class life-style. Mallet, on the other hand, found "new" workers both at Bull (a computer-building company controlled by General Electric) and Thomson, technicians or engineers who occupied a position in the company quite similar to their highly qualified pre-1941 comrades and who had new demands. It was no longer a question of defending a trade like the skilled workers of past eras. Nothing was further from their minds than the anarchic or revolutionary unionism proper to a working class in process of formation, still close to its rural origins and to the struggles against landed property and merchant capital. They were not concerned with defending minimal living conditions but with combatting economic and social management in the name both of technical rationality and the capacity—and will—of the workers to manage industry and, through it, society.

All these tendencies are important. In the May–June 1968 strikes, we again find many of the influences that first appeared in certain highly technical enterprises. Still, one must recognize their limits. For one thing, the penetration of militant action among highly developed workers, whose skills and economic level are far superior to those of the traditional worker categories, remains very weak. The great majority of staff personnel remain closely bound to management on which their careers depend. Mme Benot Guilbot's study of the Merlin-Guérin company at Grenoble showed that the salaried employees, designers, and technicians made greater demands than the workers in terms of the organization of the company but were less concerned than they about general economic and political criticism. The consequence of their orientation toward the company is that they often define themselves in terms of it. Problems of professional status, career, and defense against change and the economic threats it introduces can call into question the style of management, especially when there is an imbalance between technical management and financial management—which was the case in different ways at Neyrpic, Bull, and even Thomson at a given moment—but this smacks at least as much of Saint-Simon as of revolution. These become the demands of the new producers against the new hornets, a positive theme but one that is always in danger of becoming simple company reformism, when the ownership modernizes, becomes less proprietary and more technocratic.

The skilled workers of the end of the nineteenth and the beginning of the twentieth centuries became leaders of a revolutionary movement only to the degree that they joined with the unskilled laborers who had been attracted in great numbers by the development of heavy industries, metallurgy, railroads, and the docks and whose wages and jobs were constantly threatened. In the same way, this new aristocracy of producers has been able to move the worker movement forward to new demands only when it is pushed by the less privileged groups, who are less integrated into the company and are therefore more threatened. The disruption of society in May 1968 allowed the conjunction of very diverse worker forces and the union of objectives

concerned with self-management with more direct economic demands.

Before reviewing these diverse forces, we must insist on
the over-all change in the action of the unions. I spoke
earlier about the combination of coal-wine-civil service
work forces. In May and June, we saw a new combination:
chemical industries-automotive industry-teachers. A demand for self-management and the power to dispute company policy was substituted for a policy of redistribution
and guarantees. This change cannot be separated from a
profoundly modified analysis of economic life. Themes of
crisis and pauperization were replaced by others concerned with economic growth and alienation. The present
question is not any longer how progress and reason can be
defended against the irrationality of capitalist exploitation but rather how to claim for the workers the power to
control growth against the power of large companies ready
to sacrifice those it deems marginal, who are victims of an
expansion that multiplies privileges and inequalities.

These statements correspond particularly to the transformation of certain teachers' unions. For a long time,
they were more preoccupied with defending teachers than
with criticizing the educational system and trying to change
it. Even the minority within the socialist Syndicat
National des Instituteurs, known as the Ecole Emancipée,
defended ideas that were more open to a criticism of the
school system and was interested in anti-authoritarian
pedagogical experiences, but its analysis remained influenced more by the traditions of anarcho-syndicalism
than by the new teaching problems. Independents and
Communists among the teachers in the second degree or
in technical teaching opposed each other but their opposition—expanded corporate defense based on sometimes
remarkable achievements versus participation in more
political action—never emerged from the older forms of
unionism.

In the university faculties, the S.N.E.Sup.—a very small minority among the professors, especially in the faculties of letters where the independent union was important and was inflexible in its corporate defensiveness and social conservatism—was dominated by Communists and concentrated on quantitative demands. For it everything was a matter of square meters, millions, supplementary posts —all important considerations but a terrain on which the government's defense was least weak. This policy obscured the more profound problems and led the union to take conservative or vague positions on the problems of university reform. The crisis that jolted the union and led to the election of a new national administration which was both more militant and determined to pose the fundamental problems of the university—its social function, management, and organization—was an important element in the transformation of the union movement. It allowed this union and its principal leader, Alain Geismar to play a central role during the May crisis, before finding itself divided and weakened by the struggle between leftists and Communists buoyed up by more moderate elements.

Three Types of Worker Action

I have just insisted on the innovative currents in the union movement by opposing them to traditional practices. Now we must pull these observations together in an over-all view of the forces and tendencies within unionism. This view cannot rest on the differences among the major union organizations, for the unity of each of them is relatively superficial. If the C.G.T. is more unified in the conduct of its policies, there are profound divergences within it and the Maoist Marxist-Leninists conduct their campaigns in its ranks. The C.F.D.T. is even more diverse,

since its section of employees remains quite traditionalist
and moderate, while many of its militant workers are both
very innovative and sometimes more radical than those of
the C.G.T. Finally, the F.O., whose confederated administration (in which the influence of officials is very strong)
is moderated and paralyzed by anti-communism, is also
the refuge of the traditions of revolutionary unionism,
particularly at Nantes and Saint-Nazaire (the main centers
of shipbuilding where anarcho-syndicalism was strong
early in the century). Its chemical industry federation
took very advanced positions in May–June. Limiting ourselves to a study of the organizations would condemn us
to misunderstanding the real and multiple tendencies of
the union movement.

In fact, the unions carry on actions as varied as the economic and social situations to which they respond. In first
analysis, these situations can be reduced to three principal
types: the formation of large industries; rationalized man-
ufacturing in large series; highly technical industries. In
each of these situations, the unions present two faces that
partly correspond to differing and complementary professional situations. Union action is always concerned with
both management and opposition; it is never merely a
struggle for immediate advantages. It affirms a will and
capacity of the workers to manage the economy, the company, the plant themselves; also, it fights against capitalist
power. The two objectives are inseparable in principle
but at each stage of the economic and professional evolution of the industry they are relatively distinct.

The affirmation of the managerial capacity of the workers is particularly pressed by the more skilled workers.
They are also more interested in themes of revolutionary
initiative, while the unskilled workers are more concerned
with the defense of wages, employment, and material
working conditions because their wages and employment
are more immediately threatened. In isolation, the first

tendency runs the risk of falling into the reformism proper to the worker aristocracy. The second can be reduced to "economism" completed by support given to directly political action of the political parties.

a) In the first of the two situations I have just distinguished, union activity is marked both by professional self-defense (often pushed as far as the revolutionary conception of handling over the factory to the workers) and by action to defend the workers who are newly incorporated into the industrial economy, threatened in terms of job security, and subjected to extremely harsh material and social conditions and brutal exploitation. In France and most countries, the printers are an almost perfect example of the first tendency, while miners and harbor workers represent the second.

Even in industries that are technically and economically modern, the kind of behavior proper to unskilled workers of this first type is frequently found, usually among workers from rural backgrounds. At Flins, many of the O.S. (ouvriers semi-spécialisés, or semiskilled workers) were "beet growers" who had come from neighboring farming districts. They were not well unionized and were used to a much more rigid discipline than existed in the old worker city of Billancourt. At Sochaux also, many workers remained bound to a rural environment. These two styles of union action join especially in isolated industrial centers which are centers of rural immigration. The shock of industrialization and of subjection to a tight labor market and to owners as brutal as landed lords arouses the demands of the O.S. which are joined in that locality to the demands of the skilled workers, who are very much like artisans.

b) The same opposition between these two aspects of worker action is met in the classical large industry—the images of which fill our books—with its production lines and work/time standards. On one side, there are the great

number of specialized workers with no specific skill, who
barter their freedom to work for a slightly higher salary,
and it is they who form the mass of the movements rather
than their militants; the organized rather than the organizers, who fill up the union rosters only when a favorable
situation incites or obliges them to do so. On the other
side, there are the skilled machine or maintenance workers, small islands of skill which subsist within the mass production system; these are the most militant and the most
conscious of the class conflict that opposes them to the
owners, the efficiency experts, and the hierarchy of bureaucratic chiefs. Because they have for a long time been at the
heart of industrial production and capitalist organization,
these workers have been the principal arm of the labor
movement. They represent labor and productiveness
against the organization and its profits. They are the defenders of the working class against owners and managers.
Even today, there is no massive worker action without the
participation of these worker fortresses, these great enterprises settled in the working-class sections, whose union
leaders act on society only through the party which awak-
ens their class consciousness and transforms it into a political force.

c) Finally, in situations where science and technology
weigh more directly on production and the separation of
productive work from management is replaced by the
extension of laboratories and research-control units, the
technicians take up the role that used to belong to the professional workers or to the master workmen in the earlier
types of labor. Because they participate in the organization rather than merely in production and because they
have more general knowledge, their desire to manage
the company no longer takes the form of defense of the
worker world and productive manual labor against the
managers and money; it bears directly on the whole business. The workers no longer dream of opposing worker

cooperatives to capitalist enterprises but of transforming these into socialist enterprises managed by the workers.

Besides these, in rapidly changing sectors of industry, there are all the underemployed, those whose skills are in no demand, who are rejected by a production system which imposes strong integration on its members and would rather grant them a house qualification * than a more general formation that would allow them to adapt to change and to move freely in the labor market. These workers are defined less by any personal qualifications than by their position in the enterprise: young workers attracted to these modern and dynamic enterprises and employed during a period of unemployment for those with lower qualifications; workers over forty years old, whether laborers or salaried, who have been demoted or threatened with layoff.

If the social conflicts of May and June had been only a crisis of French society's adaptation to a change that was rendered difficult by administrative and mental rigidity, the student movement would have made its effects felt most strongly in the outmoded sectors of society, provoking a defensive reaction rather than a worker offensive. But just the opposite happened.

The Twofold Union of Students and Workers

The strike movement was not directly caused by the student action but neither can it be explained by the status of worker demands and unrest before May. It broke out with surprising force, especially in the large enterprises, and attacked the organization and management of the companies, over and beyond the material conditions of the workers. The strike was often launched with gen-

* Limited training, as opposed to more general technological training.

uine enthusiasm. The five-day notice requirement was almost never respected; most votes were taken by hand. The factories were frequently occupied by a third or sometimes a higher proportion of the employees, which goes far beyond the usual number of strike pickets.

Naturally, the manual workers constituted the principal strength of the movement. But other groups often reacted in a quite novel manner. If the control agents on the whole remained opposed to the strike and were especially anxious to act in a bloc, the administrative employees, often for the first time, participated actively in the strike and occupation of the plants. The role of the staff personnel was more complex and will be raised in a moment. The vigor of the strike caused profound ruptures between strikers and nonstrikers, who felt excluded from the factories; their influence became strong again at the end of the strike or after June 1 when the resumption of work seemed inevitable and near.

The companies whose workers moved farthest in the strike were usually those that were technically advanced. Their workers not only stopped work or occupied the premises as in June 1936 but also affirmed a will to manage the enterprise themselves; they set up independent strike committees that went beyond the earlier union organization. The first factory to enter the strike was Sud-Aviation at Bougenais near Nantes, whose director, Durochel, was locked in his office for a number of days. In the same region, the nationalized E.D.F. (Electricité de France) factory at Cheviré saw its workers decide to maintain production; at the Antar refinery at Donges, they studied its self-management. In the Paris region, the strike did not limit itself to the stoppage of production and a control of the movement by the union organizations, at least in a certain number of companies. It evolved toward the formation of local committees at the C.S.F. at Issy, especially after the resumption of work on June 19, and at Hispano-Suiza, at the Thomson establishment in Bagneux, in the Vitry factory at Rhône Poulenc, where the C.F.D.T. aroused but did not direct the committees.

In other places—at Massey Ferguson, Péchniney, and in the C.S.F. factory at Brest—the strike evolved toward worker management of the plants, strengthened by the participation of an important number of technicians and staff personnel. Similar tendencies were present in some of the large, mechanized civil service bodies, the Securité Sociale (a nationwide, autonomous organization controlled by the state), and the banks. In these highly developed sectors of the economy, the union leaders also took the most advanced positions, like Maire of the C.F.D.T. and Labi of the F.O. The union leader whose position had the widest influence was Alain Barjonet, secretary of the Centre d'Etudes Economiques of the C.G.T. for many years and a member of the Conseil Economique et Social. His activity was more closely related to the economic preoccupation of the technicians and researchers than to the rearguard combats of the industries in decline. Of all the union leaders, he had become one of the most conscious of the necessity of breaking with the rigid, old forms of militancy and of basing class action on modern economic and sociological analysis.

This tendency to take over management was mixed with other more moderate themes, which also, however, went beyond quantitative demands and wished to attack the authority system of the companies. From the beginning of the social crisis and before the Grenelle negotiations, the C.F.D.T. proclaimed, through Eugène Descamps, its secretary-general, that its principal demand was the recognition of union sections within companies and hence the creation of real worker power, capable not only of seeing that the laws were respected and of effectively negotiating salaries, but also of taking broader initiatives within the company. These themes were not revolutionary and relations between the C.F.D.T. and the student movement were ambiguous. The C.F.D.T. was the only central union that constantly showed a favorable attitude toward the U.N.E.F. and the movement in general. It had reservations about certain initiatives and declarations but never attacked the leaders of the student movement.

This sympathy can be explained by the priority given on both sides to qualitative demands, that is, to moving beyond purely economic defense toward structural reforms that would profoundly modify relations of power and authority in industry as well as in the university. Nevertheless, the C.F.D.T. did not involve itself in a revolutionary campaign and emerged from its political reserve only to the degree of openly supporting the idea of a transition government under Mendès-France. But certain local militants went further than the central leadership, without being condemned for doing so. At Flins, the role of the C.F.D.T. was essential. At Les Mureaux, they were the ones who assured, from the union's side, a close bond with the students. Until the last day, M. Rousselin was the principal leader of the union's action. During the period of the strike, relations between the C.F.D.T. and the C.G.T. became more and more distant. Whatever the immense differences that separate the attempts at worker management or the claims of the students—worker power, student power—from the structural reforms demanded by the C.F.D.T., together they constitute what has been called the managerial tendency of the new union movement.

Staff personnel and technicians were among the most interested in qualitative demands. In the nationalized enterprises and also sometimes in the private companies whose management did not seem to them capable of dealing with the great problems posed by technical change, international competition, or concentration versus decentralization, they raised the question of how the enterprises should be managed. The role of administrative staffs and the research bureaux was most important. Among the establishments where their action was very influential, we may cite the research bureau of Sud-Aviation at Cannes, the Renault technical research center at Toulouse, the French Petroleum Institute, the S.N.P.A. (Société Nationale des Pétroles d'Aquitaine), the C.E.A. (Commissariat à l'Energie Atomique), the S.E.R.E.T., the National Center of Space Studies, the O.N.E.R.A. (Office National d'Etudes et de Recherches Aéronautiques), and the C.G.E. (Compagnie Générale d'Electricité) research center at Marcoussis which set up a coordinating committee for electronics research centers along with researchers from other enterprises, the C.N.R.S., and the university. In the civil service administrations, the administrative staffs played the same role, particularly at the ministries of Equipment and of National Education. Nevertheless, apart from a small number of staff personnel who participated directly in the movement, most of those, at Censier (the new building of the Faculty of Letters) and other places, who took opposition positions acted in working committees like those the students had set up at the Sorbonne and sought to keep a certain distance from a "political" strike. (Their attacks on the authority system must not be too quickly identified with a revolutionary movement.)

Whatever the content of this tendency, it did not appear first and thus make possible a bond between students and workers. The revolt of the young workers, threatened in their job security and qualification, hostile to the constraints imposed by the large companies and sometimes led by revolutionary groups, established this bond or rather, even before the outbreak of the student movement in May, provoked the first violent conflicts in which students took part. If certain labor conflicts, particularly that of the Rhodiacéta—a party in Besançon whose influence was augmented by the film of Chris Marker, *A bientôt j'espère,* seen on television—were closer to the managerial tendency already discussed, the conflict in SAVIEM and the clashes at Caen demonstrated even better the revolt of the young workers which awakened echoes among the students.

After May 13, young workers played a determining role in a good number of companies. At Sud-Aviation in Nantes, the initiative to occupy the plant was taken by young workers, who had direct relations with the students' action, in connection with the violent clashes which took place in front of the prefecture. At Cléon also, the young workers, many of whom were under a provisional contract, launched the strike. The same thing was true at the SAVIEM in Caen, at the C.S.F. in Brest, and also in the post offices where we note the role of young employees possessing secondary teaching certificates. At Flins and at Billancourt, the young workers were visible. Those who passed along the Quai de Stalingrad to Billancourt during the strike could see a banner hung on the bridge that leads to the Ile Seguin with the inscription: "Young O.P. = O.S. with a C.A.P.," a protest against the loss of qualification by young workers who could not find employment corresponding to their certificate of professional aptitude and were obliged to hire themselves out as O.S., beneath their real qualifications.

Technical training students, who faced considerable risk of unemployment and underemployment, were very active participants in the movement alongside the *lycée* students. For the young workers, the theme of job security was the most powerful, given that they were hardest hit by unemployment, particularly in the Paris region.

The bond between students and young workers was found everywhere: at Lyon; at Besançon, where the students in the faculty of letters established an alliance with the young workers of the Rhodiacéta; at Toulouse; at Nantes, where the alliance went further and included relations with young farm workers. The participation of young workers, manual laborers, and employees in the demonstrations and barricades was important and grew steadily, as the police arrest figures show. But were they participating as *workers?* The diversity of professions represented would lead us to think that they joined the student action rather as *young* people. Nevertheless, this interpretation is not always sufficient. It is false in certain very clear cases, as on May 24 when, as we saw, young members of the C.G.T. left the union march to join the student demonstration and also during the silent demonstration for the burial of Gilles Tautin, the *lycée* student and member of the U.J.C.M.L. drowned in the Seine during the police raids around Flins.

These are the two faces of the worker-student union. It is not a question of defining the sphere of influence of the student movement but rather of indicating the categories of workers who participated actively and spontaneously in an action that went beyond the usual strike demands and sometimes led to revolutionary objectives. This action mobilized both the young and the highly qualified personnel, two categories until then not very strongly integrated into union activity. The main body of the working class, and especially the union delegates, seldom very young, maintained a defensive conception of the strike.

Union Control and Defense of the Workers

At the opposite extreme, the "old working class" participated in the strike but was not drawn into a movement that invented new objectives and new forms of action. The miners were among the first to accept an agreement with their management but did not immediately resume work in the name of a worker solidarity that is still powerful among them. Their strike was controlled throughout its course by the C.G.T. according to the standard procedures. The same observation is true of the transport workers. Nevertheless, certain aspects of the old union traditions were mobilized for active participation in the movement. This was true in Loire-Atlantique particularly. This *département* has long been marked by an anarcho-syndicalist tradition. Its history has been checkered but it was maintained particularly in the F.O. unions which broke in this regard from their central leadership.

From the last quarter of 1967 and even more so during the violent demonstration of February 14, 1968, the student movement in that area had often taken an advanced position and been in union with the militant workers. Nantes knew real people's power. The F.O. transport workers and the students barred the roads leading to the city. As at Caen, the prefect was deprived of all effective power. A central strike committee from all the unions distributed gasoline coupons, organized food distribution, and regulated prices. As in the strikes of the beginning of the century at Fourmies and in Languedoc, women participated very actively in this movement. I believe this case, even though isolated, to have been important to the degree that it showed, at the heart of a very modernist movement, the resurgence of themes and forms of action that had central importance long before the organization of a massive union movement that has become highly structured and been conquered by political formations. It is also a quite complex case, so that one should refrain from seeing in it the proof that revolutionary power had already begun.

There remain the great classical industries, where the giant companies attracted public attention. In the past, they played a pilot role and this time again they were

among the points of greatest resistance to the resumption
of work. The participation of the automobile industry in
the strike was exceptional. Despite a certain weakening
of union activity, Renault had always been a company
where there were many militants and where the management was not brutal, but Simca and Citroën were well
known for their policy of anti-union repression. Before the
purchase of Simca by Chrysler in the first years of the
Gaullist regime, a committee had to be formed to denounce the anti-union practices of this firm. At Citroën,
the unions had initiated judicial and administrative actions to protest against the obstacles to union activity
and elections set up by the management. If no real movement could be organized at Simca, there was a return in
force of unionism at Citroën, despite police-type pressures and a judicial action by the corporation. The Renault and Citroën workers were the first to reject the
Grenelle agreements on May 27; at the Renault and Peugeot factories, the most violent confrontations with the
police took place, in the course of which three demonstrators died. Along with some metallurgical and elec-
tronic companies, the automobile industry prolonged the
strike for the longest time. Finally, from the time of the
occupation of the Sorbonne until June, the students organized the most numerous demonstrations of solidarity
around the automobile factories at Billancourt and the
Quai de Javel.

Revolutionary groups played an important role in
some cases. This was well known in the case of Flins,
where a group of young workers from the proletarian
C.G.T. appealed to the students and was at their side
after the clashes of June 10–11, at the time of the funeral
of Gilles Tautin. The large number of union militants in
these large companies who were attached to the direct
expression of the class struggle and to the struggle against
the authoritarian organization of work explains the strong

spirit of combat. This was even more remarkable because of the high proportion of foreign workers in these companies whose participation in union activity was minimal, since they were more subject to pressures from the hierarchy and felt somewhat outside French society. A higher number took part this time, as many witnesses of the Flins strike report. But this spirit of combat was not as inventive as in other sectors of industry. In general, the union leaders were opposed to direct contact between workers and students, even when the latter came not to exhort to action but to put at their service their own "weak hands," incapable of holding up the banner of revolution by themselves.

The strike at Billancourt, for example, was carried out with great discipline and was organized by the unions as other strikes had been: the strike committee watched over the machinery, guarded the buildings, took care of the food supply, and arranged for entertainment for the strikers. Meetings were organized on the Ile Seguin (part of the Renault plant at Billancourt), at which laborers and employees massed around red flags. If this strike did not express itself in terms of worker management, neither was it contented with salary demands. The unions had broadened their action for several years: lowering the retirement age, gradual return to a forty-hour week and monthly salary for all personnel were objectives that went beyond salary increases. During the strike, as its national dimensions made possible the achievement of important economic advantages, the idea continually grew stronger that it would be a bad bargain to be contented with salary increases because rising prices would wipe out any advantages that had been won. This feeling led to a demand for greater increases but, even more, to the desire to win more than a favorable negotiation, a victory, that is, a retreat on the part of the owners. The rejection of the protocol established at the Rue de Grenelle meetings, which had not been foreseen by the central union leaderships (who had negotiated it without, however, signing it, agreeing only to propose it to the workers for ratification) renewed and hardened the strike. This development also modified the attitude of the C.G.T. and the Communist Party, which are extremely sensitive to the reactions of the workers in the large automobile companies.

There was no massive transformation of the orientation of the strike. It became only a means to press for the establishment of a new Popular Front, reversing the 1936 equation between social crisis and political change, since this time it was not a change of government that opened the way to a wave of strikes, but a strike movement that was to lead to a change of government. The great C.G.T. demonstration in Paris on May 29, two days after the meeting in the Charléty Stadium, supported a vast campaign for the formation of a democratic government, and was a means to pressure both the government in power and the Federation of the Left, which began to plan for a transition government.

The strike in the large classical companies did not remain entirely under the control of the unions. Begun spontaneously, in a way that had not been foreseen, it was supported and generalized by the C.G.T. only after May 16. The rejection of the Grenelle accords was the most striking proof of how far it had gone beyond the union structures. The fact that Benoit Franchon and Séguy were disavowed by the workers of the Régie Renault demonstrates how far!

Must we conclude that the movement was revolutionary and was hindered from becoming so openly only by the union bureaucracy? Such a statement is unjustified. The Grenelle accords were not blamed for not being revolutionary but for not paying sufficiently, and for remaining within the Matignon agreements that had brought sometimes fragile but spectacular results: paid holidays, forty-hour week, shop delegates. The structural reforms demanded by the C.F.D.T., associated with the abolition of the regulations governing the Securité Sociale, the lowering of the retirement age, and payment for the time of the strike would have brought the workers the consciousness of a victory. But the C.G.T. went directly from action concerned solely with grievances to a political campaign without wishing to become involved in what seemed dangerous to it, a reform of structures and a "revolutionary reformism" as André Gorz had defined it in *Stratégie ouvrière et néocapitalisme* (Paris: Editions du Seuil, 1964). The prolongation of the strikes was not due to revolutionary pressure but to the politics of the Communist leaders who rejected what they called the adventure. This rejection clearly demonstrated the separation between a labor movement committed to its integration into the political system and a wild social movement that overturned the whole system, those who ran it as well as those who were seeking a broader place in it.

Professionals against Technocrats

The contacts between students and workers were of two kinds that seem to me different and opposed. On the one hand, in the modern enterprises, skilled workers or technicians pressed their demands toward managerial power and first of all toward creating union power within the enterprise. This movement was strongest in certain sections of the C.F.D.T. On the other, the action initiated by the student movement reinforced the groups of revolutionary workers, the most important one being the Maoist Marxist-Leninists who acted within the framework of the C.G.T. and fought against the reformism of the Communist leaders. The students of the U.J.C.M.L., some of whom had gone to work in the companies before May 1968 in order to participate in the proletarian struggle, played only a minor role in the specifically student movement and showed greater reservations regarding actions that seemed to them to give dangerous priority to university struggles and to the attack on the political system. There was profound opposition between these two tendencies. The second wished to rediscover the revolutionary action of the working class. The first, with a less well-formulated doctrine and strategy, discovered a community of grievances and actions among all those who are subjected, beyond classical capitalist exploitation, to the much farther reaching domination of structures that insure their power by social integration and cultural manipulation rather than by purely economic mechanisms.

This is why the C.G.T. and the Communist Party felt threatened both on what they could call their right and their left: on one side, by the radicalization of the proletarian worker struggle and, on the other, by the bypassing of any purely worker movement in favor of action carried on by all who are subjected to the power of the large organizations. The invasion of Czechoslovakia a few weeks later was to make the opposition between these two tendencies even more apparent. While one side condemned Soviet imperialism and took up the defense of socialist liberty and the spring activity in Prague, the other side equally condemned the revisionist bureaucrats in Moscow and the Czech liberals as traitors to the proletarian revolution. Sometimes the two sides came together in common action as at Flins where the C.G.T. Maoists and the C.F.D.T. militants fought the C.R.S. together. But such unions must not cause any illusions; the student movement was not able to maintain this apparent unity of these two alliances with the worker forces. The student contribution to a proletarian revolutionary movement had little influence and represented only a notable but limited countercurrent in social history.

However, the joining of technicians or experts with the students, themselves future technicians and experts, is of the greatest importance, for it established a social force that occupies a central place in the new system of production that is being organized. Unless we use the word *capitalism* in such a vague sense that it designates only the separation between the big and the little, it is essential to recognize that economic power today belongs, not to private holders of profit, but to large organizations, private or public, nourished more by self-financing or public credit than by private capitalists holding the right to make economic decisions.

In a parallel manner, the working class is decreasingly composed of excess agriculture workers or artisans. On the contrary, thanks to education especially, a growing number of those who are born into the working class are destined to become salaried rather than manual workers, that is, employees, technicians, or staff personnel.

The sociologist Francesco Alberoni correctly indicated that the situation of workers today is analogous to that of the peasants in the nineteenth century. They are a social category in relative decline, with particular interests to defend, no longer a growing category that is the privileged adversary of the dominant class. The central social conflict of our society opposes the technocrats to employees and experts in organizations, who in turn can oppose to their control the resistance of their own education and technical skill even though they are still manipulated by the technocrats, not essentially by the fluctuations of the labor market but through their careers, status, and all the other forms of social integration. The old working class cannot ally itself with the students in whom it seems future management leaders. The new technicians and experts, on the contrary, know—especially if they are young—that the

majority of students will no longer be called to management posts but only to tasks of organization, communication, and technical execution, without participating in decision-making power.

The students will not be a new proletariat; they will occupy the same position in the "techno-structure" as the
skilled workers in industry at the beginning of the century. Along with those who already hold the functions that
will be theirs in a few years, they form a class on its way
up, struggling against the new managers who are also on
their way up. This is why the student movement today
is no longer an intelligentsia but a category of workers
which is losing its former privileges and traditional models of formation and, at the same time, is conquering an
increasingly massive place in the organization of the economy and, consequently, the social conflicts.

Since we have just defined the class situation of students,
this is the place to define as well the power that they and
other elements of their class are combatting. I have several
times used the word *technocracy*. It is less important to
comment on it than to know whether it gives a sufficient
idea of the social power against which the May Movement
directed its struggle. I have already spoken of the twofold
meaning of the student attack on the bourgeois university
system: *1*) they attacked the attempt to adapt the university to the needs of the economy, a technocratic conception
of social organization as the totality of the means to economic growth; *2*) they also attacked its defense of cultural
forms which serve as a protection for social interests and
favor middle-class students who are better prepared for the
university experience. The labor movement fought in the
same way against capitalist exploitation and the resistance
middle-class archaism put up against social and economic
progress.

The fact is that a ruling class, even while it directs society and its development by establishing its own power,

is never entirely modern; it is the heir of the former ruling class as well as in opposition to it. A new ruling class may unite itself for awhile to the popular effort against the former ruling class. This is the case with what was called the national bourgeoisie. A more recent case is the national technocracy of the socialist countries which opposes the domination of the old worker bureaucracy tied to the Soviet Union. In France, in terms of the university, the Caen Conference marked this limited and provisional convergence of modernizers against traditionalists. But when popular pressure was strong, this alliance broke. Likewise, when the new ruling class is solidly established, it enforces elitist and integrating methods that insure the continuity between the former dominant culture and the one establishing itself. In the French case, the absence of important social opposition under the Gaullist regime made possible an amalgam, solid but full of contradictions, between the former bourgeois society and the new technocratic society, just as the July Monarchy had been both capitalist and aristocratic, according to the Whig plan.

The May Movement attacked not only plans for technocratic management but also a ruling class that was both capitalist and technocratic. The famous Napoleonic authoritarianism that the reformer technocratics attacked with so much ardor and imprudence, was actually only the instrument to join the power of the middle class to that of the technocrats, who had no particular antipathy toward the E.N.A. (Ecole Nationale d'Administration) or the Ecole Polytechnique from which they came. Gaullism, whose action on our society is more real than Napoleon's was, is above all else the social framework in which the continuity from one ruling class to another is to be achieved, just as Francoism insures, under more difficult conditions, the passage from pre-industrial elites to the leaders of Spanish industrialization.

This is the very same battle as that waged against university archaism and against the practical and professional conception expressed by General de Gaulle in a TV interview with Michel Droit. Likewise, there is no complete break between the struggles the worker wages against ownership by divine or family right and those directed against the techno-structure. The reality of technocratic power lies not only in its project of modernization, but just as much in its defense of order and all the guarantees of social domination. This is why union action against an archaic ownership authoritarianism is not foreign to the struggle for collective management of the centers of production and decision-making. In both cases, it is a matter of moving beyond material demands toward a struggle for greater social power. In a modernized economy, this power is all the stronger because it is still based on pre- or proto-industrial forms.

The movement of opposition to technocracy does not combat a disincarnate image of a society directed by science and technology, but a real power that is both archaic and modernizing, that defends economic rationality but is also guided by the search for social, cultural, or military power. The action of wage-earners can reinforce this social movement. It remains, however, by its nature different from the movement against private property and profit. It can only develop outside the structures inherited from this earlier movement, structures that today are only pressure groups or elements of a political system.

Once we have affirmed the existence of a new social movement, of a new pole of organization and politicization of demands, must we also conclude that the new class conflict in which it is engaged can only take revolutionary forms, that is, that there cannot be either negotiation or institutionalization of the conflict? An affirmative answer would confuse a social struggle with the

224 THE MAY MOVEMENT

political and institutional system through which it manifests itself, which has never been accepted by any analyst of society.

From Social Crisis to Political Crisis?

Now we must move beyond the ways workers participated in the May–June movement to ask whether or not, during that period, a revolutionary process was begun only to be halted by the counterpressure of the unions and political orgainzations of the working class. Put this way, the question deserves a negative response, not only because the facts dictate such a response but especially because the question is badly framed and creates great confusion. It is not true that a revolutionary process depends on the conscious will to make revolution; that would confuse two distinct levels of reality. Class consciousness is consciousness of the fundamental conflict between two classes, one of which exploits or dominates the other by identifying its own interests with those of society as a whole. That is alienation. Even if today's entrepreneurs and technocrats give less thought to their own profit and power than to their role as creators of wealth and prosperity, they still consider the workers instruments of their own activity and beneficiaries of their efforts. The workers are manipulated quantities, production factors, or a consumer market.

The worker who opposes his own class consciousness to this consciousness refuses to be dependent in this way. He does not believe the ruling class to be simply a modernizing elite; for him, it is also a domineering group defending its own interests, which contradict his. The conflict between these class movements contradicts the whole policy of integration or fusion of the classes and all the consequent exertions of the ruling class, from repression to paternalism, from Taylor's "carrot" * to human relations programs. But if itself class conflict does not determine the political forms of the struggle. The English workers are no more moderate than their French comrades, despite the different political form of their action. A movement into revolutionary action does not depend on how strong class consciousness is but on the inability of the institutional system to negotiate the conflict.

This inability has diverse causes, three of which seem essential. In the first place, there is the lack of balance within that class of workers which, instead of being settled in a defined class situation, is moving rapidly from one social situation to another. Those whom economic change draws massively from the rural world into the industrial world or from small artisan shops into huge companies are caught up in a collective social crisis as well as a class relationship. They run into a society in which they are "marginal" and dominated, a society they contest from within and without, into which they are integrated, or which they reject. In such a society, they have little capacity to establish effective opposition or to negotiate.

The second classical determinant of a revolutionary situation is analogous but concerns the dominant class. To the degree that it is bound to an older social, political, and cultural order, it is more anxious to insure the unity and fusion of the dominant classes than to define itself in terms of the class of workers which corresponds to its practical activity. Thus, in many developing societies, contrary to the illusions created by the trust put in the national bourgeoisie, the union between the new industrialists and the old oligarchy has shown itself to be solid. In the advanced industrial countries, the union between technocrats and older forms of capitalist power, whether

* Taylor, it is said, compared workers with donkeys, who must be pushed ahead with the whip and lured on with a carrot.

formed directly or through the intermediacy of the State, favors a blocking of the social conflict and consequently the formation of authoritarian domination and revolutionary movements.

Finally, certain circumstances can wipe out the possibility of negotiations and even affect the whole institutional organization of a society. A military defeat, a foreign invasion, extreme disorganization of the political system, or an economic crisis can lead to the class conflict being replaced by attempts, on both sides, to seize power, to replace conflict with dictation, that is, to suppress the autonomy of the institutional system relative to social conflict. There is no constant and absolute equation between class consciousness and revolutionary outbreak.

The Paris Commune was born in a situation that favored a revolutionary outbreak: a working class in the process of formation, a middle class that dominated far more than capitalist profit, a military defeat, and the overthrow of the previous regime. (Attentive historians have nevertheless shown that one must not too hastily conclude that the Parisian workers were primarily moved by proletarian class consciousness.) Was French society in 1968 in a situation that favored a revolutionary break? Although there were undeniable elements of a break in France, they were sufficiently limited that a revolutionary situation could only have been created by a deliberate decision of the organized political forces.

The elements of a social break in the French situation were not essentially bound to the workers. This has been demonstrated by the fact that advanced sectors of the economy, not those midway between archaic industrialization and a more advanced economy, were the most active. We have raised the point of authoritarianism on the part of the owners. The C.N.P.F. (Conseil National du Patronat Français), whose power should not be exaggerated, has always had as its principal task the establish-

ment of a common front of owners and, consequently, the
binding of the archaic interests of industry to those of the
more dynamic groups. The liberal character it proclaimed
—at least partly in response to the public opinion aroused
by F. Bloch-Lainé's *Pour une réforme de l'entreprise*
(Paris: Editions du Seuil, 1963) —was everywhere interpreted as a stiffening of its position, a refusal to question,
beyond economic interests, a particular conception of ownership power. Its opposition to the effective recognition of
unions in industry demonstrated this attachment to rights
that cannot be reduced to the defense of economic interests. In the more modernized companies, the transformation of management had begun to modify very effectively
the monarchical constitution of companies. The lag in
management methods in most French companies has not
only had economic consequences; it has also caused a profound inability to negotiate. French owners prefer to see
concessions imposed by the government rather than to set
up procedures in their companies that would limit their
liberty to make decisions unilaterally. The Matignon accords were imposed on the owners in 1936; the owners preferred to accept major salary increases rather than have
their power questioned.

The principal element of a social break was not to be
found among the owners; it was political, connected with
the nature of Gaullism. The slogan written and chanted
during the great demonstration of May 13 was eloquent:
"Ten Years Is Enough." Gaullism seemed to so many foreign countries in the socialist world and the Third World
to be a progressive political force because it cracked the
unity of the capitalist world by opposing American domination. For most workers, especially the young, it was a
monarchical system incapable of recognizing the problems
of the French people, who interested it less than French
grandeur. Some who were a little older and had actively
experienced the events of May 1958 could never consider

the regime entirely legitimate, despite the popular vote
that had consolidated it.* In this, they agreed in a way
with the position many times affirmed by General de
Gaulle himself, who always based his legitimacy on his
identification with the national interest in the tragic situation of June 1940 rather than on his acceptance by public opinion.

Opposition to Gaullism might all the more readily have
led to a political break because the militant students were
not the only ones to have strong anti-parliamentary feelings. These had been clearly expressed among the workers
in 1958 and reappeared with great force at the time of the
parliamentary debate on the censure motion on May 22–
23. The speeches, by the representatives of the left as well
as the right, seemed strangely unreal to most of those
who listened to them. It is easy to understand why on
May 7 the mass march of students paid no attention to
the National Assembly when it came near it. Opposition
to Gaullism could not be used to restore an Assembly
regime. Here is where it might have been possible to
move beyond the social crisis to a political crisis, that is,
to indict the Gaullist regime without accepting a parliamentary solution. Whether this would necessarily have
been the first step of a revolutionary process or whether
the crisis of the regime could have been controled without a revolutionary outbreak, was and is a subject of discussion. For all or almost all on the left, the overthrow of
Gaullism was the most immediate objective. Cohn-Bendit
proclaimed it several times. Barjonet made a careful distinction between the overthrow of Gaullism, which seemed
to him possible, and the establishment of socialism, which
seemed to him impossible. The Communist leaders as
well as the leaders of the Fédération launched a cam-

* On the thirteenth of May 1958, a revolt of French authorities in
Algiers began a political crisis which ended with the breakdown of the
Fourth Republic and the comeback of General de Gaulle.

paign directed toward overthrow of the government rather than toward social revolution.

This was the limited perspective that seemed open. When they have the documents, historians will tell us what degree of real seriousness the political crisis—or regime crisis—of the last days of May actually reached. The crisis can be placed between General de Gaulle's two speeches, one on May 24 proposing the referendum and the other on May 30, accompanied by the massive demonstration on the Champs-Elysées in favor of de Gaulle and law and order. It is at least certain that the machinery of the State was paralyzed at many points and sometimes doubted its own survival. For a few days, the fall of the regime seemed likely to many, not all of whom were on the side of the movement.

If the regime had fallen, the leftist parties could have taken its place and a popular vote would very probably have ratified this. Those who strove to transform the movement into a political force certainly counted on that change being only a first step. It would have led to an intensification of social struggles and the weakness of the coalition between the Fédérationistes and the Communists would have caused a popular revolutionary force to rise up. These were not farfetched hypotheses. But the events do not show that the political leaders of the movement would have been able to intervene actively at the end of May in the political developments. The committees organized by the P.S.U. never had any importance; the meeting in the Charléty Stadium, where not all the speakers were revolutionaries, had no follow-up. Finally and most importantly, had there been a strong move toward a new, specifically political force, would the work stoppage on May 30 have had such immediate effects? The P.S.U. did not achieve notable success in the elections. The incidents at Flins and Sochaux in the first half of June were not dominated by the theme of political revolution. Even if the power structure crumbled, the political expression of the movement was not yet formed. Nothing is more striking than the contrast between the breadth of the movement and the social crisis on one hand and the practical nonexistence of its political organization on the other, despite the efforts of some individuals, some groups, and the P.S.U.

From a strictly political point of view, the movement's action culminated in those days of crisis and especially in those hours of waiting that followed the mysterious departure of General de Gaulle for a then unknown destination. But that was not the moment when the movement showed the greatest strength. Attention was turned away from it; it seemed to be the distant cause of effects it could neither control nor direct. Whether the accent is placed on the movement itself or on the political crisis, the conclusion is the same. The movement was not equipped to direct political evolution and commit it to already prepared paths. It had been too spontaneous and too hostile to political organizations to transform itself into an instrument for the seizure of power.

The Double Conflict Between the Movement and the Worker Organizations

From what we have analyzed, one can understand more clearly the relations between the Communist leaders of the P.C.F. and the C.G.T. and the leaders of the student movement. The student leaders were not interested in the political crisis for its own sake. Their actions were directed at strengthening the chances of a social revolution. But it is possible to imagine a social revolution—that is, the seizure of political power and the institutional structures by social forces outside the established processes—without these forces being guided by a powerful, well-organized party, able to define and carry out an effective strategy? Many of the participants in the movement felt resentment against the Communist Party because they expected that this party, which had been formed by the teachings of Lenin and declared itself a revolutionary party, would bring to the movement and spontaneity of the masses the support of its organization, power, and capacity for political leadership. There was no resentment against the Federation because no one expected anything from it, but there was a strong feeling of having been betrayed by the Communist Party. This was expressed particularly against the leaders of the C.G.T. During the May 24 demonstration, a large group walked in front of the offices of *L'Humanité* (the official organ of the Communist Party) shouting, "Séguy, traitor." On May 27 in the Charléty Stadium, hostility toward the C.G.T. and its secretary-general was strongly expressed. These accusations were leveled less at the inability of the great central union to foresee the social movement and help it forward than at the refusal of the Communist Party to put itself at the head and service of a revolutionary movement.

These reproaches, as violent as they were, do not explain the other aspect of the relationship between the May Movement and the Communist leaders, the hostility of these leaders toward the leftist leaders, of whom Daniel Cohn-Bendit and Alain Geismar were the principal targets, the former at the beginning and the latter more toward the end of the central period of the movement. This hostility was directed against the leftist attempt to bypass the Communist Party and the C.G.T. organizations. If the young revolutionaries accused the Communist Party of not standing at the head of the revolutionary action because of the hope they had placed in it, some of them from the outset considered the party and the C.G.T. obstacles to revolutionary action.

The Communist Party, like the French government,

certainly tended to see the "Chinese" behind the action,
especially in the early stages of the movement. But if this
did not unduly alarm the government (because whatever
bothered the Communist Party could not really displease
it), it increasingly disturbed the P.C.F. The groups of
Trotskyite or anarchist inspiration had always been condemned very vigorously and the crisis of the U.E.C. and
the cell in the Sorbonne faculty of letters, which resulted
in the formation of the J.C.R., was recent enough to provoke the party's anathemas against the "little groups."
Committed to its policy of coming to power through the
formation of the political union of the forces of the left,
it was more determined to destroy deviations on its left
than on its right in order to maintain the unity and power
of the party.

From the outset, the Nanterre "enragés" waged a violent struggle against the Communist students. Students of
the U.J.C.M.L. expelled the deputy, Juquin, from the faculty when he came to present the theses of his party on
the reform of the administration of national education.
This was only a more visible incident than others. Cohn-
Bendit attacked the Communist leaders with particular
vigor. A little while before the Night of the Barricades,
a meeting of the March 22 Movement in the Nanterre
amphitheater (rebaptized the Che Guevara) was the occasion of a long confrontation between the Communist
students and the March 22 militants. This hostility was
taken up by all those who for years had been defamed,
attacked, and denounced by the Communist Party. From
the assassination of Trotsky to the communiqué issued at
the beginning of May by the municipality of Nanterre
against "the German anarchist, Cohn-Bendit" and the
articles of Georges Marchais and Réné Andrieu in *L'Humanité,* the uninterrupted series of Communist attacks
was for the first time in a long time answered publicly,
before a mass of students rather than in the secrecy of

small groups. The opposition of the local and national
Vietnam committees to the more prudent attitude of the
Communist Party, the conflict between those who cried
"Peace in Vietnam" and those who answered "Victory in
Vietnam," reinforced the mutual hostility between the
Communists and the leftists.

Nothing could have been more opposed than action
focused on the strengthening of the party and its democratic centralism and a movement entirely aimed at a new
development of the worker struggle and the revolutionary
forces. Before May 3, the Nanterre "enragés" did not foresee how far the social conflicts and the disruption of society that they caused would extend. Action against the
Stalinist bureaucracy was no longer important in their
eyes. The important thing was to open a breach in the
wall constructed by the party structure that was keeping
prisoner the spontaneity of the masses. Only later did
Cohn-Bendit speak of the "Stalinist slobs" but even before
the Communist leaders were not deceived about his feelings toward them.

After the first street demonstrations and the first casualties, the Communist Party moderated its attacks. On the
day after the Night of the Barricades, the C.G.T., like the
C.F.D.T. and the F.E.N. (Fédération de l'Education Nationale), decided to move forward to the thirteenth the
great demonstration planned for the fourteenth. Not without misgivings, it agreed to the presence of people like
Cohn-Bendit in the march and also agreed that the union
and party leaders would not have their usual place at the
head of the demonstration. This was a considerable victory for the "enragés" who, a few days earlier, had been
expelled from the traditional May 1 march by officials of
the C.G.T. when they wanted to join it with black flags.
But the spread of the strikes, which had not been foreseen and were not controlled by the C.G.T., as well as
the new violent street demonstrations on May 22, after the

decision to expel Cohn-Bendit, and on the night of May 24–25 again heightened the tone of the Communist attacks. The rejection of the Grenelle agreements and the Charléty Stadium meeting on May 27 brought them to the high point. More and more clearly, the Communist Party accused the leftists of having knowingly made a play for power and of being agitators, who wanted nothing more than to defeat the party of the working class by bringing down on it the weight of a deceived public opinion and a hostile government.

When the students went to Flins to aid the strikers at Renault at the time when the C.R.S. had reestablished what was officially called freedom to work by chasing away the pickets, extremely violent attacks were directed against Geismar, whom the Communist press painted as a trouble-maker, while it remained silent about the police repression, the attitude of the working-class population which demonstrated its sympathy and support for the students, and about the exact conditions of the death of the *lycée* student, Gilles Tautin. The militant students of the March 22 Movement, meanwhile, were pursuing their activity in the working-class sections and in the plants, while the Maoist Marxist-Leninists were organizing committees to support the struggles of the people. They were all trying to reach local militants, to establish relations especially among the workers in the small companies closed by the strike, and to arouse active local participation in discussions and political actions.

Although their success was limited on the whole, the C.G.T. naturally saw these attempts as an effort to bypass its action and organization. It was all the more encouraged in its resistance because it was conscious of being, in the midst of the crisis, a force of central importance that would even grow stronger, a conclusion backed by soundings of public opinion. Along with the Communist

Party, it mobilized its forces to reinforce the pressure for
an eventual leftist government.

There is nothing to be gained from becoming involved
in ideological arguments or from opposing the adventur-
ism of one side to the bureaucratization of the other.
Everything that has just been recalled will be better clari-
fied if we replace spatial metaphors—extreme left, center,
right—with a more historical view. The Communist Party,
like social-democratic parties in other countries, has been
the political expression of a labor movement bound to
the problems created by great capitalist industrialization
and accompanied by weak social control, punctuated by
crises, and dominated by the power of the owners and
financial groups. The Communist form of the labor
movement has also been bound to a lag in French society
due to the economic and political importance of the agri-
cultural sector and also to the weight of the State, sometimes innovative and sometimes conservative, but also the
channel through which social reforms have been obtained
that economically undynamic and socially reactionary
owners would not negotiate.

Paradoxically, it is this institutional and cultural aspect
that suffered least from obsolescence in France, while society has been profoundly transformed, economic modernization is well on its way, and the large companies and
certain sectors of the State have joined in what is called
economic planning. The power of the Communist movement remains great as an instrument of the combat of the
"superstructures" while it has lost its creative power on
the level of the economic "infrastructures." This causes
what Barjonet calls the subjectivism of the Communist
leaders. The May Movement is not to the left of the
Communist Party but ahead of it; it belongs to the next
generation. Its youth comes less from the age of its militants than from the newness of the situations and con-

flicts they express and on which they act.

Gradually, the worker problems have been institutionalized. From the moment when peaceful coexistence replaced the Cold War and the Communist Party began to
emerge slowly and hesitantly from its Stalinist hiberna-
tion, everyone could realize that the problems that it was
posing in terms of revolutionary struggle had reached the
point where they could be treated institutionally. If the
Communist Party had not maintained its rigidity in
consequence of its former revolutionary role, the institutionalization of labor conflicts would have progressed even
more quickly. The May crisis moved it forward another
step. At the same time, the social and cultural isolation of
the proletarian class lessened. This does not by any means
signify that there were no longer any labor problems—
which no serious sociologist has ever said—but that there
was no longer a class movement unifying these problems
and moving beyond them in its over-all activity, opposed
to an economic power and resting essentially on the manual workers of industry, the victims of capitalist exploitation. Worker problems became diversified and particularized at the same time as, in a society in which the
proportion of salaried non-laborers was rapidly rising,
they grew to concern other social groups. Parties and
unions adapted to this new situation and moved away
from global social opposition.

At the same time, the Communist Party remained too
closely connected with revolutionary traditions not to
be frightening. During the elections of June 23 and 30,
the government was able to present to the alarmed good
people the image of a Communist conspiracy in which
the Communist Party was identified with those it most
detested, the "adventurists" of the May Movement. This
campaign lost the Communist Party, and the Fédération
as well, votes on its right wing.

On the other hand, the party is too committed to its

institutional activity—both on the national level through its search for a grand alliance with the moderate left and on the municipal level where it pursues an active policy of collective alliances through which it seeks political control of the population—to be the bearer of the new movements that are being formed. These indict the power and constraints of the large organizations more than the profit of the entrepreneur or the individual owner; they combat social integration, cultural manipulation, and imperialism more than low salaries or the cyclical crises of classical capitalism. This impotence costs the Communist Party votes on its left, which either abstains or votes for the P.S.U. This party is more a collection of currents of opinion than a political force capable of directing the social movement it expresses. Revolutionary action is too novel and too dispersed to form a real organization for itself, especially at the time when the election of the president by universal suffrage led to the formation of vast coalitions rather than ideological parties.

A Revolutionary Movement Without Revolution

The May Movement which launched into creative action minorities of students, researchers, and teachers, workers and technicians, intellectuals and artists, did not become a social revolution. But neither was it merely the remnant of antiquated revolutionary forms, which are incapable of moving with the tendency toward the institutionalization of older conflicts led ambiguously and hence weakly by the Communist Party. At this nascent period of a new stage in industrial societies, it was the first crisis through which new demands and new objectives were established. Coming close to revolt, it was nevertheless also the birth of an opposition which might or might not end in a revolutionary outcome, depending on the behavior of the dominant economic forces, the institutional system, and other social forces. It suggested the contours of the new dominated class and of the cores which will defend it against technocratic power.

The May Movement, erected against the established order, wished first of all to be faithful to a revolutionary tradition. While its tactics were as far as possible from the tactics of Lenin, it used the language of Lenin. It leveled accusations against the Communist Party because it wished to be the agent of communism. If it can continue and reflect on itself, if it can elevate its theory to the level of its tactics, it must recognize itself one day, not as a new stage in the proletarian movement, but as a new stage in the class struggle, as different from the older struggle as the Commissariat of the Plan and IBM are from the Comité des Forges (Ironworks Committee), one of the most conservative pre-war employers' associations, and the families who owned the textile mills. The student movement could not have fulfilled this role of bringing forth a new class movement if it had remained within the university. By moving to the factories, it won an importance corresponding to its vision and surpassing its hopes, but it also came into confrontation with what was closest to it on the political horizon but farthest from it historically. Only the consciousness of this contradiction is capable of leading, through reflection and action, to the formation of new social movements. Only this consciousness can indicate a way out of the artificial choice between integrative reformism adorned with the plumes of modernity and an antiquated revolutionary inspiration which itself leads to a new fashion of social integration in a society whose ruling forces are dynamic, full of imagination, and sufficiently sure of themselves to tolerate in their midst a camouflage that disturbs their adversaries.

For the present, the May Movement was not the deed of conscious and "organized" workers but of unorganized militants whose consciousness was formed, despite many ideological and utopian detours, through action. It was closer to the utopianism of 1848 than to the contemporary republican movement, which is more solid and better backed up by thought and the conquests of the French Revolution, but nevertheless is so much less in touch with the future than the first demonstrations of worker power. The movement mobilized only a small number of individuals, but it awakened public opinion both within and outside its boundaries. In a few weeks, it swept away the integrative ideologies which considered great social conflicts impossible in a dynamic and prosperous society. One no longer spoke only of industrial or technological revolution; the movement restored life to the whole revolutionary idea. This is what neither its adversaries nor those who wished to serve it could understand.

If we return from this conclusion to an analysis of the political situation, it is correct to say that the movement had no political outcome. Neither the Communist campaign for a democratic government—that is, a union of the left dominated by itself—nor the sympathetic efforts of Mitterand and Mendès-France were the political expression of the movement. From the point of view of the political system and its possibilities for governmental change, the impotence of the movement is evident. That utopian language spoke about a simultaneous political and social revolution is a fact, but one that weighs less heavily than the fact of the absence of political action within the movement. The slogan, "The Elections Are a Betrayal," which could easily have led to sabotage of the elections was not used by any group in that sense: the revolutionary movement did not attempt to establish an insurrectionary power. The fall of the Gaullist regime would have created a situation more favorable to the movement's development but it would not have been its victory. It was unable to express itself politically.

That this considerably limited its historic importance is true; May 1968 is a less important historic event than the Paris Commune. But isn't it strange to consider important only what succeeds politically and what does not achieve political power as only profligacy and farce? In some cases, a social movement and a political crisis join forces and create a revolutionary situation. Much more often, these two orders remain relatively separate. A purely political change like that of May 1958 is not without importance because it was only political; neither is a movement like that of May 1968 an incident without consequence, merely an economic mess and bad theater. But a social movement would in fact be of little importance, if it did not affect the political system. Who can say that the May Movement was such, when after all it disrupted Gaullism, provoked the collapse of the Fédération, and brought to light the ambiguity of Communist policy?

It was not through intellectual weakness or practical impotence that the movement did not form a program and that the attempts at political organization within it had so few results. After the meeting in the Charléty Stadium, and especially after the demonstration that marched from Montparnasse to the Austerlitz Terminal on June 1, the formation of a revolutionary movement was debated by Jean-Pierre Vigier, A. Barjonet, Gilbert Mury, Alain Krivine, leader of the J.C.R., and the March 22 Movement, among others. But this attempt was cut short. By June 1, Geismar, Barjonet, and Mury no longer figured among the founders of the Comité d'Initiative pour un Mouvement Revolutionnaire. On the same day at the Sorbonne, during a long debate, Cohn-Bendit, supported by the March 22 Movement, opposed Daniel Ben Saïd, of the J.C.R., who favored the organization of a revolutionary political force.

The May Movement was a social force and as such it enjoyed its most important political significance; by its very existence, it criticized a political system that declared itself independent of social realities and conflict and defined itself by the exigencies of growth and the national interest. The movement did not, could not, and did not wish to take power; but it recalled that the present political power does not govern the common good but imposes, by means of institutions and administrative organization, the domination of a few over the whole of society. It set aside the problem of power.

VI

The Antisociety

The May Movement, after a few weeks of mass actions, had not yet succeeded in transforming political life or unleashing a social revolution. It began to consume a major part of its energy in violence or in self-expression—words. Many consider this self-expression the great event of the month of May; this is not my point of view. The May Movement appears important to the degree that it revealed in practice the new social conflicts of a society that had been profoundly transformed. Consequently, the cultural revolt that erupted starting from the occupation of the university faculties and the Odéon cannot have central importance, since it did not commit the movement to active conflict.

It may be exciting to say that the imagination took power and that what was said in the amphitheaters and written on the Sorbonne walls was an important part of the great May contestation; but such a statement has

obvious limits. In French society, power is not headquar-
tered in the Sorbonne courtyard or in the Odéon. For a
number of weeks, students and non-students were the
masters, not of French society, not even of its university
system, but of its walls. They were strong enough that the
government could not dislodge them without serious violence, with unforseeable social and political consequences. We cannot speak of a Student Commune, for the
students never had possession of the command posts of
society. The Sorbonne courtyard was the place to which
the strength of the movement retreated when it could not
be absorbed by the worker struggles, the street demonstrations, or the renovation of the university.

The occupation of the university faculties was a victory.
The Censier annex of the Sorbonne—a modern building
constructed on the site of the former leather market, on
the boundary of the Latin Quarter and the Gobelins—
was occupied a few hours after the Night of the Barricades, on Saturday, May 11, at 6:00 P.M. The occupation
of the Sorbonne took place right after the great demonstration of May 13 which the March 22 Movement had
prolonged by political discussions on the Champ-de-Mars.
The prime minister, just returned from abroad, had
spoken on the eleventh and announced a political change,
measures of appeasement intended to restore a more lasting order than the police repression of the previous night.
But this effort could not restore calm. Who could imagine
that the Sorbonne, when it reopened, could resume its
normal activities because of a few "liberal" reforms? The
occupation of the heart of the university of France and
then of other faculties—some were already occupied,
especially Nanterre—was the beginning of a student move
for the creation of a new university and gave them a geographic center for the movement, where everyone met,
planned, and expressed themselves.

The Sorbonne was the high point of the movement's

self-expression, not of its action. This judgment is harsh and needs clarification. The cultural revolution is also an expression of the new class struggle. But, at the time of the strikes and the political crisis, its direct expression, separated from the worker and university struggles, could not have the same force it had at the beginning of the movement. Each week, it became more and more a demonstration of the crisis and gave up its revolutionary meaning in order to become either pure revolt or reformism. It no longer transformed the social situation; it acted in response to the dissolution of the university system and of a great part of the fabric of society. It did not produce the revolution, it consumed it.

On the other hand, the resistance of the State allowed the cultural revolt to nourish revolutionary action. At the Sorbonne and the Odéon, this State resistance was artificially removed with the result that the revolt tended to play itself out rather than to nourish action. But there is no clear dividing line between the cultural revolution tied to class action and the revolt of the antisociety. Hence, within the climate of May–June, we must discover the specific meanings of three things: the action, the destruction of archaism, and the mask of impotence.

Participation in the Action

The first positive aspect of the occupation, one that was able to strengthen the movement, was the concrete experience of freedom of political organization and expression for the students and all those who participated in the movement they launched. The sterile walls and "functional" rooms of Nanterre, Censier, and Halle aux Vins came alive. The university, usually crowded but lifeless, overflowed with activity at every hour of day and night. The university faculties, which had never supported student life, became places for it. The creation of child-care centers was more than a new student "service"—it indicated the will to help the students live as completely as possible within their university. At the Sorbonne and the other faculties, the militants of the movement ate and slept, took care of their needs, organized themselves, and debated—in other words, they lived there.

Whatever the meeting or discussion was, the rooms were full. Attention was intense and enthusiasm was quick to manifest itself. The students took possession of their working places. It is not exact to say that they ran them themselves because the university did not "produce," that is, the libraries, research centers, and laboratories did not operate. But the students were no longer just people who received teaching and prepared for examinations. They were citizens and, even more, comrades. Everything that had been repressed by the university organization—political ideas, forms for expression and intervention—broke into the light. The books that were spread in the Sorbonne courtyard were intended to be working tools for militant political action.

It is pointless to ask whether a university can fulfill its fundamental tasks in this way. The question is either naïve or badly intentioned, since that was not what it was all about. Quite simply, it was a question of holding up for discussion the political bases of an action that sought, among its other objectives, to transform the university system. Science must not be confused with the university institution and organization. Those professors who cried about the shipwreck of science when the old university edifice crumbled bore witness to an ideology just as constraining as that of those students who denied that there were any problems proper to scientific and intellectual production. The occupied faculties ceased to be outside society. They were violently placed at the center of its struggles. The authority of the administration and the professors had for so long been proposed as self-evident and beyond opposition that the student take-over of the buildings was less a reversal of the situation than their entry onto the scene of political debate and process. Perhaps student power will become a counterpower or a part of the decision-making power in the university. Starting from May 11, it imposed itself alone, because it alone had been excluded.

Internationalism

Beyond this fact, which has wide implications even though it was limited to the university aspect of the movement, the most striking aspect of participation in the movement, both within and outside the university faculties, was its internationalism. Foreign students living in the university dormitories or near the faculties, participated actively in the movement, as did the foreign workers in the companies. They took part not only in its professional activities but in its political activities. The importance of this fact is indicated by the government's reaction. Hundreds of foreigners were expelled and the new Minister of the Interior showed himself particularly determined to combat what he considered subversion organized by foreigners. The government was not alone in arousing hostility in national feelings against the German citizen, Cohn-Bendit. He was a bad example to choose. Over and beyond the demonstrators, when radio listeners and television viewers heard this student—who was indeed a German but entirely French as well and better able to handle our language than many deputies and Ministers of the Interior—they were hard put to be shocked by his participation in the Paris student movement.

The participation of foreigners was not important

simply because a few foreign nationals who were completely integrated into French culture, like Cohn-Bendit, played an important role in it. Its importance was due to the fact that foreign students, intellectuals, and workers were involved precisely as students, intellectuals, and workers. They found an opportunity to demonstrate political demands and objectives that shared the same revolutionary inspiration as the May Movement but were directed at the political and social problems of their own societies. Notices in Spanish on the Sorbonne walls called Spaniards or Argentines to meet in a particular room. African students organized meetings to attack neocolonialism. Several international student dormitories were occupied by their residents under conditions, it is true, that varied widely but which will certainly have effects on student activity in different countries. At the end of the last great demonstration, on June 1, before the Austerlitz terminal, an Italian student, introduced by Sauvageot, addressed his French comrades in Italian.

Just as the movement at Nanterre had been strongly influenced by the German S.D.S. and the activity of Rudi Dutschke, so the May Movement aroused echoes in many countries: Germany, Argentina, Italy, Brazil, Belgium, Yugoslavia, Switzerland, Mexico, etc. The foreign students and workers rediscovered the internationalism that has always accompanied and nourished revolutionary movements: in 1830 and 1848, at the time of the creation of May 1, and following the Soviet Revolution. This spirit had clashed with the integration of the workers into national societies with increasingly vast decision-making systems much more unified than formerly, and also with their integration into consumer markets directed by the same commercial propaganda. The participation of foreigners was more than reinforcement during battle: it was a sign of revolutionary consciousness.

The Form of the Action

Beyond the mobilization of novel, hitherto hidden or repressed forces, the very form of the action was the most important consideration for those who participated in the movement. As we have already said, the strength of the March 22 Movement lay in its lack of organization and its constant appeal to spontaneity and to a personal and collective responsibility that permitted it to transcend the very limited area of action of the Trotskyite or Maoist "little groups." How far this rejection of central authority went was illustrated when journalists who had come to the Sorbonne for a press conference with Cohn-Bendit met a group of March 22 militants who declared, "We are all Cohn-Bendit."

After May 13, the movement organized into action committees in the university and in the working-class sections; there were also joint student-worker committees. Former leaders of the U.N.E.F., like Marc Kravetz and Jean-Claude Peninou, played an important role in creating them. This was not a novel form of organization. Especially in the working-class sections, many members of the action committees had already participated in committees dedicated to peace in Algeria or some other political objective. These small groups were well suited to the militants who, unintegrated in any broadly based political organization, strove to escape their isolation by attracting all those who were ready to work militantly for a precise objective rather than join a highly organized structure. The P.S.U., a conglomeration of various currents of opinion and small, highly cohesive groups, furnished many militants to these committees, which were much more widespread than in the past. A great number were formed outside the university, in the civil service and the research agencies. In all of them, the same priority was given to precise action; there was the same hostility to "bureaucracy," the same concern to encourage maximum participation by the greatest number. Beyond this basic agreement, there was very little unity. The coordinating bodies at the Sorbonne, in which the organized political groups acted in a much more precise fashion, had, for this very reason, only a very limited importance. In certain cases, a personality dominated an action committee, in a particular university faculty, for example. But while everyone knew the names of Cohn-Bendit, Geismar, and Sauvageot, it cannot be said that any individual "directed" the occupied Sorbonne, just as no individual dominated the action committee of Nanterre.

To the very degree that organization and coordination were weak and thus the complete opposite of the practice of the Communist Party, the richness of expression and information was superabundant. Newspapers, posters, and graffiti appeared everywhere. Of the noncommercial papers, which were often ephemeral—*Le Pavé* had only one issue—and were usually sold by individual distributors, one especially, *Action,* had particularly great influence. Published with the support of the U.N.E.F., the S.N.E.Sup. and the F.E.N., it was created by older militants of the student movement as an instrument of the struggle; its first page was a poster, its editorials were calls to action, and its news was oriented particularly to the worker struggles. About 350 posters were published by the People's Workshop of the Beaux-Arts, that is, the former Ecole des Beaux-Arts, which was one of the great centers of organization and information at the service of the movement, especially at the time of the confrontations at Flins. Distributed everywhere, often reproduced by improvised means—for example, in the street opposite the Epée-de-Bois theater near the Albert-Châtelet Centre, where the March 22 Movement met for a while—they were usually appeals for unity between students and workers, denunciations of police violence, and attacks against Gaullist authoritarianism. Finally, there was the graffiti, which, even more than the newspapers and posters, were the libertarian expression of the rejection of social and moral, even more than political, repression.

The Anti-Spectacle

In these graffiti and their appeal for liberation from repression and manipulation, we can best read the most profound cultural theme of the movement. They embodied social and political demands formulated in the early hours of a new movement, appeals to spontaneity and to "needs" interpreted in a utopian fashion rather than appeals to abstractions. To the degree that a movement becomes organized and moves closer to power, it appeals to reason and to history, opposing them to the irrational power of its adversary. The May Movement was formed in a society already dominated by the economic rationalism of technocracy. It answered statistics with words, forecasts with affirmations, strategy with pressure. The statistics showed that everything was getting better and better, that the university system was growing, that the general living standard was rising. Passion did not argue with these statistics; it exposed repression and alienation and encouraged the determination to struggle.

Its speech was not argumentation, discussion, and negotiation but the juxtaposition of statements, appeals, and condemnations. Often one heard meetings refuse to allow someone to respond after his statement had just been discussed. This disturbing procedure expressed the desire not to delay the movement in a discussion but to broaden it by letting each new statement be responsible for marking a step forward from those that preceded it. There was also a desire to weaken the influence of those who were used to speaking and discussion, who could so easily impose their influence because of their ability or their technical competence. The debates in the meetings and the action committees were long, loaded with repetitions, tortured, and often gave a strong impression of not getting anywhere; after an hour's absence, one could pick up the thread with no trouble. This was because these discussions were self-expression more than deliberation, liberation more than reflection.

But can anyone who has heard union meetings or sessions of a faculty council forget the much greater richness of the May debates? They tended not to find solutions but to clarify problems. In their very disorder, they committed each one who spoke, not to an established body, but to a collectivity of individuals at once more different from each other than in a bureaucratic assembly and more united with each other by the consciousness of a common responsibility to act in a new world defined by action, not by rules, traditions, or statistics. French society has always opposed to the power structure both retreat into tradition, custom, and family or private life and an intelligentsia free in its declarations, actively committed to unite philosophical reflection, political criticism, and literary judgment.

In May, the movement forced many people out of their habits and their retreat, particularly the students who had lived entirely centered on their private lives. The central power in France would not be so ponderous and so closed if the social and cultural barriers and divisions were not so strong throughout the country. Reinforced by the nature of the central power but also combated by it, these barriers turn this society into a theater in which the various social categories place themselves one above the

other, from the orchestra to the balconies, the more
privileged seeking to isolate themselves in the best seats
and boxes, while the government and the whole political
system puts on a theatrical which those who have paid for
their seats are proud to be able to freely applaud or hiss
and to criticize on leaving, without feeling concerned by
the performance.

This comparison comes to mind because a university
amphitheater, as the name indicates, was also a theater in
which the professor was play-acting. There was much
theater in May: at the Odéon, which no longer wished to
be one after its occupation by a revolutionary action
committee on May 15; at the Sorbonne; in the streets,
where the debates took place. The first took place on the
Boulevard Saint-Michel where, even before the Night
of the Barricades, Cohn-Bendit challenged Aragon, the
surrealist and revolutionary who had become a candidate
for commissar of letters in the heyday of Stalin and
Jdanov, while maintaining, like so many Frenchmen, his
own private intellectual life. This theater wished to
destroy spectacularly the separation of the actor from
his public, as the Living Theater, whose ideology is
far removed from that of the May revolutionaries, in
its own way destroyed the idea of theater as spectacle.
The Gaullist regime had enormously increased the role
of spectacle in political life: press conferences, televised
speeches prepared like recitals, the presentation of the
successes of the year, the creation of a dramatic climate
simultaneously exalting, tragic, and aloof. In May, those
who entered political life invaded the theater and settled
in the unoccupied territory whose partitions had been
destroyed. Those who remained outside the movement
and came to observe it out of curiosity might be shocked
to see a badly directed spectacle but, in fact, it was neither a classical play nor, as has been lightly written, a
psychodrama. It was an anti-spectacle, closer to the Club

des Cordeliers * or a soviet than to the meetings of political parties or popular celebrations.

Against Authoritarianism: The CAL's (Comités d'Action Lycéens) †

The movement showed its creative force not in the quantity of its proclamations but in its capacity to indict the forms of authority. Reaching far beyond the faculties and industrial companies, this questioning of authority was very intense and almost general. It was opposition that entailed little danger in many cases. It was the rejection of superannuated institutions, an effort to rock them rather than a daily struggle to overturn an oppressive authority that was a real power. For this reason, one can say that very often revolutionary proclamations covered up an effort to modernize that was both very healthy and also quite far removed from revolutionary objectives.

From the Vichy government and the traditions of corporatism, France had inherited professional organizations, dominated by well-known persons, which almost always defended particular interests in the narrowest manner possible. In May, young professionals started to assault these organizations that barred the way to change. Architects, lawyers, magistrates, and doctors attacked or even occupied the local headquarters of their council or order. We have already said that the action of staff personnel was of this kind rather than an element of the strikes in the industrial companies. This was less a proclamation of the rejection of all authority than a desire for professional renewal, for the replacement of smoke-filled rooms dominated by old men in favor of open committees better

* Club des Cordeliers, one of the most lively centers of the "Montagne" during the central part of the French Revolution.
† High School Students' Action Committees.

able to defend the professional interests of the majority and to express in modern terms the role of the professional in society.

In some cases, the opposition was even more spectacular and, at the same time, less important. At the beginning of 1968, the defense of Henri Langlois—the creator of the Cinémathèque brutally closed by the government—provoked a lively reaction and the beginning of political criticism, the scuttling of the Cannes Festival, and the protest meetings of the actors, but despite the efforts of a few, there was no real action involved, since interests and ideas quickly clashed after a moment of high spirits. Some writers invaded the Hotel de Massa, headquarters of the professional Société des Gens de Lettres, and succeeded at least on that occasion in stating an intelligent criticism of a simultaneously reactionary and commercial image of the writer's trade.

Only when this opposition encountered the strength of a real organization, in the schools and the radio-television industry as well as in the university system and industry, did the cultural revolt acquire any practical importance and begin to nourish, instead of reflecting, a social and political movement. Two great battles against authority were waged, one in the *lycées* and the other at the O.R.T.F. Almost the only thing they had in common was that they went far beyond the kind of opposition that involved neither danger nor real consequences. In the secondary schools, cultural opposition was profoundly connected with the formation of a social movement; at the O.R.T.F., it clashed with political power. It is noteworthy that the most radical indictments outside of the university faculties were produced in areas of formation and information which until then had been outside political participation —the secondary schools because they were run by the State and the family; the agencies of public information because they were run by the State and secondarily by

unions lost in the labyrinth of questions of status, a labyrinth that they themselves sometimes helped to complicate.

One cannot speak of the movement in the secondary
schools in isolation from the university faculties, to which
they were so close and among whose students their militants mixed immediately at the time of the street demonstrations of May 3–10. Despite this community of action,
the movement of the secondary school students kept a
strong specificity, if only because it attacked an essential
and clearly defined institution, the *lycée*.* Agitation in
the secondary schools showed itself almost as early as in
the university faculties—the secondary school action committees (CAL) appeared in November—and attracted
the attention of an astonished and dumbstruck public
on the occasion of the expulsion of a student from the
Lycée Condorcet who had been accused of political activity within the institution. The opposition political groups,
particularly the local Vietnam committees, the J.C.R., and
the E.S.U. (student branch of the P.S.U.) recruited adherents in the older classes of the secondary schools just as
they did at the university. This parallel is easily understood if one recalls that the median age of those who earn
their *baccalauréat* has risen in the course of the last years,
so that many secondary school students are more than
eighteen years old and more adult and independent than
many students of the preceding generation, when the role
of the family was stronger and the importance of teen agers
was more limited.

While the secondary school action committees participated in the movement as a whole, in a few days they had

---

* It should be remembered that the *lycées*, especially the most important ones, are more than high schools. After the baccalaureat, the best
students stay in the *lycée* instead of going to the university, to prepare for
the examination for entrance into the *grandes écoles* or the Ecole Normale
Supérieure. An important *lycée* in Paris is more similar to Columbia or
Harvard College than to a high school.

overturned the authoritarian organization of the *lycées*. Because the secondary school did not lead to professional life, criticism of its social function centered entirely on criticism of its methods. Even more than in the university faculties, pedagogical problems were general social and political problems; for the function of the secondary school was to form a social elite by the employment of constraining intellectual methods, by applying strict discipline and methods of evaluation reduced to marks and classification. However, this first picture must be immediately completed in two ways.

In the first place, the *lycée,* a Napoleonic creation but entirely nourished by the experience of the Jesuits and the Oratorians, has not been the instrument of a social class in the same way as the English public schools. Its goal was not to form gentlemen and to prepare a certain type of social behavior. There were no collective activities in the *lycées,* only individual work and an almost exclusive insistence on intellectual formation, given over a long period for the most part by a body of professors recruited on the basis of *agrégation,* hence at a high level of university training. The secondary school wished to be and was a means to rise socially through studies. Through it, the lower middle classes could raise their children to the ranks of the bourgeoisie in the liberal professions and as professors and civil service officials.

This means that in the case of the secondary schools as well as of the university faculties, to speak of a bourgeois education is both true and too summary; it neglects an intermediate term in the relation, the State. Teaching was determined by the State which in the nineteenth century was assuredly a State that belonged to a bourgeois society but also exercised its own action. Hence, the form of the studies was as important as the content of the instruction and it has certainly evolved less. The secondary school movement had lasting consequences because it

first of all indicted a system of education built on authoritarian organization, with its compositions and classifica-
tions which create an atmosphere of competition rather
than of search for personal diversity.

In the second place, today's *lycée* is far from corresponding entirely to its principles. As with the university,
this is due to the fact that the number of secondary school
students has considerably increased, one minor reason being the increase of births since the war but the essential
reason an important increase in the proportion of those
who attend school. The bourgeois character of the secondary school came primarily from the fact that it used to be
content to transmit abstract knowledge, because the students received from their families the indispensable com-
plement of education and above all the necessary motivations to successfully make strenuous efforts and bear harsh
constraints. A great number of today's secondary school
students neither are nor can be in this situation. As a result, the teaching they receive appears to many of them
as a body of tests which have no meaning and offer no
reward.

The more highly educated teachers, especially the
agrégés, also strongly resent this imbalance and feel
themselves socially humiliated by this mass approach to
education. They often either become defensive or seek
more prestigious levels of teaching. Some of them, the less
highly trained teachers as well, showed themselves quite
at one with their students and quite disposed to work
with them to seek a new balance that would permit a less
brutal pedagogical relationship. This reaction is quite
analogous to that of the staff personnel in industry, especially in the modern industries in which they are numerous, who began to feel closer to the wage-earners than to
management. In many secondary schools, the teachers
participated actively in the movement, which testified to a
more lively consciousness of the university crisis than

was shown in general by the professors of higher education.

In the overcrowded and crumbling university faculties, the intervention of the students had considerable difficulty in getting beyond generalized criticism and the presentation of general themes of social transformation. It was difficult to focus criticism on particular points because the reality was elusive. A secondary school, on the other hand, is much more like a workshop. A class is a real social unity; a few dozen students spend a great number of hours together. The action of the CAL's was very realistic: numerous propositions, often very well-worked out, were presented, touching on the organization of the teaching, the nature of the courses, and the methods of evaluating results.

This realism could easily become, indeed often became, a quite narrow kind of reformism. The secondary school students wished to prove their seriousness and felt dominated by the power of their institution. The action of the CAL's, which was more integrated into the real life of a working collectivity than the action committees of the university faculties, also had to struggle against isolation, against the situation of the secondary school students as "minors." That is why political activism was very strong. There was often a bitter struggle between those who supported the reform of studies and those who wished to concentrate on exterior political action. This was aggravated by the opposition between Communists and leftists and finally by the creation of the UNCAL (Union Nationale des Comités d'Action Lycéens), which opposed the CAL's and was more angry than they. The importance of the CAL's resulted from the fact that, beyond those opposed tendencies, a principle of unity guided their action: the struggle against an authority system. This struggle was not against the representatives of authority—the administrators were ignored rather than fought

—but against authoritarianism as it concretely manifested itself in their lives. It was not a cultural rebellion
or a flight into words but a will for social transformation
bound to political criticism and action.

This connection is essential. The role of authoritarianism in the *lycée* is to give it the role of a seminary, in
the ecclesiastical sense of the term. The social order defined principles and rules and inculcated them into those
who would later rule it. When the CAL's opened the
secondary school to the life of society, to its values and
dominant norms and, above all, to its political and intellectual conflict, it destroyed the integrative role of education and augmented its innovative role. It was not a
matter of integrating the school into the community, as
the Parent-Teacher Associations do in the United States
(their role is not always conformist, in any case), but of
integrating the school into all the intellectual and social
movements through which society establishes itself by debate and conflict.

Such a radical criticism of education and its social function went far beyond a lightening and modernization of
the study programs. It did not situate itself on a psycho-
social level and did not reason and react first of all in
terms of communication but in social and political terms
as well as in terms of personality development. It was
much less a matter of transforming the school environment than of transforming the relationship between the
young person and society. He was being taught to enter
society; he wished to learn how to change it.

Public Information

In the secondary schools and university faculties, freedom of political information, expression, and organization was both demanded and imposed, primarily because

the apoliticism of the institution was only a cover-up for the maintenance of the social order and the existent social powers, which did not wish to admit what they actually were. The strike at the O.R.T.F. had an entirely different, even opposite, meaning and nevertheless was part of the same movement. It was not a matter of politicizing public information but of serving political freedom by telling the facts and by resisting the constraints imposed by the State. This was a liberal objective in the best sense of the word but one that came into direct conflict with the State, since the conflict broke out over the refusal of the O.R.T.F. management to cover the political and university events of the beginning of May.*

This strike was all the more exemplary because it clearly gave priority to the problems of public information over those connected with the professional situation of the contracted correspondents and stringers of the O.R.T.F. Although it was supported by 90 percent of the technical and administrative personnel, the action of the journalists was most widely known, not only because the public knew the names, voices, or faces of many of them, but because by their very function they most directly defended freedom of information, which few Frenchmen were ready to affirm had been respected. How many Parisians followed the events of May 3–10 on the France-Inter network? Television, even more violently criticized, given its greater influence and its practically assured monopoly over the entire territory, behaved dur-

---

* In France, the state holds a monopoly of all radio and T.V. programs. A series of private companies broadcast from nearby territories: Monaco, Luxemburg, Andorra. The French Government owns large parts of the stock of some of these companies but does not control the activity of most of them. The most important of these companies, Radio Luxemburg and Europe n°1, have their studios in Paris and draw the majority of the French audience. For technical reasons, the State monopoly on TV is practically complete, except for some regions along the Belgian and the Swiss frontiers.

ing the whole beginning of the crisis in such a manifestly
scandalous manner—neither informing nor presenting
the viewpoint of the students and demonstrators—that
the crisis broke out very sharply. It would not have been
as profound or as long-lasting and would not have involved such harsh sanctions if, through the television coverage, the whole political system had not been indicted
and if, beyond this, the political struggle had not been
intensified by the internal problems of a constraining
administration that was disorganized and shaken up by
reforms that had not touched the essential problems.

The relation of this strike with the May Movement
was very close, as shown by the demonstrations of solidarity with the organized strikers—"Operation Jericho"—
around the Maison de la Radio, and also by the fears of
the government, not without foundation, that the demonstrators would attempt to take possession of this building
or of the television studios on Rue Cognacq-Jay. Even
after that phase of the movement, when the S.N.E.Sup.
defined the preconditions for the resumption of independent university activities, it continued to insist on the necessity for a transformation of the O.R.T.F. and an annul-
ment of the sanctions, licensing requirements, transfers,
and anticipated forced retirements that hit many of the
strikers and, especially, about 100 journalists.

It was also a complicated relationship, for the O.R.T.F.
strikers were demanding the objectivity of public information and its freedom, rather than its commitment to
the service of a revolutionary movement. They did not
speak about a class television, they opposed national television to government television rather than opposing
bourgeois television to socialist television. They wanted
to have the same independence as their colleagues in the
BBC rather than tie their strike to a political movement.
Consequently, there seemed to be a very great distance
between the student Sorbonne and the O.R.T.F. strikers.

But this very distance, which did not impede active
solidarity, illuminates one of the most important aspects
of the May Movement. It was a revolutionary action that
sought to provoke a break with the past and wished to
revive the class struggle and, at the same time, it was
opposition to a social and political order in the name of
liberty. The two strengths of the movement, as we shall
see, were both united and in conflict with each other
within the committees and meetings that prepared the
transformation of the university. The closer one came to
the center of the movement—groups of militants committed to political action—the greater priority was given
in May and June to the revolutionary struggle. On the
other hand, the more one considers the effect of the movement on particular institutions, the more it is the reversal
of constraints and domination and of all forms of authoritarianism that came to the fore. The O.R.T.F. strikers,
whose movement remained independent, showed the
strength of the movement of liberation and indeed of
serious liberalism that gave rise to the action of the militants who were horrified at the word "liberalism" and
were more concerned with worker or student power than
with political liberties.

In calling for "objective" public information, the
O.R.T.F. journalists were not only concerned with the
political problems connected with it. They moved beyond
a narrow conception of political life. The governments of
the "right" were not the only ones to have restricted
freedom of information; the government of Guy Mollet
during the Suez Crisis and the Algerian War had inter-
fered with it in a very partisan manner. Consequently, it
was a matter of struggling against control by the political
structure, whatever it might be, and of recovering an
objectivity which would not cover up conflicts but
would show them and would have no other rule than to
respond to the expectations of the public.

At the beginning of the O.R.T.F. strike, the little group of journalists was regarded with suspicion by the great mass of the technicians of the administrative staff. It was the journalists, nevertheless, who supported the strike the longest and who bore the principal burden of the sanctions imposed by the government. This proves that the defense of objective public information, far from being an apolitical objective, revealed the essential problems of a society in which power acted more by manipulation than by economic exploitation. Freedom of information is necessary for the formation of a political life and for society not to be identified with the government. The O.R.T.F. strike, apolitical in the sense that it did not fight against one party in the name of another, showed that opposition based on political liberties and social democracy belongs to the debates of the past and has no more meaning when social democracy is fighting against a State structure that imposes a kind of depoliticization that masks its self-interest and its rejection of this very fact and of all debate.

Criticism from the professionals in education and information should be broadened and lead to criticism from those in that more complex form of information, science. Results here are less convincing, inferior to what they were in Germany, for example, but they were not negligible in an area intermediate between scientific research and information. This was true, first of all, because the workers in research agencies participated very actively in the movement. They were too close to the social sciences not to feel concerned by opposition originating among sociology students. Whether they belonged to the public or private sector, they depended too directly on the State and its commands not to question the use made of their competence. As specialists in urban problems or the use of land, in studies of public opinion or consumer affairs, they first of all asked what and whom their work was serving. They sometimes pressed their criticism further, questioning the very nature of the intellectual operations with which they were charged. Because they carry out studies rather than research, they have to place themselves in the situation as it really is, in the social system as it actually functions, without questioning the limits and constraints of its functioning. Does not their very role lead them to treat people purely as customers, asking the reasons that lead them to purchase a particular commercial product, a particular type of home, a particular political party, as if these choices could be correctly and sufficiently defined by the solutions or responses offered by citizens at a given moment?

This kind of questioning among the technicians of the social sciences is found even more among the specialists in education, as the Amiens Conference had already brought out. The Institut Pédagogique National was one of the most active centers of discussion and opposition. A movement was established, C.A.I.R.E. (Comités d'Action et d'Initiative pour la Renovation de l'Enseignement) that was determined no longer to consider pedagogy as a technique for adaptation and social management but would place priority on problems of personality over those of professional preparation and socialization. In the same way, the personnel in supervised education criticized the excessive control of the administration of justice over their work.

The bad conscience of these experts, whose university training often did not correspond to their real tasks, did not lead all of them to demand a more "practice-oriented" university system. Many assuaged their consciences for a long time through political opposition of no great consequence. That explains why one of the first appeals in the Billion for Vietnam campaign was launched by social science technicians, from whom Georges Perec, author of Les Choses, organized an outspoken group. The May

Movement permitted them to criticize their own role
and the constraints that deformed it and made it pointless, insufficient, or unhealthy. Did not the opinion polls
seem strangely unable to grasp political movements beyond the choice of a party or a candidate, satisfaction or
dissatisfaction with some particular measure or personality? Had these polls grasped the formation and activity
of the student movement any better than the university
administration or the government? When a movement
breaks out within society and contests its authority, organization, and goals, and when social and political life no
longer appears to be determined by the conditions and
stages of national economic development but to be the
expression of conflicting interests and forces, choices and
power, any "objective" description of social reality can
only appear to be determined by a conformist ideology.

Now we can grasp better the importance of this revolt
against the social order. Beyond its action in the university and its participation in the worker struggles, the May
Movement touched a great part of French society. It accomplished this not only by provoking the formation of
action committees in very diverse sectors of activity during an exceptionally widespread and prolonged strike,
but even more by shaking up all the forms of authority.
Its influence was exerted less in terms of a program than
in terms of questioning and opposition. In the face of an
official society that wished to identify itself both with its
own growth and with the State, with statistics and strategy, it revolted against all forms of repression. This revolt
matched the analyses of Herbert Marcuse more than it
was influenced by them. This was an uprising against
the domination, not of prosperity and mass consumption,
but of authoritarian rationalism, understanding by that,
the intellectual and political reduction of all social life
to a technical structure in which politics would intervene
only on the level of international relations. It was a pro-

test against the dominant ideology's understanding of social change and of the industrial society that poses a directive line in history, a line that is described by modernization, new management methods, the institutionalization and compartmentalization of conflicts, and an increased participation due to consumership and instruction in progress. This protest was always twofold: through shock tactics, violence, or the pressure and organization of the workers, it imposed debate and obliged society to recognize that where the rulers wished only to see the necessary and the reasonable, there still was choice and political power; at the same time, it directly combated the constraints imposed by authoritarianism in the university system, the professions, and the O.R.T.F.

The repression that it denounced was not directly police repression but the kind of repression that knows how to appeal to the police when it is threatened: repression in the name of order that calls itself reason, repression in the name of modernity that calls itself the bypassing of conflicts, the repression of the State that takes itself for society. French society was reduced to the experience of policies called common sense and choices said to be imposed by the logic of progress. Some wished to see only modernizing change on one side and resistance to change nourished by archaic traditions and doctrines on the other. Of course, these constraints, repression, and authoritarianism were not brutal and nothing would be more absurd than to paint a dramatic picture of the condition of French youth. Problems of employment and the insufficiency of the university system are not the same thing as totalitarianism and undernourishment. But only a very poor analysis would reduce human conduct to mechanical facts, as if only serious pressure and extreme material deprivation could provoke uprisings.

Characteristically, French society was able to maintain great cultural rigidity, based on the continuity among the

ruling classes fostered by the State, while at the same
time rapidly transforming itself; in the end, it was not
capable of preventing this contradiction from exploding
because it was "liberal." This caused the gravity of a crisis
that affected the technical or economic foundations of
society less than it did the forms of social organization,
human relations, authority relationships, and the methods of education—the crisis of an archaic society with a
modern economy. It exploded brutally because it was neither foreseen nor grasped and because the State was as
incapable of understanding it as it was of repressing its
consequences. The result was its rapid spread and the
crumbling of those institutions that seemed most solid
and influential.

By its statements, the May Movement made many people realize that the state of things was often shocking and
that every social system exists only by repressing interests,
feelings, and styles of conduct and organization that are
virtual elements of society or of personality. A society pre-
vails only through its capacity to confront itself, to be
open to what it rejects, to live with its conflicts, its dreams,
and its contradictions. The May Movement was a night-
mare for those in power. Let them remember that a being deprived of its dreams becomes insane.

Crisis and Rejection

Revolt against repression can be creative only if it is
critical. What it says has meaning only in terms of the rejection it opposes to constraint and prohibitions. If it in-
dulges in monologue, it encloses itself in speech which is
meaningless and paralyzing. The great misfortune of the
May Movement was to have sole possession for a few weeks
of a few acres of stone and cement where it could feel that
it was, all by itself, a new society. While the most active

militants were moving toward industry and business and others were involved in the work of transforming the university system, the secondary schools, and the university faculties, still other energies were consumed in endless talk to no one. Perhaps one should not attach too much importance to what happened at the Sorbonne. But its fever aroused so much enthusiasm that one is within one's rights in wishing to moderate it and to say at least that what was the most spectacular was also the most illusory. What would we think of the Jacobins and the Cordeliers if we did not know that the political evolution of the Revolution was being debated there and that the movements formed there were characterized by decision and crisis?

It has been said and written that in May the imagination seized power but it was only an imaginary power. Because they no longer wished society to be a spectacle, they mistook a spectacle for society. What was done or said at the Odéon? After a few hours in that furnace, how many people committed themselves to act, how many took risks of which they would not have dreamed or would not have dared face the night before, how many were transformed? Revolt on the part of what has been repressed or by one who has been alienated does not amount all by itself to the creation of a new society and culture. The student revolt was important only because it was less than a revolution assuredly, but more than a revolt. In any case, it was a movement that wished to go beyond its protests and strip itself of itself by directing its attacks beyond the university system and against the economic and political system.

This critical reaction is assuredly very subjective and more must be said. But first, personal feelings and impressions must be allowed to react against the illusion, the emotional evidence, of revolutionary fire, that supposedly would have burned on the barricades and at Flins in the same way as at the Sorbonne and the Odéon. It is natural at the moment of the event, which surprised a

sleeping society, for one to react in a simplified manner.
The rights of analysis do not stand alone and an observer
who had not taken part would have missed what was essential. At a time when the Sorbonne was the refuge where
the wounded came for escape and care; when the very existence of the student assemblies had brought down the
former university authorities; when one was at one moment in the courtyard of the Sorbonne and a few hours
later between Flins and Les Mureaux—how could one not
be primarily aware of the unity of a complex and diverse
movement that was quite clearly defined by what it rejected.

"Excesses" were constant from the beginning of the
movement. Let us go back first to the events at Nanterre,
recalling the observations we have already made. The first
student demonstrations at the beginning of 1968 were
organized around the issue of the blacklists that the administration was supposedly using. After January 26, the
walls of the faculty were covered with statements treating
the dean as a Nazi and a Gestapo agent. I am speaking of
excesses not in the name of moderation and justice, but
primarily because these accusations had no relationship
with a reality that may be distant for young men of twenty
years of age who should, nevertheless, have a more mature
political judgment. There is an evident contrast between
these excesses in words and action and the political violence of a Cohn-Bendit, who never went further in words
than in action and who was never gratuitous. In May,
when the marchers shouted, "C.R.S. = S.S." or "De-
Gaulle—Fascist," it was the same kind of exaggeration beyond political reality.

A utopia is the expression of political energy that has
not yet been able to transform its ideas into combat but is
creative. On the other hand, the shock or insult that ac-
companies revolt is rather the sign of social pathology than
an instrument of the struggle. Those who wrote, "I had a

good time with the paving stones," were not the ones who took on political action. These remarks are not meant to express regret for excesses that tarnished the image of the May Movement, as if these excesses were only regrettable and were only the deeds of a few marginal persons. The climate of crisis and social rupture was an essential aspect of a nascent movement, just as the work of modernization and updating that was carried out in many professional groups. But one cannot be satisfied with fusing within a chronological unity, cultural crisis, class conflict, and institutional modernization, just because the actual event was defined by their simultaneity.

The cultural revolt both continually aroused political action and opposed it; the first is the shot fired over the wall and the second is the heat released at the point of impact. The union of the red flag and the black flag was the very symbol of the May Movement. Rejection led to contestation and political struggle, but everything that a society represses cannot be transformed into a movement toward a new society. Revolutionary action is not the affirmation of the antisociety, but the revelation of the contradictions of a society and the consequent separation within that society itself of what is "progressive" from what is reactionary. If social life were reduced to alienation, the natural man could be opposed to society, as the pleasure principle is opposed to the principle of reality, but no transformation of society by man would be possible and one would be locked into a vision of society that could nourish despair or celebration but certainly not political action.

In the case of the student movement, expression of the rejection and revolt constantly went so far beyond the revolutionary program that one cannot explain what happened as the formation of a revolutionary movement. That is why from the beginning, when we analyzed the university crisis, we refused to see the university system as only a bourgeois institution: it was also an institution that was simultaneously rigid and crumbling, an institution whose principles, rules, and practice were in profound discord. The student revolt was not solely an act of social contestation but also a reaction to absurdity and nonsense. The very nature of the university system, the fact that its constraints, discipline, and manner of repression were always very weak and hesitant, compared to what a worker or employee knows in his company, the hesitation of public opinion and of the government in the face of a movement in which so many children of middle-class families were participating, all this contributed, along with the student occupation of the faculties, to allow the revolt a self-expression that went outside the paths traced by political action and helped to demonstrate the autonomy of the cultural and social crisis relative to the class conflict.

The opposition that I am seeking to indicate between a social combat and crisis reactions must nevertheless be a limited one. They are the two complementary faces of the same movement, or rather the social combat is the political concretization of the initial break; their unity lies in opposition to this social system, its forms of power and organization. The May Movement was created by the "enragés," just as one finds at the origin of the German movement the spectacular provocation of Kommune I, or at Berkeley, after the great push of the Free Speech Movement and before the massive actions against the Vietnam War, there was the so-called period of obscenity. The action originates in the sociocultural break. It does not stop there, unless it has not mobilized all the forces of the break. If utopianism played a central role, this was because it was midway between a social movement and simple rejection.

The social crisis provoked two responses that were apparently opposed but went equally beyond the social movement that was in the process of formation: the push

toward modernization, perfectly acceptable to the technocrats; on the other hand, the proclamation of the antisociety that consumed itself in its own talk. Because there
were so few possibilities for political action and because
the revolutionary movement was unable to create a revolution, the antisociety held great attraction, which contributed to the weakness of the movement. In the next
chapter, we will see that in the final phase of the movement in the university there appeared irrational reactions
of pure rejection that could lead to terrorism but were
otherwise impotent. From beginning to end, there was a
great temptation to deny the existence of problems and
exigencies connected with production. Since the movement formed and developed primarily in the university,
one sometimes witnessed the reappearance of the most
sloppy forms of thought: the rejection of all constraints
required by experimental work and the apology for the
abandonment of the human sciences to sentiment and
ideology.

The antisociety was not the movement itself but its response to the impossibility of action and to the complacency of society. A social movement both lays bare and
fights against the internal contradictions of a society; the
image of an antisociety is brandished only by those who
find themselves outside society. The May Movement was
both within the technocratic society and outside it, just as
the university itself was. It fought for a new society at the
same time that it proclaimed the antisociety. The red flag
crossed the black flag. Were this rejection and social break
—which appear to me to be the reverse of utopianism and
the opposite of a social movement—nothing more than
that symbol suggests? Why not reverse the analysis and say
that the revolutionary proposal was only a clumsy political expression of what was in fact a crisis of civilization,
the opposition of alienated youth to the production-
oriented society that a wounded industrialization and pros-

perity now deprive of all historical reality, since it has attacked their goals? Rather than a social conflict giving the movement its meaning, the cultural crisis would define the event.

When Malraux reflected on the events of May, he saw, above all, this crisis of civilization, a general weakening of the traditional hierarchies in a society defined for the first time by its programs and future rather than by its past, by its works rather than by its faith; the outcome of that long-term tendency that sociologists call secularization which takes on particular strength in a society that has long been attached to local and family life, to the beliefs that cement the whole social order. Is not the France of the village, the family, the monarch, and the Church meeting for the first time a generation born in a world in which symbolisms are being erased and replaced by the signs of technology, power, and sex? Youth no longer receives an inheritance and is no longer acquainted with order; it possesses a civilization but no longer belongs to a society. We are witnessing a reversal of the usual place occupied by youth. Even yesterday, this was a group in social apprenticeship; today, it is for a longer and longer period uninvolved in the rules of productive work and is freed earlier and earlier from the influence of the family. As that adult society more and more plans, organizes, calculates, and submits to bureaucratic and hierarchized organization, to the same degree the society of the young is marked by the immediate, by anti-history. It discovers new codes of conduct and personal relationships, new relations with objects, sex, authority, and organizes itself according to primary groups, bands, or undifferentiated masses but never in stable organizations.

This interpretation goes far beyond the vague idea of a generational conflict. It even contradicts it in a very useful manner. The youth movement is not directed against the preceding generation; it is too detached from it for that.

It only fights against what is present—imperialist war, technocratic power, the mutation of needs into consumption. If it is enraged, the reason is that it has received nothing from the past, that it lives in a new world in which the principles and rules of the past seem to it devoid of meaning, incomprehensible, and absurd.

The acceleration of change makes the present uprising of youth more violent than that of the romantic youth who also experienced, following the French Revolution and at the beginnings of industrialization, a first step into a new society. But this movement that has the force of the *Chants de Maldoror* or of *Une Saison en Enfer* responds, not to a crisis in society, as at the end of World War I when the Dada Movement and then surrealism broke out, but to a more complete transformation of society and culture. If, perhaps, a civilization of scarcity has ended and a new image of man and human behavior has appeared, was the May Movement primarily the anguished discovery of the death of man, that is, of a certain idea of man?

I believe that it was quite the opposite, almost entirely oriented toward the problems of a society, not of a civilization. The death of the philosophy of man was also the birth of sociology. The interpretation of Malraux is that of a philosopher, of a man witnessing the disappearance of the civilization from which he received his heritage. The youth movement is not meditation but action. If man is what he does, he is also what others make him, what society, its products, its organization, its centers of power make him. From the moment that essences disappear, everything in social life becomes social relations, everything is political. Today what would a collective, purely cultural revolt be but a political step backward?

The movement was no stranger to the reactions of youth who wished to be outside production and power; it fought against them as a form of alienation; it saw in them the work of those who possess power and who reduce human

beings to manipulated consumers. The movement
mounted by the young was the criticism of a group manu-
factured by society, just as the labor movement was the
criticism of the workers' condition by a group created by
capitalist industrialization. Most constantly, the students
showed themselves determined to cease acting merely as
students and to provoke everyone to action against the
power that dominates the whole of society. The whole
action of the movement sought to transform a crisis of
civilization into political action and by this very effort the
influence of this crisis was weakened.

The invention of new cultural patterns and the formation of a new image of man cannot be accomplished by
such a social movement. They require a certain distance
from the conflict of which the movement is the agent, a
certain fusion of social action with the new forms of production and material life, for a culture is not a deliberate
creation. The double sense always attached to the word
culture—cultural models and unconscious practical behavior—indicates that it is a combination of the influence
of social life on man and the influence of human groups
on society.

The May Movement was one of the elements through
which an historic change and a crisis of civilization could
have been transformed into a new culture. But had it been
primarily the consciousness of this crisis, it could have
created only poetry, not politics. Its action would have
been only of the imagination. It was utopian, that is, it
politicized the imaginary. If the young, both students and
workers, were the principal protagonists of the movement,
this was not in order to affirm themselves outside the
bureaucratized society of adults. The reason was that at
the beginning of a new society—whose social conflicts are
not yet organized, while those coming from the earlier
society are already strongly institutionalized—the young
are the group most ready to throw themselves into global

contestation because they are free of the constraints imposed by the everyday economic struggle or professional
career. The young anticipate most easily the problems that
belong to their future. They are more free to invent forms
of new action that are not limited and, unlike their elders,
are not paralyzed by the necessary defense of what has
been achieved. But whether the action of the young was
modernization, political contestation, or cultural revolt,
it was always defined in terms of the whole of the society
that was to be transformed, not rejected. The militants
of May were not the defenders of youth; they constantly
defined themselves, on the contrary, as workers and sought
to affirm their freedom by struggling against their masters
or against the mask of the apolitical. They sought—more
than social participation and less than a culture—power.

Adaptation to Change or Social Transformation

The May Movement was simultaneously a will for social
participation and the rejection of a social order. It is easy
to oppose these two attitudes as contradictory and to state
that the strike at the O.R.T.F. and the permanent agitation at the Odéon had nothing in common. But while,
indeed, the movement stretched from liberalism on one
side to cultural insurrection on the other, it can best be
understood not by considering these extreme manifesta-
tions but by seeking what allowed it to move in such
different directions at the same time. Its unity was above
all political. Too much significance has been attached to
this term for it to go without some clarification.

Societies like ours are primarily changing societies.
They argue about their principles less than about their
growth, about their foundations less than about their
objectives. Their fundamental political choices, consequently, concern differing conceptions of social change.

For some, change means rational adaptation to an environment. It would mean reinforcing the capacity of the production systems to make decisions, to plan, and to achieve. This position is very far from the conservatism of those who think only of safeguarding heritage and principles and what has been achieved but who reject all debate about the ends of political action. Freedom of choice, say those who hold this position, is quite weak in reality and much more profound changes are caused by growth itself than by any transformation of distribution. They contend that one must renounce abstract rationalism, adopt a more experimental attitude, break down rigidity, insure the mobility of all the factors of production and of information through all the levels of manpower.

Among the defenders of this general position, some insist particularly on strengthening decision-making capacity at the top, and on the necessity of forming elites who have a broad overview of the organizations that they direct, who would be new entrepreneurs of the Saint-Simon type, motivated by austere devotion to the progress of production and the rational modernization of society. Others insist more on the need for participation. Like a company undergoing change, society cannot be locked into laws, rules, and organizational charts whose seeming clarity masks rigidity and the incapacity to organize change. A growing number of individuals and groups must possess strategic autonomy. Change must be argued and negotiated. The balance must always be kept fluid and must be questioned by the initiatives and demands of individuals and groups. The important thing is to organize the discussions and negotiations. We know that attitudes toward change are more favorable when those involved can be informed about it in advance, prepare themselves for it, and discuss how it is to be applied and what its consequences will be. This tendency, that we can call psycho-sociological, may do nothing more than cover up propaganda at the service of those in power, but this criticism is frequently made too quickly and neglects the essential. For this tendency, in a country with traditionalist and authoritarian habits like France, clearly opposes the concentration of authority at the top and fights against an oversimplified image of social rationality. If the first tendency is particularly concerned with posing and achieving technical and economic objectives, the second recognizes the existence and autonomy of the problems posed by social change. It admits the existence of special interests, of motivations and attitudes that must be combined and associated, rather than melded, in order to allow, through constant discussion, the active participation of individuals and groups as basic working units, instead of imposing from above decisions that present themselves as the expression of a natural and scientific necessity.

The May Movement revolted against the first tendency, which we shall call authoritarian technocracy, but it equally fought against the second, which I shall name liberal technocracy. For it rejected development of participation on the basis of a social model that was taken for granted as "natural." Participation must be subjected to contestation just as the activities of the company committees, or similar organisms, must always be subordinated to the demands of the unions.

Beyond the styles of functioning, it questioned the orientation of society. It could not be content with opposing a counterplan, for that would have been to place itself on the ground of the rationalizers. It was rather a matter of creating forces of social contestation that would make it clear that so-called economic rationality is inseparable from a system of power and management. This opposition could not avoid being passionate and making light of economic growth, since the constant reference to economic growth is the denial of conflicts of interests and the real relations of power. But it was not only emotional and essentially strove to transform contestation and social disruption into political initiatives. It did so by moving far beyond the methods of psychosociological intervention in its determination to create real groups, not just networks of interpersonal relationships within a framework of objectives and institutions to which they had to adapt, but groups that would bear real proposals for social transformation or, more exactly, would oppose one social determination to this other complementary and opposite social determination of the technocrats, who would finally be recognized for what they are, not bearers of social rationality but a ruling class that is both modernizing and domineering.

The revolt against the "one dimensionality" of the industrial society governed by the economic and political structures could not break out without involving some "negative" aspects, that is, without opposing the immediate pressure of its desires to the constraints—accepted as natural—of growth and modernization. But the May Movement cannot be reduced to this negativity which is both destructive and revelatory of social conflicts. It was both a scandal and a movement for social transformation. Sometimes the scandal enjoyed itself and its liberation from prohibitions, sometimes the social transformation weakened into reform and adaptation. But the importance of the movement resulted from the fact that essentially the bond between negativity and creative utopianism was maintained, although they were never fused.

The worker movement has always been the defense of immediate interests, that is, an appeal to the past at the same time as a "progressive" program for social development. The movements of social and national liberation in the colonialized countries are likewise both a determination to achieve economic development and the affirmation, or sometimes the recreation, of a national tradition. This tension between the two aspects of social action is the direct consequence of the duality of the actions of the ruling classes, who are both the agents of social change and the defenders of private interests and, consequently, defenders of a particular social order. This double dialectic defines all social evolution, considered not as the more or less mechanical effect of economic and technical changes but as the relations and conflict between those who innovate in the economy and dominate the society and those who present their demands and wish to transform society.

Official France perceived itself only in the form of curbs and quantities. It vigorously resisted social negotiations both in the public administration and in the private enterprises. Consequently, it experienced more clearly than other nations a kind of contestation that, launched by the fire of cultural revolt, opposed the passionate determination to reveal the political nature of social facts and relations to the naturalism of the managers of the industrial society.

VII

The University
in Question

The nature and effects of the movement emerged most
clearly in the context of the university system, where its
principal thrust was toward the creation of a utopia. This
word should not mislead us; utopians are usually individuals who seek out some corner of the world and some social
collectivity to remodel according to their ideas. In this
case, just the opposite happened: the utopia had the
strength of a social movement. The community shed the
habits of its daily existence and sought to invent not a
model university but an intellectual and social force to
transform the university and its relationships with the
whole of society. Its action was both powerful and fragile.
It needed to be translated into new institutions, but the
May Movement was no more able to take power in the
university than anywhere else. "Constructive" projects
risked stifling the determination to transform for the sake

of possible reforms. The risk of "recuperation" was great. Contrarily, to the degree that hopes for profound social change were disappointed and the university itself escaped or slipped into reaction, the energy of the movement risked being wasted in simple revolt and social disruption.

The student movement was not a political organization that sought to maintain its direction by skillful strategy that would enable it to avoid the Charybdis of recuperation and the Scylla of nihilism. Its nature made it unable to negotiate, since it was neither a pressure group nor a structured political force. It was essentially the collection of the various initiatives it aroused and it had neither the means nor the will to draw into doctrinal unity all the actions sparked by its early acts and combats and the social crisis that they occasioned. When the students returned to the faculties that had been closed or when they occupied almost all the university buildings, a collection of social, cultural, and political forces engulfed the university: modernizers, adherents of the political opposition, and social rebels, all mixed together yet distinct, brought to bear on a particular institution all the forms of social transformation and all the forces aimed toward it that had arisen during the street fighting or later as a reaction to the Week of the Barricades.

The movement changed scale. At first it had been the action of a few dozen, then a few hundred Nanterre students mostly from the departments of human sciences and philosophy; in the course of the battles against the police, it became a mass of thousands of students, young workers, and teachers. After the occupation of the faculties, the whole of the university organization was held up to question, from the secondary schools to the C.N.R.S., the professional schools, and the major establishments of higher education, including all university faculties. This extension was not simply diffusion and was not essentially due to the intervention of the Nanterre and Sorbonne students in other university establishments. The movement born at Nanterre was not bypassed; it had neither the will nor the capacity to direct the movement as a whole. Neither did the U.N.E.F. Although the secretary-general and governing office of the S.N.E.Sup. played an essential part in the movement, this organization was not a coherent and maneuverable battle corps. The violent disruption of the established order unleashed a multiple movement of rejection, critical analysis, and transformation of the university.

We must follow as precisely as possible the history of the creative and exhausting tension between the negation of university order and the invention of a new university. First, we must understand under what conditions the movement succeeded in integrating these two complementary and opposed tendencies in practice; then, under what other conditions, on the contrary, it was led by one or the other tendency alone and failed to achieve a transformation of the university and the student condition. Where the student movement gave absolute priority to extra-university struggles and the professors and administration fled or rejected negotiation, no transformation was achieved. Where the movement set itself only professional objectives and met a powerful organization that was able, after its first panic, to regain lost ground and make only very limited concessions, the same negative result was met. But sometimes participation and contestation managed to join forces in the student action, aided by the university organization's capacity for negotiation.

For a variety of reasons, one may express preference either for the social break or for the purely professional reforms, but these feelings do not prevent us from answering the central question: under what conditions did the student revolt, nourished by a revolutionary movement, succeed in introducing social change into the university system and what kind of change was it?

The Occupation of the Faculties

The dimensions of student participation in the criticism and transformation of the university system were immense and unprecedented. Even at the time of their greatest power, during the Algerian War when the students sent a contingent into the *djebels* to join the Algerian guerrillas, the U.N.E.F. had never mobilized masses comparable to those which participated in the debates in the faculties. The public transportation strike and the shortage of gasoline were, nevertheless, formidable hindrances, especially in the case of the outlying faculties. But many students and teachers spent more hours in their faculties during one month than they had spent during a whole year. Others remained silent, preparing for their examinations, taking advantage of this unexpected free time, rejecting what seemed to them subversion or masquerade. If, as some contend, all those who were absent were resolute or terrorized opponents, then it would have to be admitted that most decisions taken even in "normal" situations are unrepresentative impositions, for it is rare for a high proportion of the members of an association to participate actively in decisions. Even simply in terms of numbers, the student participation in the university action was exceptionally high.

The movement involved whoever approached it. The clearest case is the Paris Faculty of Law which was not in the hands of revolutionary groups. It organized serious, regulated elections with secret balloting for representative commissions charged with introducing reforms. The silent majority had a simple means in that case to show its numbers and to overturn the terrorist groups by its vote. It would have been easy to insure the victory of the most moderate projects. Nevertheless, it was the plan worked

out by the strike committee—renamed the Panthéon-
Assas-Nanterre Movement for the location of the law
school in Paris and for Nanterre—that won a clear victory.
(Let us add that proportional representation allowed
minority tendencies to make themselves heard.)

How many times, at Nanterre during March and April,
did someone oppose the tiny minority of the "enragés" to
the immense majority of reasonable students? This opposition was true, if one was satisfied with a superficial and
conservative image of public opinion. However, in a situation in which these "enragés" had neither power to co-
erce others nor even any assurance of assuming any importance, their influence grew constantly and, indeed,
more and more rapidly. During the second half of May
at Nanterre, departments that had taken almost no part
in the movement, in which the professors exercised an
influence that was certainly not revolutionary, committees were formed which started from very profession-
oriented positions but were rapidly radicalized. The opinion of individuals cannot be arbitrarily isolated from the
collective conditions under which they are formed. To
recognize only individual opinions expressed outside of
all collective context is to maximize the influence of established situations and of those who hold power. Often,
when a collective action is being prepared or worked out,
what begins as mere discontent or rhetorical claims and
dreams can become solid opinion and attitude, the real
disposition to define objectives and the means to their
attainment.

The decisions taken in the general assemblies of the
departments or faculties were usually reached by acclama-
tion or show of hands, not by secret ballot. Must this be
seen as an intolerable offense against democracy? Yes, if
democracy is defined as the functioning of an institutional
system established by a constitution. On these grounds,
one must consider antidemocratic all movements that

have wished to change an institutional order and, by doing so, to transfer power. If the early labor movement had proceeded within industry (rather, next to it since its activity was repressed within it) by secret votes in order to decide on the creation of a union or on the organization of a strike, it would never have moved beyond being an ideology or a small political group. For legal violence and the power of the owners, which did not depend on votes either by secret ballot or show of hands, weighed heavily against the workers. They became conscious of themselves, through organization and the action of active minorities, by repressing the constraints that hindered them from expressing themselves and from discussing and preparing their action. The constraints that weighed on the students were not of the same order but they were not less powerful. The student was defined as an apprentice and a minor, as someone on the receiving end who is being prepared to enter adult life. Before action could be possible, a collectivity had to be formed where previously there were only individuals either isolated or bound individually to the institution and the teachers, and the student had to emerge from his situation as someone taught.

One may be opposed to any change via social disruption but, in a given situation, this is a political position like any other. Those who are opposed for whatever reasons to this style of social transformation have no more right than others to speak in the name of all. Let them make their appeals, form movements, and act, and we will see better the exact nature of the forces that they can muster.

There is another question. Did not this movement—led by active minorities oriented toward revolutionary action that often met in the university only deaf hostility or a void—make fortresses out of the occupied faculties; did it not create a coercive and even terrorist power, following the example of many revolutionary movements? The answer to this question cannot be simple; it has at least two aspects. First of all and most simply, was terror-ist power actually exercised against institutions and per-sons? Let us consider persons first. In most of the faculties, where there were no incidents before the middle of May, the professors had had no opportunity to take or ask for sanctions. Their feelings were not well known to the stu-dents. After the occupation of the faculties, many of them withdrew or participated only very occasionally in the new activities. I do not believe that a single case can be cited in which a professor was forced to participate in assemblies or votes or to express self-criticism, or in which a dean was mistreated, locked in, or attacked.

At the Sorbonne, many titular professors withdrew, continued their individual work, or strove to keep some contact with their students. At Nanterre, the tension was most severe and prolonged. Some professors were very clearly committed against the student movement, calling for sanctions and publicly voicing threats. A serious inci-dent took place: the classroom of a professor who had begun to teach again after the reopening of the faculties was invaded and he was insulted and threatened. This professor had written an article in a journal in which he accused the militant students of being "thugs" and "men-tally retarded" and he asked for sanctions against them (admirable treatment for the mentally ill!). This article aroused such strong reactions because it appeared at the very time of the meeting of the university council of which the author was a member. We recall this incident, which had no aftermath, to stress that no professor was hindered from being present or absent according to his choice or from taking part in the meetings. The case of Dr. Pierre Soulié is different. The chief of a cardiological clinic serv-ice, he objected to the action of one of his high-ranking collaborators, who organized a demonstration in defense of the demonstrators who had clashed with the police. His action caused a revolt by a good part of the clinic service but Dr. Soulié continued to exercise his hospital functions. He experienced no repression but did not wait long before he imposed it.

At no time did the student assemblies pronounce the downfall of a teacher. As to the institutions themselves, there could have been terrorism only if power had been seized, which, it seems unnecessary to recall, never happened. Within the Sorbonne, the rector, so often reviled by the students, was able to continue to live and act with enough liberty that he was able to intervene again at the time of the closing of the Sorbonne by the police. The dean of the Faculty of Letters, who had a few months earlier renounced the normal time for his retirement, was replaced by the first assessor not to be chased from his office. In fact, he intervened with courage at the time of the closing of the faculty. The Secretariat was not invaded by students.

At Nanterre, the occupation did not extend to the administrative building for a long time. The personnel, caught between union participation in the strike and the fear of clashing with the administrative authorities, took refuge in the occupation of their own area. The determination of the occupation and action committees to control the material resources necessary for their activity caused conflicts, since the dean's administration refused to make any concessions. But the long and complex discussions showed at least that there was no violence or terror. A little after the beginning of the occupation, a move to set up a new executive authority for the faculty was expressed by a very small number of teachers. Since this was opposed or ignored by the majority of both students and teachers who participated in the movement, it had no effect. Also at Strasbourg, where the proclamation of autonomy announced an even clearer break with the former authorities, it was a matter of an occupation and the organization of debates and political action more than of a revolutionary power reorganizing the functioning of an institution.

For it was not a matter of management or decision-making, since the faculties were materially dependent on the Ministry of National Education. Indeed, the administration of the faculties was often ignored and left aside rather than destroyed or expelled. The important thing for all the tendencies within the movement was not to create a university commune but either to create political agitation and mobilization or to arouse participation in new projects to be ratified later in agreement with the teachers.

This brings up the hesitation which the theme of university autonomy met. Raised first at Strasbourg and calmly accepted by the minister, whose acceptance was immediately rejected, it reached Nanterre where it was more the proclamation of a de facto occupation than the creation of any new organization. Autonomy was opposed by many of the most revolutionary militants who did not want their movement enclosed within the limits of any institution and thereby removed from more general political battles in the name of this limited liberty. The determination to have no other relationship with the government except battle ruled out any question of managing an institution that, for all its autonomy, would remain dependent on the ministry. If there was so much talk on all sides about cultural revolution, it was less through parallelism with the Chinese movement, from which some forms of expression were adopted but whose nature was profoundly different, than in order to indicate the priority given debate over content and political mobilization over a seizure of power limited to the university.

If there was no seizure of power, there was a de facto power vacuum and plentiful opposition within the movement, the general assemblies, and action committees to the maintenance of the traditional organs of decision-making, especially the faculty councils. Action differed widely from one faculty to another, but frequently the councils ceased to act and were replaced by plenary assemblies in which all the teachers participated and in which the titular professors were mixed with a greater number of *assistants* and *maîtres-assistants*. The less directly the faculties or establishments had been touched by the movement from its beginning, the more the traditional management organs retained the capacity to meet and to take decisions, even if only about the representation of professors on the representative bodies that were being formed.

In the Paris faculties of letters, at the heart of the movement, the impotence of the councils was greatest. The Sorbonne, as a faculty of letters, was too swallowed up in its new role as center of the university system and the movement was too oriented toward political tasks for the reorganization of the faculty to become a concrete object of debate. At Nanterre, which is more isolated, the assembly of teachers, in which some teachers no longer wished to participate, attempted at the beginning to negotiate and named a group of twelve persons charged with establishing contact with those who organized the occupation movement. This was an attempt with which some Communist teachers were associated—all through the crisis they took a Centrist attitude—but it was an attempt that was immediately opposed and which failed in a few hours.

The Transformation of the University

The movement enjoyed de facto existence rather than organized power. Before May, political activity had been prohibited within the university; then it broke out everywhere: propaganda stands, posters, headquarters of various movements. The Marxist-Leninists of the U.J.C.M.L. were very visible, even more than the anarchists who settled on the second floor of the Sorbonne in the rather out-of-the-way offices of the Ecole des Hautes Etudes. Anyone who entered the Sorbonne during those days knows that there was no movement organization and, still less, any methodical program to transform the university. Immediate political actions used up all available energy from moment to moment. At Nanterre, for example, in early June, the commissions that had barely been convened were dissolved when an appeal was broadcast over loud-speakers asking the students to go to Flins. The fear of bureaucratization made coordination of efforts and continuity of discussion very difficult. Many times, a decision taken one day was annulled the next. It is therefore impossible to define a particular conception of the university that was worked out and applied during those weeks.

Nevertheless, certain ideas can be extracted from the discussions; their unity will be clearer if opposed to earlier tendencies toward a particular type of change that had partly provoked the student revolt. The university system found itself overwhelmed by the wave of students it had allowed to enter without giving much reflection to the problems posed by their arrival or to the transformations of its own organization that this change ought to have occasioned. The consequence was an attempt to free the university from a burden that it could not support. This attempt took three main forms: *1)* The creation of short courses, the IUT's (Instituts Universitaires de Technologie), already in use in the scientific areas and planned for the "tertiary." Within the following five years, these were to absorb a more and more important proportion of the new students. *2)* Selection, which would probably have been introduced in ways similar to the English or Scandinavian system. This might have been accompanied by the development of a category of part-time students involved in professional life, something uncommon in France but very common in the Soviet Union. *3)* Isolation of the first cycle, that is, its "secondarization," relieving the faculties of a good number of their students and placing the beginners within a framework very similar to that of the secondary schools.

Aside from the creation of the IUT's, which had been carried out but had not yet had any notable effect on the flow of students, there were only ideas and plans. The lack of a clear policy led many students to think that the only real measures that would be taken would involve a quota system that would replace or reinforce the very primitive measures of selection practiced up to that point, which consisted of eliminating a great number of students in the middle of their studies. The general attitude of the student movement was to refuse to adapt the contents to the container but rather to transform the container. There was a deeper disposition to deliberately accept the mass university, to press for a transformation of the numerical increase into democratization, and to reject the distinction between a base destined for limited professional studies and an elite.

The rejection of selection was the simplest position to define. Since the student did not face a real choice among different types of educational establishments and training, selection either signified nothing immediate or it simply expressed a barrier to his entry into the university, unless the university machinery were modified. But this was not the reasoning advanced and this idea is closer to the declaration attributed to Edgar Faure in July than to the student declarations during May. But it explains the peremptory rejection of a plan that was both contrary to the inspiration we have just defined and devoid of all real reformist sense.

More interesting and original was the constantly advanced idea that from their first years of study all students should participate in intellectual initiatives and responsibilities. In point of fact, many students will occupy the middle ranks in education, business, and civil service. But instead of "adapting" education to these professions —which would in fact limit many who advance socially through studies in the professional schools, while those who have a higher level of expectation because of family background would be directly committed to academic studies—the students demanded in principle that the university rid itself of cultural traditions and inequalities and be obliged to assign students to actual work experience. This was not to be done under artificial conditions based on a class culture rather than on technical demands but under real conditions so that their ultimate direction would result from their experience, not from their social situation when they entered higher education.

This touches on an essential pedagogical problem. The democratization of education is closely connected with active methods of teaching. When education was simply a matter of transmitting socially well-defined cultural forms, the student could be an attentive, serious, disciplined pupil, respectful of his models. On the other hand, to insist on an apprenticeship of intellectual work and to give less importance to content in favor of effectively practiced methods means placing students in a position of equality and judging them on what they do rather than on what they have received from their social milieu.

This general viewpoint led people to take very definite positions and led above all to a sharp attack on the examination system that went beyond criticism of the attitudes embodied in the present set-up. For it was not only a particular type of test or a style of marking that was rejected but the whole situation of examinations which manifests and practically constitutes the student condition. During an examination, the student is placed in specific conditions completely foreign to those of intellectual or professional practice. Does the reading for *agrégation* or the questions on the medical internship examination have

anything in common with the conditions of research,
teaching or diagnosis? The examinations were not criticized because they are badly organized but because they
are occasions when power relationships come to light,
when the student is forced to act in ways imposed on him
and is judged in terms of his adaptation to an organization
rather than according to his particiipation in work of
knowledge.

An even fresher idea was the rejection of strict specialization. One of the most frequent criticisms of the Fouchet
Plan is that it raises barriers between the various disciplines rather than lowering them. In the country where an
outstanding and laborious intellectual effort has forged a
close link between history and geography through the
educational work eminent scholars such as of Vidal de la
Blache, Albert Demangeon, and Roger Dion as well as
Lucien Febvre and Fernand Braudel, have we not seen it
made difficult even for quite young students to move from
one discipline to another. The breakdown of the boundaries between the disciplines and departure from the de-
partmental structure were two of the most constantly
expressed demands. They were voiced with particular
vigor in the faculties of letters where it was a matter of
completely changing the definition of the area of studies
proper to these faculties. They should become faculties of
the sciences of man and give the students direct contact as
soon as possible with general methods of analysis, whatever may be the particular object of interest of these
students. Important progress had been made in recent
years in order to introduce mathematical training into
areas where it is more and more utilized but is it not time
to do the same thing in the modes of thought and analysis
of the human sciences?

When one recognizes the profound unity between these
reforms of educational content and the desire to democ-
ratize, it is easier to understand the meaning of certain

student propositions concerning the opening of the faculties to those who are not officially students. This idea was presented as a political theme, but why establish an opposition between the political desire to establish a union of workers and students in their struggles and the effort to transform and forward education itself? The clear desire of the student movement to emerge from the student situation and to bring the workers into the faculties, student residences, and university restaurants was viewed as nourished by a "workerism" that was more sentimental than realistic. Such a judgment fails to recognize the meaning of these proposals. Breaking the isolation of students means first of all rejecting the opposition between manual and intellectual work and consequently breaking the bond between the university and bourgeois society. This break can be achieved in other ways under other conditions, but since the massive growth of higher education has brought about only very limited democratization in contemporary France, it was necessary for the student movement to proclaim the end of university isolation to make possible practical measures of democratization.

The last fundamental theme was the recognition of political freedom within the university system. The isolation of the university was condemned in every regard. Is it true that the needs of the economy, as interpreted by the existing social order, in the name of which many wish to transform the university system, are not in fact political themes? When economic, political, administrative, and even union leaders are invited to be heard within the university, why should there not be established a union between students and laborers or other workers within the framework of common political and cultural activity? Since the university must be returned to the center of society, why should it be bound only to the structures and why should social and political demands not be expressed there?

These three general themes—scientific practicality, democratization, and political liberty—are interconnected and constitute both a modernization of the university and a social and political choice. One may reject this choice but it is difficult to deny that in rejecting it one is making a contrary choice which is also political. Is it necessary to fragment higher education and professionalize it or, on the contrary, is it necessary to insure the greatest freedom of circulation of men and methods within the whole society by reconciling diversification and unity?

In raising the themes of university reform put forward by the movement, I have not spoken in terms of organization and functioning. *Autonomy* and *representation,* key words to some who were touched only indirectly by the movement, were considered ambiguous terms by the militants of the movement. They were no more for or against them than they were against atomic energy which can be both peaceful technical progress or atomic bombs. Autonomy and codirection could create a new corporatism that would differ from the old only in that the students would be more integrated into it. The most active students could be absorbed by committees, commissions, and technical groups where they could express many new ideas but where the power of their movement to express social and cultural contestation would be lost. On the other hand, autonomy would allow long-distance conflicts with the ministry to be replaced by more direct conflict that would mobilize more participation and perhaps facilitate certain transformations by limiting them at first to individual institutions. Representative management, for its part, is a defense against the return of routines and authoritarianism and hence is a means of raising the level of information and responsibility and consequently of involvement for many students, in terms of their professional situation and the general problems that it manifests.

The essential thing was the refusal to think primarily in institutional terms and to reject the opposition between functioning and movement, organization and policy. This refusal is above all a reaction against the sluggishness of professional preoccupations and institutional forms. For even at the moment of its widest extension within the faculties, the movement could not be unaware of its relative weakness. Most of the professors, at least in Paris, slunk off and fled the discussion or proclaimed the fundamental principles of the institution; on the other hand, the spirit of simple reform, which was positive on many sides but limited the movement rather than leading it into contestation and conflict, spread more broadly than the movement itself. The important thing is not to confuse the distrust of institutional solutions with nihilism. The May Movement carried a more conscious and worked-out conception of the university than most projects discussed in the commissions of the learned.

The Teachers

There was no corporate resistance or solemn protest on the part of the professors against the occupation of the faculties because they were divided, hesitant, and troubled. Attitudes changed but they can be summed up during the main period of occupation—that is, until the political withdrawal of the movement—in one word: retreat. In general, the professors and teachers, especially in the faculties of letters, had little desire to defend the university organization. They were conscious of their bad working conditions and their impotence in the formation of an ineptly structured mass university. They felt injured by the weakening of the faculties, the development of the C.N.R.S. and the major para-university establishments. Finally, many of them were attached to individual work which did not dispose them to be actively interested in administrative problems. In contrast to the faculty of sciences, for example, where there were teaching departments in which important problems of administration were raised and a veritable general staff functioned around the dean, the directive structure in the faculties of letters was extremely spare. For most professors, the council was only an electoral college. Very few general problems were dealt with or even raised.

We have spoken of the crumbling of the university system. The term is accurate if it indicates an absence of coherent policy and reactions; it is not accurate if it leads one to suppose that before May there had been effective management by the professors. The movement revealed a void that many professors recognized but felt impotent to fill. Many, therefore, observed without hostility the creation of new relations with the students within the framework of sections and departments in which they felt they could be effective. They balked when others acted on a higher level, treating problems of the faculties, the Ministry of National Education, or society and even considered the professors as representatives of an administrative and social order of which they did not themselves feel part. They did not defend an institution that did not satisfy them, but they were led to defend their personal role and therefore to combat a de facto power that seemed to them illegal and, to some, scandalous. Very few dared to express their fear or their opposition. In very many cases, this silence is explained by the feeling that everything would work out: after all, it was only a passing revolt, a storm after which calm would return, wise reforms would be introduced, and excesses would be forgotten.

In the case of Nanterre, where the conflicts lasted longer than in other places, the professors who were most hostile to the movement were not the ones to intervene. Isolated and disconcerted, they retired to their homes or avoided emerging from the framework of their departments. At the Sorbonne, the reactions of the Nanterre extremists could not show themselves until after the occupation of the faculty, in a situation in which they had little chance to achieve practical consequences; this explains the more marked retreat of the body of professors at the Sorbonne.

In many of the provincial faculties of letters, at Lille, Poiters, Clermont-Ferrand, Aix, and Dijon, for example, reactions varied from distrust to open participation in research projects, without any absolute break within the body of professors. Reformists and conservatives had different conceptions of the university institutions for which they had responsibility. One cannot say that in all the faculties there were clearly opposed camps. One who appeared conservative in a "hot" faculty could well have been liberal in a "cold" faculty: the clearest example is that of many professors and the then dean of Nanterre, who continuously defended ideas and made judgments that would have appeared very reformist in another situation.

If many professors were mortified, distrustful, or hostile, the reason was not only that the initiative was taken by those who had not held it before, the students, but also that the whole university hierarchy was overthrown. The ministry was empty; the minister had retired in fact long before his retirement was made public; its offices were silent. No forceful condemnation was forthcoming to encourage the conservatives. Above all, the titular professors did not feel supported by the *assistants* and *maîtres-assistants*. We have recalled that at Nanterre in April a great number of *assistants* had taken a collective position for the first time on problems that did not concern their own professional situation. After May 3, in the faculties as a whole, the mass of *assistants* tended to split up. While some stoutly defended the existing institutions to the degree that they were absorbed in an effort to carve a place for themselves in them and were dependent on their professors and their jury to achieve such a place, others shook off a guardianship that was often simple but sometimes weighed very heavily. They demanded to be represented on the mixed commissions; they often felt closer to the students than to the professors and utilized the new situation to win more independence and to obtain more rights within their departments and faculty. Some, particularly in philosophy and the human sciences, involved themselves more completely in the movement and participated in its political action, exercising real influence in the working commissions.

The creation of plenary assemblies of all teachers was felt, at the Sorbonne particularly, as a direct attack on the prerogatives of the professors. If the titular professors were tied in with this mass of young teachers, wasn't co-optation of the professors a real and immediate threat? Wouldn't this give the greatest influence in university affairs to those who were only beginners and had not yet proved themselves? The professors reacted very strongly to this point and the share on the representative assemblies assigned to the *assistants* was often reduced. But it is probable that the very marked split between the different categories of teachers, which the considerable increase in the number of *assistants* has deepened in recent years, will not be maintained. To the degree that the *cours magistral* (formal lecture) seems to have condemned, the distinction between that course and the *travaux dirigés* (studies directed by *assistants*) will necessarily also be called into question. The appearance of the *assistants* as a particular category, defending its own interests but also representing a strategically central element in the life of the departments, will almost certainly be one of the results of the May Movement that will be hardest to wipe out.

If many professors withdrew into distrust, many *assistants* strove to hold a middle position that corresponded on the whole to that of the Communist Party which had many supporters in this group as well as among the professors. The Communist teachers sometimes took a critical position toward the official attitude of their party and some of them signed or supported the letter of the Communist intellectuals of the Central Committee in which the importance of the May Movement was recognized and the attacks against it condemned. Nevertheless, the fact remains that these teachers placed themselves in the uncomfortable position of recognizing the student contestation and, at the same time, defending the functioning of the university institutions. For no one was more anxious than they to resolve the problems posed by the social movement by the introduction of rules, guarantees, and procedures based on original analysis or new objectives. They were at ease only within a union framework that was strongly organized in professional terms. Ready to indict the political regime, they distrusted the "leftists" and wondered how their pressure could be contained and transformed into professional demands or into a campaign for the formation of a new government. They were at ease only in the demonstration of May 13 and, despite their number, did not play an important role in the weeks that followed.

Finally, in the faculties where the movement had its greatest power, a few professors committed themselves more or less profoundly on the side of the movement. A few historians and professors of English at the Sorbonne, a few professors of French, philosophy, and sociology at Nanterre took very definite positions and participated very actively in the general assemblies and the action committees, and felt at one with an indictment that went beyond the quest for updating. At the faculty of science, an important group of professors also took militant positions; they later made up the "Dedonder ticket" at the time of the elections for the representative body charged with transforming the faculty. Because I belong to this small category, I must say here that I do not believe that it exercised an important influence over the events, at least in any immediate terms. These professors were able to defend the movement and its vulnerable militants. They participated in the working out of a new conception of the university system. They could not identify themselves with a total criticism of the university without falling into ridiculous self-criticism for which no one asked them, in any case. What they rejected was abstract and partisan opposition to the idea of the university and to the movement that was transforming its reality. Social concern and intellectual unrest pressed them to the same combat. Without being decisive, their action was certainly more important than that of the very small number of teachers who called for the destruction of the university. These professors and others now have a responsibility to take measures so that the university may no longer be so incapable of changing and accepting conflict and innovation.

Because of the inflamed situation at the Sorbonne, such a position could not be worked out effectively. At the Faculty of Law and Economics, a plan of transformation was worked out that recognized the place of both participation and contestation. It followed lines that were assuredly more limited than those proposed by the "reformist revolutionaries" in the faculties of letters but the proposed plan was nevertheless very different from the exclusive orientation toward representation and co-management seen in other places where opposition was less lively.

Both teachers and students of the law faculty were able to operate on the level of the entire faculty. The new organizational forms they worked out were not defined outside of a general perspective in which both the spirit of the educational program and the form of the studies were questioned. For the moment, themes of modernization, like the development of econometry, were defended side by side with a more critical attitude that demanded that professionals in law and economics be open to the research of the social sciences and to the problems of contemporary politics. One may call this success mere technocratic modernism; although there is some truth to this judgment, it cannot be reduced to a simple condemnation.

In fact, student action has the best chance of developing and of establishing itself in the future in the sectors of the French university system that are in the process of modernizing—and the progress of economic studies in recent years is beyond argument. The revolt originated in the more archaic sectors of the university, the faculties of letters, but like the labor movement, which has never drawn the core of its lasting strength from the declining sectors of industry, which are capable of revolt or defensive pressure but not of inventing forms for the future, so the students' action will work out its future in the modern faculties and will only develop if the university system modernizes.

Besides the example of the Faculty of Law, one can cite the example of another modern sector of the educational system where the political and innovative capacity of the May Movement showed itself: the economic and social sciences section of the Ecole Pratique des Hautes Etudes. For twenty years it had been a center of intellectual initiative and imaginative direction. Despite the dispersion of its centers and seminaries, it witnessed active agitation and worked out, through a tripartite commission, projects of reform that were neither simple adjustments nor propositions indifferent to the problem of intellectual creation and to the problems of management of an institution tending toward constant renewal.

Such efforts show that the movement was not condemned to be only negative or rejecting. It could connect its opposition to the development of the university system without being contented with "maneuvers of recuperation," purely organizational measures that neither criticized nor transformed.

Recuperation

This term covers quite distinct orders of facts, depending on whether one considers the central or the peripheral elements of the movement. In the former, its meaning was most simple. When the May Movement in all its forms determined to politicize university problems and the student action, to increase the participation of the largest possible number in social struggles, and to criticize the general principles of university organization and its recent reform, recuperation consisted in returning the students to their former structures, giving priority to the most immediate professional problems, and leaving untouched the functions and prerogatives of the teachers. The occupation of the faculties brought the movement up against the pressure of those students who were primarily concerned with finishing the school year, passing examinations, and obtaining their diploma. Essentially, these students were neither very sympathetic nor very hostile to the movement as such, but were often disposed to participate in reforms and to establish compromises that would allow them as quickly as possible to reach their new working situation and thus improve their chance for professional success.

As the example of the examinations clearly shows, the policy of recuperation always consisted in dissociating the general problems of the student condition and university organization from the more limited and immediate questions of the functioning of departments and the daily participation of the students. This was an attitude exactly comparable to that of industry leaders who thwart union activity and call for worker participation in the hygiene committee or safety committee, that is, in company committees, at the same time proclaiming that technical and professional questions must not be mixed with political considerations. Thus, in the hot centers of the movement, general themes like representation and codirection were vehicles of recuperation. To counter a movement of revolutionary inspiration, it called for priority to be given to the "common good," allowing all to join their efforts to arrive at practical and reasonable solutions that would respect everyone's legitimate interests.

In a faculty like Nanterre, to give a concrete example, while the student movement was turned outward rather than concentrated on the faculty itself, the departments that were considered most conservative moved fastest toward plans for codirection. Representative commissions were created. For the opening of the following school year, they worked out plans for reform that could not go very far, since they were limited to the smallest unit. Both at the Sorbonne and Nanterre, the departments most bound to the movement rejected the creation of these representative commissions, not only because the manner of designating membership was contested, but because they led students and teachers to close themselves up in the narrowest professional problems. At the Sorbonne more than at Nanterre, this refusal had important results. After the first wave of enthusiasm for representative organs, there was a reaction; at the time of the closing of the Sorbonne the restructuring of the faculty had not been accomplished and the forces favoring a complete break won over the simply reformist proposals.

At Nanterre, the evolution was both more complex and easier to follow. Despite the lively resistance of the departments of sociology, philosophy, and even psychology, representative commissions were created in most departments following a vote by categories instead of by head. A suggestion by a professor led to the creation of a coordinating committee made up of representative delegations from all the departments. This committee rapidly moved in a direction counter to those who wished to restructure the faculty starting from the most practical and immediate common preoccupations. The sociologists and philosophers found themselves supported by other student delegates in the effort to give priority to the general problems of the faculty. At that moment, revolutionary "reformism" came closest to taking concrete form. This success led to a rapprochement, at least in attitude, between the coordinating committee and the action committee. Most of the professors known for their distance from it had taken part in the first meetings but now ceased to attend them. The student movement, however, was too deeply distrustful of university reforms and besides had not gone through the long preparation that had been possible at the Faculty of Law. The result was a general failure of both the efforts toward recuperation and the revolutionary projects. At the moment it was closed, Nanterre was in the same void as the Sorbonne.

We must expand a bit on this very limited summary of the facts because they took place in the centers in which the movement constantly designed the forms of its power to attract a following. The Paris faculties of letters were not the only ones to have experienced a reaction against the move toward recuperation and codirection. If we wish to consider the university faculties as a whole, the situation of which the Sorbonne and

Nanterre were the most visible examples (to which must
be joined Strasbourg, the Besançon Faculty of Letters,
Lyon, and Nantes) was clearly a minority experience. In
a great number of faculties, schools, and institutions, reforms were discussed, studied, and approved; committees
of faculty and students were set up. Is it possible to call
all these cases recuperation? It is not a matter of making
a favorable or unfavorable judgment on what was done
but of asking whether these actions, which could not have
taken place without the agitation sparked by the May
Movement, reinforced and accompanied it or, on the
contrary, utilized the situation created by it to accomplish transformations opposed to its objectives, especially reforms carried out in the name of the adaptation of
university institutions to what were called the needs of
society. Our question is not partisan. One may consider
such recuperation either positive or negative but it is necessary to judge the transformations introduced into the
university in terms of their relation to the May Movement.

It is impossible to give a general answer to the question. The various experiences can, however, be reduced to
three situations: one in which an effort of adaptation and
modernization corresponded to the already limited demands of the students and hence accompanied and prolonged the movement at its periphery; a second in
which modernization based originally on the movement
moved further and further away from it and ended in
results that differed from the orientations of the movement.

a) The first situation, one in which modernization
met with such strong obstacles that it was transformed
into revolt, took place in many faculties outside of Paris.
If we recall that the social origin, the life-style, and the
professional plans of the students of many provincial
cities are very different from those of Paris, and that
the provincial faculties benefited from the increase in

students, one can understand why the May crisis was the occasion for young teachers and students to work for the transformation of their faculties. The faculty council in the provinces is not what it is in Paris, for in these faculties there are many *mâitres de conférence* and *chargés d'enseignement* who are still preparing their theses. The council is often very small and the average age of its members is quite high. Many of these members have worked for a long time in weak faculties that favor reflection on the part of a few but prefer routine, even nepotism, for others. For years, young teachers have been meeting the opposition of the older teachers as they worked for new relations with the students and a better organization of work. The Faculties of Science and Letters at Lille are good examples of this situation. It would be unjust to speak here of recuperation since the movement, weakly represented in this situation, did not enter into violent conflict with this modernizing tendency. There were tensions and clashes but no real break; for example, through the small group of teachers who were sympathetic to the action of the movement and the larger group of those who thought primarily in terms of improving working methods and pedagogical relations. The university authorities and particularly the deans were able in many cases to play an important role in a peaceful transformation.

In such cases, the debate was limited to a reform of the mechanics of the functioning of the faculty. In the years to come, will the changes that were introduced allow more profound debates on the content of the teaching and on the social function of the university system? It is doubtful. For now, it would be vain to oppose the effectiveness of these reforms to the confusion of the Paris explosion, for the former are only a by-product of the latter. One can, indeed, wonder whether a university system in which basic problems are not raised is not also a university system reduced to a secondary role; useful indeed, but not responding to its principal function, the critical elaboration of new models of thought.

b) Entirely different is the case of those sectors where modernization ran up against a potent system of power, authority, and organization that resisted changes. The Paris Faculty of Medicine, in particular, experienced unexpected disturbance. While the movement had active participants there, more among the *fondamentalistes* students in the basic course than among the clinicians, the participation of the students in the transformation of the faculty was at first directed by practical and professional objectives. At the same time, many *agrégés, assistants,* and clinic professionals intervened very actively in order to transform the organization of the faculty and to strengthen the CHU's. The real meaning of what was undertaken can be seen if we oppose it to the earlier medical-hospital organization.

The 1959 reform, prepared with great breadth of vision by the commission presided over and led by Dr. Robert Debré, effected a certain modernization and a decisive rapprochement between the university organization and the hospital functions. But if it broke down the former order, it had not yet succeeded, on the whole, in making a new system function, since resistance from the profession and administrative impotence combined to prolong a crisis situation. What was taught corresponded very little to the needs of the practitioners. While scientific knowledge on a higher and higher level was demanded, knowledge of the patient and the hospital was not improved nor was the connection of the medical disciplines with the human sciences, particularly psychology, taken into consideration. Continuity in the power of the great masters was maintained, simply modernized and often reinforced. There was a change from mandarin to director that maintained often if not always the mentality and forms of authority of the old, reinforced in the new leadership by more highly developed technical tools.

From this resulted the alliance between two forms of opposition: the students, who spoke in the name of the practitioners, and the medical-hospital staffs. The White Paper of the medical students presented an image of medicine focused both on the consciousness of the physician-patient relationship and on problems of public health, an emphasis that had nothing in common with the tired ideology of liberalism that had served to combat the social security system and every other attempt to construct a public health policy. The medical staffs, for their part, combated forms of personal power that were obstacles to scientific progress and to the good functioning of the hospital service.

In this distinctly unprogressive faculty, it was the students who took over the direction of the reforms. They even chose the teachers who participated with them in mixed working groups. Nevertheless, after a first phase of euphoria, tensions appeared. The teachers and hospital staffs, caught between the student demands with which they shared certain objectives and the hospital organization in which many of them were integrated, often found themselves in difficult situations. It was not certain that they would achieve the transformation of work methods and organization on which they were set. Some progress was won in the domain of medical training: attachment of the preparatory year to the Faculty of Medicine and no longer to the Faculty of Science; the principle of participation of all students in hospital activity. Perhaps, one day, we will see the human sciences penetrate more than they do today into the Faculty of Medicine. The psychiatrists have waged a very active campaign in this direction, going so far as to propose a new faculty, in which psychiatry and psychology would be associated and psychoanalysis would finally receive an institutional recognition that has so far been denied it.

These reforms did not touch the essential problem, that is, the extreme concentration of decision-making power in the medical and hospital organization. The great leaders had not emerged weakened from the earlier reforms —quite the contrary. More and more, the service that is central unit of the whole organization and its chief— teacher, researcher, and supervisor simultaneously—are more and more absorbed by the effort to obtain credits and obtain the tools for work, while the hospital continues to be a weak unit, governed by the old administrative methods of the Assistance Publique, the hospital administration in Paris. This medical leadership, among which are eminent men, achievers of scientific and medical work of high quality, is also often deformed by the concentration of power; very often these men resemble the builders of financial houses of cards of the 1920's more than the major directors of modern enterprises. This leadership allowed a few institutional reforms bearing on the organization of medical studies but opposed, sometimes brutally, any basic questioning of the hospital organization, most often by its refusal of any contact.

The medical students mobilized in terms of professional themes, both because they were for the most part far removed from any political contestation and because they thought they could obtain immediate reforms. They were also more at ease with problems of teaching than with the problems of hospital activity. The limitations of this type of action appeared very quickly. Hence, after a first phase of intense activity and a second when the displaced authorities reestablished themselves, there appeared a more combative movement that had recourse to mass pressures. This movement intervened at a moment when the strategic situation was much less favorable than in June and its future is uncertain. Whatever it may be, the development of the movement at the Faculty of Medicine is the opposite of a passage from revolution to reform. Everything began with the spirit of reform, broadened into a realization of the problems of medicine, and ended finally in open conflict.

c) There is a great contrast between this modernizing and critical activity and the direction taken by the reform proposals in the para-university sectors, the C.N.R.S., and the major professional schools. These tended rather to reinforce the separation between the mass sector and the elite sector of the university organization and at the same time to establish new corporate professional defenses. This judgment may seem too summary but it should draw our attention to what sociologists call the "unexpected consequences" of a social action.

The movement that began in the faculties did not directly affect the C.N.R.S. The situation of researchers and technicians is very different from that of students. Also, the unions were very solidly established at the C.N.R.S. and its leadership was as well a modern administration led by men who, when they defended the interests of university research, strove also to improve the situation and careers of the researchers. The serious problems that were raised were of the kind that a union knows how to discuss. A sensitive point was the role of the chiefs on the commissions of the C.N.R.S., hence their influence over the careers of the researchers. Consequently, an action committee that acted primarily as a prolongation of the union concentrated on strengthening the role of the researchers themselves in the management of research. Very serious studies were made which led at the beginning of July to the Assises Nationales de la Recherche, as a result of which the organization and the status of researchers were strengthened.

The movement awoke more profound reverberations in the C.N.R.S. human sciences section which, as a whole, has been quite weak within the organization. In some laboratories, there was intense participation in the political action of the movement and in the efforts to reach the worker world, accompanied by intellectual debates and the ultimate creation of varied management commitees that sometimes tried also to serve as means of reorienting social science research in the light of the social crisis. This remained a minority tendency even within the human sciences division and allows us to speak of recuperation, that is, to note without any spirit of polemics that the forces of contestation revived by the May Movement were not the ones that led to reform. The result will probably be a crisis in the union.

This remark is even more true of the transformations introduced in some of the major professional schools. They certainly permitted the modernization of programs and methods of training and courageously attacked the excessive role of the competitive examinations. But in opening themselves to the entrance of students through means other than the competitive examinations, through the *maîtrise* of the faculties especially, the professional schools contributed to the reinforcement of a superior division of the educational system and the relegation of the university faculties to the teaching of beginner students who were not destined for the highest levels of training. The students of the professional schools scarcely emerged from an isolation which runs the risk of increasing once the doors are opened more broadly.

In the preceding chapter, we saw that outside the university system the actions sparked by the movement were continued in waves of modernization and also in opposition that was better able to affirm itself than to accomplish any profound and irreversible social transformation. In

the same way, within the university system what we have
called recuperation is a mixture of modernization and
participation leading to greater social integration rather
than to the reinforcement of a movement to transform
society. Consequently, it had as a counterpart a negative
attitude of opposition that must be considered now and
which is as far from preparing for the creation of a new
university as is recuperation.

Decay and Reaction

The May Movement, considered in itself and not in
its more or less long-range effects, did not seek dialogue
in the university any more than anywhere else. If it
spoke with itself a great deal, it spoke with its adversaries and partners very little. While ideas and a general
orientation can be drawn clearly from its activity and its
proclamations, it did not seek to work out a strategy of
reforms, to find allies, or to negotiate. In fact, where the
movement had most power, it accomplished least in
the way of reforms. The Sorbonne and Nanterre, after the
crisis, were a shambles in which almost everything had
been destroyed and almost nothing had been recon-
structed. In May and June, the expression of rejection
and the obsession with repression often dominated the
general assemblies and the action committees. Nothing
would be more false than to present a reassuring image
of the movement and to say that, despite a few excesses,
it was constructive and gave rise to new forms of organization. This would be as profound an error as the opposite, which sees only gesturing and uncontrolled frivolity
in the meetings and harangues.

A social conflict is not a debate over ideas between
two persons who are defending well-defined viewpoints
and who must finally arrive at a reasonable compromise.

The student movement, we must repeat, did not combat a power directly opposed to its own. It was never in
the situation of the market where the buyer and the
seller are face to face on supposedly neutral terrain. It
stood against the identification of a particular social domination with society; it denounced the material and
ideological private interests that hid behind a mask of
objectivity, neutrality, scientific agencies, and economic
necessity.

When the university authorities wished or were able
to break with their complacency and were ready to
negotiate, discussion and negotiation were organized. In
June, the Faculty of Law and Economic Science, in the
person of its leaders, adopted the attitude that it would
not refuse to talk and discuss. In the Paris faculties of
letters, the situation was entirely different. Whether some
teachers proclaimed lofty principles and rejected any discussion with the barbarians or more were trapped re-
luctantly in the ruin of a disorganized system to which
they were bound, the student movement did not find itself facing either men or bodies ready to discuss or negotiate. At the Faculty of Medicine, the body of professors,
which holds considerably more power, rejected even more
directly all negotiations; the teachers who were close to
the action committee were considered a handful of
agitators.

These remarks should not be misunderstood; it is not
a matter of saying that the movement wished to negotiate and found no one to deal with. Formed in the
situation that we have described, it was itself oriented
toward contestation, not negotiation. Its strength and its
weakness have the same source: it wished to tear away
appearances and reveal conflict and domination. It was
not yet ready to organize itself for pressure and discussion. It created action and it gave life and the power
of involvement to a utopia—it could not carry on institu-

tional action. In the university, as in other places, the result was that once the initial encounter was past, and to the degree that this political impotence became clearer, the energy of the movement tended to consume itself, often in disorganization, sometimes in sectarianism. These reactions flamed out in the general assemblies, all the more vividly as despair and bitterness replaced hope and the ability to move forward.

This cultural contestation that rejected the institution of the university or wished to consider it only as a weapon in the political and social struggle, could lead to terrorism. Just as it is impossible to claim that the movement caused a reign of terror through its action committees—that is, imposed its decisions and its line, manipulated the public, eliminated its adversaries by force and sanctioned deviations—so it is also necessary to recognize the existence of terrorist intellectual and political tendencies. Precisely because the student movement did not take power in the university system, because reformist activity largely outflanked it, because from the beginning of June, the political defeat of the movement was evident, it was in the course of the weeks of retreat and internal crisis that a stiffening appeared, all the more clearly as the chances of victory grew weaker and reaction more clearly regained the advantage.

In some faculties, restructuring was not possible; a void replaced conflict. The revolutionary movement deprived of revolution swirled around and felt trapped. An organized political movement can make a retreat, go underground, work out new forms of action, and plan its strategy. The May Movement was pure offensive; it could not make a successful retreat. A group like the March 22 Movement, quite the opposite of a party, had no raison d'être other than to entirely exhaust itself in its initial attack. The absence of organized political action, so essential to the definition of the May Movement, brought about the disorganization of June. In its turn, this aroused the appearance of dogmatism. Because there was no longer any future for the movement, it broke up and lost itself in the most obvious mistaken tactics. The assemblies fell apart and the discussions bogged down. The obsession with an enemy attack reappeared and the fever sought to exhaust itself in the preparation of munitions which no one will use. In some faculties of letters, at the Sorbonne more than at Nanterre, some groups responded to this gradual weakening by a doctrinal hardening which only increased as they felt more and more isolated. There was talk of the destruction of the university, of the transformation of the faculties into "red bases" to attract and shelter revolutionary workers and to function as centers of permanent agitation. Some felt that this would lead to the chaos from which a socialist society could be born.

Against everything that attempted to co-opt the revolutionary forces that it had loosed, certain elements of the movement wished to maintain or create a permanent crisis that would go beyond contestation. Terrorism is not an extreme form of contestation. Claude Lefort was right to stress that the May Movement did not act in the name of a model of future society. It acted from instant to instant, calling for the spontaneity of the workers and students, creating scandal, and responding to blows. In its own eyes, it was less a stage of a history that has already been mentally written than a revolutionary revolt, a social rupture and liberation. Hence, when the established order regained its strength, when the reforms moved away from the current that had made them possible, and the revolutionary moment had moved into the past, programs and doctrines reappeared and proclaimed that the only task of the university must be to consume itself in the service of the social revolution of tomorrow.

First at Nanterre and then almost everywhere, the

movement had condemned the bourgeois university system and had risen up against it. Now there appeared the
idea that the university must be a class university rejecting a political science and basing its social role and
its own progress on a political orientation and on class
interests. The text published by the delegates of various
faculties who met for a weekend in June at Nanterre
was dominated by this idea. The very form of this closed
door meeting that neither aroused nor sought any participation by the students of Nanterre is characteristic of
the change that had taken place. It was no longer a matter of forming alongside the official university a critical
university that would oppose it but would also be capable of transforming it by criticism; it was a matter of
transforming the university into a weapon, into a paving
stone. It is just as wrong to fail to recognize this hardening of position as it is to see it as the nature of the
movement from the beginning, as if the movement had
advanced step by step toward the most terrorist formulas,
the innocent joining in passing. These innocents, in be-
lieving they could bring about reform or even open the
university to the problems and conflicts of society, would
have been only innumerable Fierlingers * of a new
Prague coup, directed this time from Peking rather
than Moscow.

In a situation of retreat or chaos, danger comes less
from doctrinal hardening than from the disorganization
of collective action. The appeal to spontaneity had been
able to form a group out of the mass; the absence of
openings risked dissolving this group into a mob, excit-
able and manipulable in the midst of which leaders
might compensate for the impossibility of acting by the
rhetorical extremism of their rejection of society and by
calling forth immediate and emotional reactions. The

* Fielinger was the leader of the pro-Communist wing of the Czech
socialist party in 1948.

danger did not come from the movement but from the difficult transformation of institutions, too weakened to be rebuilt and too inert to direct their own change. One cannot isolate the terrorist tendency that showed itself in the student movement from the context of June and the reversal of the situation that was to lead to the closing of the occupied faculties. It marked the agony of the movement.

Starting from the moment when the resumption of work seemed certain—though still delayed by the resistance of the strikers in the major companies—and when preparations were going forward for the elections—of which there was general agreement that they would more or less clearly reinforce the regime—there was a gradual reappearance of the forces and tendencies hostile to the movement in the university. The first notable sign was the articles by Raymond Aron published in the conservative, influential *Le Figaro* from June 11 to 15 and on June 19. They were all the more important because their author was well known for the criticisms that he had addressed to the university system and which had contributed to his decision to quit the university at the end of 1967. They were vehement articles, resented as an unfair attack by all those who had participated in the actions sparked by the movement; they received the grateful assent of those whom Raymond Aron had judged without indulgence in the recent past.

The Fédération des Syndicats Autonomes de l'Enseignement Supérieur, especially the very conservative union of the faculties of letters, were slower to show their sentiments. They issued statements that would have horrified their members a few weeks earlier and which had no purpose other than to prepare the ground for an anticipated counterattack. This attack was aimed first of all at the assemblies of teachers or the mixed assemblies, which had dispossessed the faculty councils of their traditional functions. (Later, in July and August, this union expressed itself in a more direct manner but at that time its irritation was directed against the Minister of National Education rather than against the student leaders who seemed less immediately dangerous.)

The members of the S.N.E.Sup. were dramatically divided. Alain Geismar played a twofold role, as a union leader and a leading personality of the movement as a whole. He felt the consequence of this situation, resigning as secretary-general to devote himself with more freedom to revolutionary action. The union congress in June saw strong opposition to the directions taken by the national leaders. This opposition was led by the Communists but was supported also by the provincial union leaders, who were hostile to the action committees and anxious above all to stabilize and institutionalize the conflict. Nevertheless, the "Geismar tendency" won out and opposition between the two organizations of teachers continued to grow. (The Communists gained control of that union in 1969.)

Despite a few outcries, there was no energetic reaction. At the end of June, extreme right-wing groups appeared that held some noisy demonstrations and committed a few acts of violence. But there was no organized countermovement, first of all, because a movement cannot be created simply out of the rejection of the contrary movement or simply with the objective of affirming principles and traditions. Besides, why bother? Was it not better to wait, to let the government reestablish order and empty the faculties before reestablishing to the fullest degree possible everything that had been compromised. Finally, at the end of June, the idea spread that many faculties would not be able to reopen their doors on the official date and that new serious troubles, perhaps more violent in the university than those in the streets in May, were to be expected. It was consequently imprudent to take too many risks and to expose oneself to misadventures.

The government itself did not precipitate matters in June. The movement could not prolong the crisis very long after the social conflicts were over. It had acquired lasting strength only where it had been able to organize new institutional forms. What had succeeded at the Faculty of Law had failed at Nanterre and had not been possible at the Sorbonne. The approach of vacation, the cancellation of some examinations and the official postponement of others, along with physical exhaustion, emptied the faculties.

As a measure of prudence, the closing of the Sorbonne was planned with some preparation: the exaggerated importance given to the minor incident of the Katangais, whom the students themselves succeeded without serious incidents in getting rid of; closing of the Odéon, which even the most active militants of the movement accepted; finally, the mounting of an incident. A young man wounded near Saint-Germain-des-Près was moved during the night into the Sorbonne; he was immediately sent to the Hôtel-Dieu. This sufficed to cover a new entrance of the police into the almost empty Sorbonne. The assessor acting as dean, Raymond Las Vergnas, the secretary-general, a professor, and some students protested in vain. The rector, who had initiated the crisis by calling the police, ended it by letting them enter. The closings succeeded one another rapidly, met with relief, sadness, or bitterness, but they did not provoke any serious incident.

While some students tried to regroup for the summer, unable to realize fully the summer universities that they had prepared, which could have been important only in an entirely different social and political situation,

the university world regained its old reflexes and looked
to the ministry, hoping that a new minister, known for
his political ability, would find the means to escape from
the impasse and guarantee the reopening of the faculties
in the autumn.

The University After the Crisis

After several months of crisis, and of the cessation of
usual activities, meetings, debates, and projects, what was
the state of the university system, particularly of those
sections that were most overwhelmed by the action of
the movement?

a) Those who believed that they had lived through a
crisis, a kind of illness, were deceived. Formerly, there
had been almost no discussion about the university; it
was sacred, respectable, mysterious, disturbing indeed,
but beyond analysis and understanding. Now the university was in question and its organization, which rested
more on its inability to change than on its virtues, would
not be reconstituted. Politically, on the lowest level, it
was tempting to place the principal responsibility for
the crisis on the teachers. From the president of the
Republic and the ministers to the opinion of the conservatives, it was a question of who would most violently
condemn these fools, attached to an obsolete teaching
course, closed to all intellectual innovations, defenders of
the status quo, limited by their privileges. Society had
entrusted to them the best of its youth; they had not
been able to teach this youth to love its work and its
education. The businessman who has failed is merely
ruined; the priest, army officer, or professor who have
been unable to preserve the social values with which he
has been entrusted and which he was supposed to defend,
is disgraced.

Perhaps this is an extreme expression of the condemnation by the ruling groups of the professors. Nevertheless, I doubt that the independent union that spoke in the name of the professors, their rights and dignity, met a very receptive public. It realized this itself and strove to rally conservative opinion by raising the specter of disorder. This condemnation did not come only from shocked public opinion that resented the professors for not having been able to keep the tempest in the university teapot; it came also from the rulers. The old bourgeoisie was not bothered about the university; the new one is very unsatisfied with it. It furnished society neither its leaders nor its middle management; all it knows how to do is to perpetuate itself. Most public and private administrators and leaders kept their distance from the general questioning of power and authority, but they were ready to take advantage of the crisis both to liquidate the resistances of the past that had been weakened by the student assault and to prepare a university system that was better adapted to the needs of today's society.

While those responsible for order were busy pursuing the revolutionary students—and the Minister of the Interior exerted himself in this pursuit with ardor and conviction—serious reforms were worked out. Their objectives were not those of the May revolutionaries but they did recognize realistically some of what they had won, and they especially recognized the crumbling of the old order. The team set up on the Rue de Grenelle by Edgar Faure is not to be suspected of submitting to the desires of the university conservatives. There was to be no restoration and the *emigrés* will not ever again find the tarnished delights of the old court. There will be no restoration of the old order, except possibly in the medical field because this is largely outside the university organization. It is improbable that the reforms introduced will reestablish calm and harmony or even that they will overcome traditional pockets of resistance. But if they succeed in modernizing the university system, they will allow all aspects of modern society, its creativity as well as its new social conflicts, to develop within the university.

b) Politics has entered the university and will never leave. This means two things. First, students can no longer be considered minors. Their participation in political life is no longer only an intellectual interest in the problems of the society that they will enter at the end of their studies. It is primarily a discussion of their own social situation. There will no longer be a barrier between the internal organizational problems of the university and general political choices.

Secondly, it has a complementary meaning: the university is not only a forum but a center of production. Earlier, students were preoccupied more with doctrines and political thinking than with social action. Now they can no longer avoid taking into consideration the problems of scientific and intellectual production. To continue indefinitely and completely artificially to see an opposition between the revolutionary spirit and the reformist accomplishments would be absurd. Such an opposition, which deforms the experience of the worker movement as well as that of the independence movements in the Third World, has no more meaning in the present university situation. The fact is that during the revolutionary offensive in May, more ideas for reform and more criticisms of the tired practices of the past were stated than in the preceding ten years. Those who can talk only about the essence of the university and the principles that underlie the existence of every university are not reformists; they are counterrevolutionaries. Those who wish to see the university only as a weapon to be used to bring down the dominant social order are not revolutionaries but terrorists. The future history of the

movement within the university will be a search for
two kinds of action: general political criticism and the
will to control and develop the university as a tool of
production. The university must be recognized both as a
political institution and as a center of scientific production. This is not just a moderate, middle-of-the-road
position that allows us to respond to these two complementary and opposed exigencies.

The tension of the crisis will remain and must be institutionalized in some way. Now, when the modernization of the university does not run up against any
major resistance, the primary debate concerns political
activity within the university. *Within* the university
means that the university cannot be reduced only to
political activities and choices, but that one can no more
separate intellectual production from its social utilization
than one could separate industrialization from its capital-
istic or socialist style. What will be contested in the future will be less and less the transmission of a cultural
heritage and more and more the social use made of
this production power.

Members of the university world, used to very little
participation in the management of their common affairs
and enclosed in personal work and tranquilizing authority relationships, will have to learn to make decisions and
to negotiate. The professor as such is not the custodian of
scientific knowledge. He is someone who teaches, who
belongs to a professional group, a particular social
milieu, and a particular line of thinking. The more the
choices that affect university life are argued through,
the more thoroughly broken will be the false image
of the professor that confuses the impersonal authority of
knowledge with the personal authority of the teacher.
Where the university has been avered incapable of
standing at the head of scientific research, political debate may favor intellectual innovation.

I do not hesitate to raise in this connection the situation in Latin America, an example the conservatives always hold up as a bugbear, saying, "Is not the participation of the students in the governing of the universities responsible for the weakness of Latin America in this area?" Quite the opposite. These universities, long situated in societies dominated by both the oligarchy and the bourgeoisie, societies lacking much industrial and technical development, were in love with discourse more than with research. Organized according to the German system of chairs and dominated by their professional schools, they utilized an underpaid body of professors, who often sought in the exercise of a profession the resources and social prestige that the university did not give them. They were shaken only by economic development and the rise of technicians, employees, and workers. In the name of the new forces, the students broke, first at Cordoba in 1918, the closed university of the bourgeoisie and its coterie. Their action was positive until the growth of the urban population outstripped industrial development, creating a serious problem of underemployment and revealing the imbalances connected with the growth that was foreign-dominated and dualist. The students struggled for a nationalist economic development and opposed foreign domination; in doing so, they fought for the progress of the university and for the professionalization of knowledge. When they failed, it was because their society failed to liberate itself from old and new oligarchies that are integrated into foreign economic domination. The crisis of the Latin American universities are those of their society. The students are caught in them. Who will dare say that they are responsible for underemployment and the foreign domination they are striving to escape? The French university faculties often resemble the traditional Latin American universities enough that we can hope that here also student pressure will produce innovative results.

c) Neither the disappearance of the old university order nor the penetration of political debates and action into the faculties sufficiently defines how the university will be able to function as a center of intellectual activity. By themselves, the new forms of university life, autonomy and codirection, are no sure pledge of progress. The May Movement was quite right to want to go beyond reforms in terms of representative government and even rejected them, since its objective was to contest power and the social order. It is also possible that codirection, when it limits contestation, also weakens the university itself in terms of its activity, that is, it diminishes its capacity to innovate. The risk is that the co-managed units will be more capable of organizing consumption than of foreseeing investments, so to speak. They might take as a rule the increase of satisfaction for all concerned groups rather than try to perceive and strengthen intellectual tendencies that clash in any general way with accepted ideas and habits or that disturb established programs.

The question arises: must one compromise the university's future in order to reestablish peace today?

a) In the first place, one must recognize that growth and change always suppose an insurmountable tension between participation and initiative, between consumption and investment. There is no such thing as entirely self-directed development. This is why class conflict is a central element of social dynamics. All attempts to deny its existence, either in the name of the common good of the community or in the name of an entirely creative spontaneity, are only utopias that sometimes may be fruitful but do not govern the transformations of society and often even oppose them. Just as student opposition cannot be absorbed by schemes of codirection, so also intellectual innovation cannot entirely be the work of representative commissions. The university community must be subjected to the pressure of innovations and must consequently allow an area of free expression and initiative for those who differ and those who explore. Nothing would be more dangerous than to sacrifice everything to great schemes of restructuring that would quickly render the universities as stifling as police stations. They must learn to live with political struggles and also with intellectual debates and scientific experiments.

b) These proposals would be proven false if they remained on the level of formal opposition between an integrated system and a system based on tensions and conflict. In order for there to be conflict, there must be relationships, not separation. Contestation must raise the level of participation, at the same time that it fights against integration. In a parallel fashion, intellectual innovation must criticize the established order and programs by raising the level of the knowledge to be shared at the same time that it fosters participation. The partners must be both in touch with each other and independent of each other. When Jacques Sauvageot called for student power and more specifically for the right of the student assemblies to vote and to offer initiatives, he was reacting very positively to the dangers of "recuperation." His demands were complementary, not contradictory to those of the intellectual innovators who have the same need as the political forces not to be entirely absorbed by collective negotiations; but this complementariness also supposes the existence of collective negotiations and of codirection.

In terms of the immediate situation, the members of the university have a basic responsibility: if they really reject a deceptive codirective power, they can and must defend intellectual innovation. Collective pressure must compel them to find their independence, not in their privileges or in their authority, but in the power of their scientific and intellectual creativity. Because they will no longer be unopposed governors of the university, they will be more able to be producers. Because they will no longer have to be the only ones to maintain order, they will have to be inventive.

It will be asked, how can the same organization permit both codirection and the tension between opposition and innovation. In order to answer this question, one must introduce an element of university life—indeed, of the life of every organization—of which the present debates are unwilling to speak. This is executive power. The development of the assemblies, like that of all forms of participation, has as its corollary the development of the executive. This term can be misunderstood: it is more a matter of the capacity to negotiate than of the power to make decisions, more concerned with strategy than with objectives. While the assemblies draw together in common management, a strong executive allows the conflict among the forces that are present to develop without destroying social activity. The university had neither a legislative nor an executive branch; it had only a senate of notables, who had no power and did not have to negotiate. In order to live with the independence that it is receiving, it must provide for itself both the means to reach limited understandings between the different parties and the means to allow opposition between forces that can be dynamic only when they are tense.

The university was an administrative service; it must learn to become a society. Neither brutal opposition between student power and professional power nor their complete confusion within the illusion of the common good will permit it to move forward. The mixture, still necessarily confused, of opposition, scientific research, and codirection is the only thing that can restore life to the university.

The University and Society

In May and June, there was political agitation, mobilization of the students, and the presentation of reforms. Separation of the political aspect from the professional aspect of the student efforts misses the essential point. It is sufficient to review the texts gathered by the Centre de Regroupement des Informations Universitaires (Center for the Collection of University Information) * to realize that university problems were not treated merely as those of a particular institution and neither were they neglected as secondary to the political struggle. The students spoke of culture as the workers used to speak of labor. Because this was the area of their own experience and especially because this area is or was at the heart of a particular vision of society, the students proclaimed not a program of reforms but a utopia.

A utopia certainly, for it is no longer a question of making the university function on those foundations which were impossible to replace in 1848, 1871, or in 1917, that is, to replace industrial organization with an anarchic self-government. But this utopia was not the rejection of knowledge, the horror of learning, or the apology for immediate experience as a substitute for academia with its demands and limits. It was creative primarily because it was critical. By breaking down habits and submissiveness, it brought to light the disorder and decomposition of teaching and the nature of the social relations of work, which, even more than good

* *Quelle Université? Quelle Société?* (Paris: Editions du Seuill, 1968).

intentions and complacency, dominated the university. It was creative especially because it designed not a model university, but a model of society which is directly opposed to one in which the opposition between rulers and ruled is inseparable from the opposition between those who possess knowledge and those who are its passive agents. What was demanded and proclaimed was neither the modernization of the university nor even its simple democratization. Just as the idea of industrial democracy was the reformist theme opposed to the proletarian revolution, so also participation, codirection, and social broadening of student recruitment were only limited measures. In isolation, they oppose the will to suppress the teacher-taught relationship and to replace it by relationships that some—for example, the "Nous Sommes en Marche" group—called permanent education. This does not mean the recycling of adults but the continuous movement of creation in which university workers of all ages and functions are united, taking for granted a necessary technical division of labor.

I prefer to say that the principal objective was the dissociation of knowledge and power. The one who possesses certain knowledge and the one who does not— without the differences between them being abolished —must be placed before the same problem: the creation of new knowledge and the criticism of knowledge that has already been acquired. Consequently, some wished to abolish the separation between research and teaching. This, in fact, is the essential problem of the university. The more they are dissociated, the more teaching is reduced to the transmission of a social and cultural heritage. The more closely they are associated, as they tend to be in every creative university, the greater the risk that the power of the experts will weigh heavily on the students. If the student action had only been directed against the old bourgeois university, it could have

been content to take up again the modernizing themes
of the Caen Conference. But the student action was much
more than that: it looked toward a university that is
being born, one that is an essential force of production.
Hence, it attacked the forces of power that are being
born rather than the archaic, mandarin forms that are
crumbling in any case.

The movement's university action was not the return
to institutional reforms after the failure of a revolutionary attempt. It was the passage from complete break to
the projection of revolution. Perhaps the reforms will
be able to avoid a break between the reformed institutions and this projected revolution; perhaps there will
be new forms of brutal conflict between them. But it is
inconceivable that structural and methodological changes
can integrate the revolutionary project into the functioning of the university. This project will disappear
only when the nature of production, of power relationships, and of social conflicts change; when a new society
appears that is as different from ours as ours is from the
capitalist society of the last century.

The student movement was not from its outset a will
for university reform; the mark of its success is that it
demonstrated in action that the transformation of the
university is one with the transformation of the entire
society. This is quite different from the naïve suggestion:
let us first change society; only then will the transformation of the university be possible. The university is not a
reflection of society; it is society, because it is from now
on at the center of society's changes.

What will this new university be? How will it carry
out its role? The progress of knowledge is inseparable
from the critical reflection of society on itself, on its
intellectual operations as well as on its social and political organization. Freedom of thought, criticism, and research are essential to the development of society. A

purely technical university lacks intellectual creativity and aggravates the imbalances of a society that is deprived of self-reflection. A purely political university either smothers in talk or is locked into intellectual dictatorship where it is itself in jeopardy.

The crisis that the French university system has just undergone is too profound for us to be content simply with opposition of progress to archaism. We must take a broader view and, first of all, rediscover beyond the recent situation what the role of the liberal university was, keeping ourselves from caricaturing it. Starting from there, we must ask what conditions allow the existence, that is, the liberty, of the university. A certain type of liberty existed in the French university system. To say that it did not any longer correspond to the needs of our society risks oversimplicity unless we define the new types of liberty that our society requires. The May Movement did not bring a practical answer to this problem and did not construct a new university, but it allowed this question that is essential to the future of our societies to be posed in new terms.

First, let us step away from the criticisms that we and so many others made against the university, for to criticize its poor performance and its constraints is no longer sufficient. One may say that the press makes bad use of its liberty when it brutalizes the reader with sensationalism; the argument loses its force when the liberty of the press is threatened. Very many of those who are opposed to publicity over the radio or television are ready to listen to the foreign radio stations when grave events take place. Listening to advertising can be boring or disagreeable, but to be deprived of information is intolerable. It is the same with the university: whatever position one may adopt, one cannot confuse bad functioning with intellectual oppression.

To say that university teaching was actually class

propaganda, the imposition of an ideological model, is excessive and false. That the French university was influenced by the bourgeois society and culture is beyond argument, but that its role was reduced to an ideological defense of the bourgeoisie can be affirmed only by the most extreme Jdanovists and leads to baseless aberrations, as if there was a body of capitalist knowledge and a body of socialist knowledge that were completely separate. Bourgeois society is not a monolith; it defends private economic interests but must also insure production in scientific and technical progress. It is based on social domination, but it has very often accepted or tolerated forces of opposition within it. The university was and is, simultaneously, an instrument to reinforce the dominant social and cultural order, an instrument of scientific creation and a relatively independent center of criticism and cultural change. After all, Herbert Marcuse and Theodor Adorno, Louis Althusser and Henri Lefebvre, C. Wright Mills and Paul Sweezy either lived or now live in universities, where they teach and publish.

It is improper to say that cultural and intellectual repression was overwhelming in the French university and that there existed no freedom of thought and expression. Justifying a revolutionary action by the necessity of rejecting intolerable constraints can be an ideological rationalization of action but it certainly does not constitute an explanation in the present case. Let us go further still: just as it is absurd to reduce the role of the Church in traditional France to the image given to it by the Voltairian and Freemason petite bourgeoisie, so the liberal university was a marvelous creation for long enough for one not to turn its caricature into derision.

Was the university action of the May Movement the destruction of the liberal university and its replacement or attempted replacement by an ideological and entirely politicized university? This implied judgment ap-

pears to me entirely false and testifies to a complete
lack of understanding of the crisis and movement that
we have experienced. It retains only a notion, an ideal
model, of the old university, only the conditions of
struggle in which the new university tried to be born.
Let us move to the first and simplest point. In practice,
the model of the liberal university was fully shattered.
For a parallel, one could admire the *grandeur* of the
parliamentary debates under the July Monarchy or at the
beginning of the Third Republic and recognize that today's parliamentary debates have the lowest quality and
importance, without having the right to conclude that
we have passed in one century from liberty to despotism.

The liberty to debate ideas in the university was a
franchise liberty like that of the parliamentary debates,
a liberty that is not to be despised and is not empty of
content but remains abstract and tied to a separation between ideas and social practice. The ideological debates
in the university were a more or less effective mecha-
nism of change within the social elite and the dominant
order. They did not question the university institution
itself or its social role and working relationships, which
remained much more directly bound to the need for the
renewal of the dominant class and of the instruments by
which it governed and maintained its control over
society.

This leads to the second point that deserves more attention. The primary factor in the transformation of the
university is the development of scientific knowledge,
what I have already called the production role of the
university. This is an old role in the natural sciences; it
is much newer in the sciences of man and society. The
passage from the exposition of ideas and debate over
them to scientific practice poses new problems. Because
they are susceptible of technical applications, the sciences of man acquire both greater intellectual independ-

ence and graver social responsibility, because the society
or social being that they analyze are not natural objects,
but constructs of social practice, that is, of social and
political relationships. The more practical or empirical
the sciences of man are, the more they risk being ortho-
pedic.

So long as one discusses the functions of the human
spirit, the danger is slight. However, when one is studying the conditions and balance of a social system or the
adaptation of individuals to cultural values and social
norms, the risk is very great that society will be taken
as a datum, a fact, and so there is a risk of adopting—
consciously or not—a conformist orientation loaded with
practical consequences. For this reason, sociologists and
psychologists have criticized the ideas of aptitude, opinion, resistance to change, deviation, etc. How can one
fight this confusion of scientific technique and social
ideology except in practice, that is, by introducing into
the university itself the social conflicts that are part of
the society in which the university acts and produces?

The contestation and criticism must be intellectual,
but they must touch the university institution itself.
Without the existence of the labor movement, would the
economic and social problems of labor have been studied
in the same way? Without the revolt of the dominated
countries of the Third World, would we have escaped
the ideological conception of underdeveloped or peripheral societies, a concept that leaves aside the facts of
domination? From the moment university work takes on
a technical and practical responsibility, it also has a
political responsibility. In this new situation, defense of
the old forms of university independence takes on a different meaning. Before, it insured certain possibilities
of debate, criticism, and change within the dominant
elite. Now it aims at subjecting university work to the

conditions of the social order in which it acts. The liberal attitude becomes a reactionary position.

In turn, this raises political contestation and movement that is no longer only a movement of ideas but is itself direct social and political action. If the social order is incapable of internalizing this practice, that is, if the university is incapable of dissociating techniques and ideology, knowledge and power, a counter-university will rise against the official university. In final analysis, this counter-university can only be purely political, exactly as the labor movement clashing with the violent opposition of the owners and the State could only be destructive and could not take on the demands of economic conditions of the social struggle; it is not an "idea" of the university.

Under these conditions, does the university action of the movement risk being reduced to the political struggle within the university? I shall say, first of all, that the student movement is purely political only to the degree that the university itself is more ideological than scientific. Establishment ideology has power proportionate to the rigidity with which the liberal model is upheld; in such a situation, open and violent political struggle is all the more necessary. The desire for scientific progress was more strongly realized in the sections of the university that were on the way to modernization. In the faculties of letters, on the contrary, where taste, opinion, and the cultural forms inherited from the university of the bourgeois society still reign, political criticism won out and in the face of the deceit or passive resistance of the university personnel, was aggravated to a point tending toward terrorism or nihilism.

Everywhere in the world, the scientists in the university, not the ideologues, defend most strongly the demands of intellectual liberty and criticize the constraints imposed by power. What today threatens the liberty of the university is the incapacity of the university to assume its scientific role, for ideological criticism is without power if it is not connected to the progress of knowledge and analysis. Science is not in itself democratic but there exists a possible alliance of producers and democracy against power. Science needs liberty to innovate and criticize dogmatism, just as democracy needs science to destroy the self-interested deceits of those who identify their power with reason.

In the face of the massive politico-economic structures, the university must be the critical conscience of society; this supposes that it is not itself governed in an authoritarian manner and that within it there are debates that give real meaning to its independence. Scientific activity may be at the service of the established order, unless it insures the criticism of its social function and its intellectual operations. This in turn supposes political activity in a state of tension with the intellectual creative activity but necessarily inseparable from it.

In the May Movement, in which some see only disorder and derangement, I see first of all the birth of a concrete and responsible liberty, a liberty certainly lacking the conventions of respect for the rules of the game, but, in contrast to the past order, concerned with the diversity of persons and ideas—a liberty in terms of critical confrontation but also in terms of intellectual and administrative responsibility. This liberty was no longer only for a few great personalities but for all, which made it shed the liberalisms of salons and clubs and gave it the strength of the liberation movements.

The future has not been played out. But if the university shows itself incapable of recognizing political liberty within itself, it cannot expect to regain its earlier pseudotranquility. Either it will open itself to contestation or it will be broken by it—it will be reduced to the conservative function that even most professors do not wish to assume, while counter-universities or simply destructive attacks will demonstrate the power of the repressed.

Reorganization of the University

Since the summer of 1968 the transformation of the university system has been pursued amid great disorder but, nonetheless, in such a way that less than two years later an entirely new system is taking form. The guiding law on higher education prepared by Edgar Faure and approved almost unanimously by the Parliament in November, 1968, rests on three principles: the universities must be autonomous, multi-disciplinary and governed according to a cooperative formula. This co-government was the easiest to introduce. It was first done on the level of the old departments renamed U.E.R.'s (Unites d'Enseignement et de Recherche/Units of Teaching and Research). The students hold about half the seats (on condition that 60% of them vote).

It has been much more difficult to establish the new universities, since the resistance of the old faculties, especially the medical faculties, has been stubborn. They were set up in Spring 1970 and provisional assemblies were elected to prepare their governing statutes. The most difficult problem to resolve concerned the University of Paris. Long discussions led to the break-up of the old faculties and the formation of universities which, even though they are not complete, are still more or less multi-disciplinary. The Paris region now has thirteen universities. Six of them are on the outskirts: some of these are Nanterre (Paris X), the university formed around the old Faculty of Science of Orsay (Paris XI), and the two universities created at the end of 1968, Dauphine (Paris IX), which is a kind of business school and Vincennes (Paris VIII) where, in a very strained political situation, interesting inter-disciplinary experiments have been carried out and a considerable number of students who did not graduate from Lycée have been admitted. The seven others come from the break-up of the Paris faculties. Paris I includes U.E.R.'s of law, political science, history, geography and philosophy, grouped around economics. Paris II is predominantly juridical. Paris III is centered on languages and contemporary civilization. Paris IV represents the conservative majority of the old Sorbonne: French, classical languages, history etc. Paris V includes several medical units, pharmacy, sociology and part of psychology; Paris VI corresponds to the major part of the old Faculty of Science. Paris VII includes scientific and medical units as well as units concerned with the human sciences and languages.

Beginning in 1971 the Conseil National de l'Enseignement et de la Recherche will be established to be in charge of budgetary and administrative decisions concerning the distribution of resources and activities among the universities. This system combines the autonomy of the universities (they will elect their own presidents) with a certain coordination. This will be guaranteed by the existence of the Conseil National and particularly by its authority to decide which diplomas will be nationally recognized. These will be the only ones that can be recognized by another university and that will permit one to register for the competitive recruiting examinations. All these changes have been accomplished by the professors themselves under some pressure from the Ministry of National Education.

The new Paris universities are clearly divided into two categories. Some resist the new direction and seek to imitate partly or totally one of the former faculties (Universities II, IV, VI). The most active representative of this viewpoint is the dean of the Paris Faculty of Science, Professor Marc Zamansky. An active, authoritarian man, opposed to the break-up of his faculty and to co-management, his attitude grew more rigid during the spring of 1970. He came into open conflict with some of the professors and the student representatives of Paris VI—where he has not succeeded in being elected president. Universities I, V and especially VII are more clearly inter-disciplinary. The professors were freely distributed among these universities based on a mixture of professional and ideological considerations. Paris IV is generally considered right-wing and Paris VII left-wing.

The organization of these new universities will involve material difficulties. One favorable element is the stabilization of the number of students—for a few years—which makes the reorganization less impossible than it would have been a few years ago during a period of rapid growth.

The principal difficulty comes from the inability of the Minister of National Education to effectively control such wide-ranging change. An important administrative reform introduced at the beginning of 1970 is supposed to bring this office out of its old paralysis. But it is not likely that he will be able to act very effectively.

This administrative obstacle is not the main one, however. French society continues to have no ideas or plans for the future of the university system. The government, the Parliament and the "silent majority" see it only as a source of disorder and seem unaware of the long-term problems posed by the re-organization of higher education. But this lack of ideas and plans may actually favor the birth of autonomous universities and consequently the diversification of higher education!

During 1968 to 1970 the student movement separated itself from university reform. In 1968–69 some universities experienced extreme disorganization. The political movement took refuge in the university system. Ideology was substituted for both professional work and active politics.

During autumn 1968, particularly at Nanterre, various groups tried to revive mass action. Their failure quickly became evident. Whereas the meetings in the spring had raised the degree of mobilization, those in the autumn ended in confusion.

This situation encouraged the rector and the new dean of Nanterre, Professor Jean Beaujeu, to undertake a policy of repression: the exclusion of students who had taken part in the agitation at Vincennes and the formation of a university police force which committed serious brutalities and was withdrawn only after a hunger strike by a group of students of anthropology and under pressure from Edgar Faure himself.

These reactionary efforts were not isolated. During the 1968–69 academic year many professors thought that it was time "to put things back in order," but this attitude rested on such obvious errors of judgment that it caused the conservatives nothing but embarrassment.

University agitation, in which a certain number of young professors played an important role, no longer had any future. It ended only in the disorganization of education in some departments and in struggles between very confused points of view. The futility of this kind of agitation was soon evident. Also, the most revolutionary elements, which formed the Marxist-inspired groups like the Gauche Prolétarienne, began actions outside the university in spring 1970: in the factories, the shanty towns, among the immigrant workers. They rapidly experienced violent repression. Their principal leader, Alain Geismar, was imprisoned in June 1970.

Since 1968 the prevailing behavior patterns in this crisis-ridden and sometimes chaotic university were tied to their disorganization—major absenteeism, lack of coordination in teaching programs, sporadic violence. Moreover, especially in 1968–69, there were political struggles for control of the student group: prolonged struggle at

Vincennes between Communists and leftists, struggles between the extreme right and the extreme left at the Paris Law Faculty, attempts by the Communists to return to power at Nanterre. There was much more violence during this year than there had been during the preceding years. The period 1969–70 has been much more calm, since it was dominated by the revival of political actions outside the university and by the gradual formation of the new universities.

Only at Nanterre in March 1970 did violent incidents break out following a long period of decay, the main victim of which was a reforming dean, Paul Ricoeur, who was personally attacked by bands with no political affiliation. Under pressure from conservative elements and in order to respond to this disorder, the dean called in the police who acted with great violence. Since then, Nanterre has continuously sunk deeper into crisis, exhausted by its role as avant-garde in the university movement for the three previous years. The attempts of the Gauche Prolétarienne to occupy the Censier annex were rapidly stopped by the police. The revolutionary groups—which still enjoy some public sympathy, especially when they are being pursued by the police—no longer have much ability to mobilize. To use a comparison that comes naturally to mind, the student movement in 1968 resembled the situation in June 1848; in 1970 it resembles even more Blanquism, that is, discontented intellectuals addressing themselves to the most underprivileged groups and not reaching the working masses or the student masses.

Conclusion: This Is Only the Beginning

Return to Social Conflicts

Following the Second World War, world politics were defined by the confrontation between the capitalist bloc dominated by the United States and the communist bloc dominated by the Soviet Union. At the same time, the political and economic decline of the older European capitalist powers paved the way for the development of nationalist movements in Africa and Asia and the rise of populism and anti-imperialist movements in Latin America. China was absorbed in its own popular revolution. Social problems, during this period, were submerged into national and territorial concerns. The Yalta agreement redefined the opposition between two types of society into conflict over zones of power and political influence. Most major conflicts were over boundaries:

Greece was forcibly brought into the Western camp, Czechoslovakia into the Eastern camp. The two empires clashed in Korea. Yugoslavia detached itself from the Soviet bloc and other countries followed its effort to remain unaligned. The Jewish and Arab nations fought over Palestine. Cuba moved out of American domination; the Dominican Republic did not succeed in doing so.

The great social conflicts that had marked capitalist society grew weak and the labor movement was divided by the opposition between East and West, communism and socialism. Tied to the State in the East, more or less integrated by collective bargaining and various other forms of participation as well as by rising living standards and changing life-styles in the West and, associated with populist movements or newly independent governments in the Third World the labor movement lost its international character, and was institutionalized and particularized. It demonstrated most strength when it attached itself to a national movement or to revolt against political domination. The 1947 and 1948 strikes in France are one example; worker participation in the Budapest uprising is another. While the empires and nations clashed, their societies remained peaceful, not because everyone was satisfied but because new cleavages and new conflicts had not yet been formed.

The relaxation of the Cold War, the atomic balance of terror, and the decline of nationalism in the Third World, crushed by the growing economic domination of the major capitalist powers, revealed new social conflicts after this long period of political change and struggle. The first example to appear was revolutionary activity on behalf of the most disinherited, the peasants of the Third World, encouraged by the gigantic example of the Chinese Revolution. But while such action had had major results during the preceding period of nationalist

and social struggles, now it had very limited effectiveness, even when it awakened the passionate support of
broad sectors of public opinion.

In the industrialized countries, opposition to the social
order first took the form of accusation and the refusal to
be integrated. Industrial society appeared closed, "one
dimensional," in the words of Marcuse, and at first those
who were marginal—Marcuse's "outcasts" and "outlaws"
—seemed the only possible supporters of contestation.
In Germany, a first step was taken: the criticism became
intellectual but it was still rejection; it was not yet
discovery and development of the internal contradictions
of the new society. The passage from the exaltation of
rejection to action that brought out and exploded these
contradictions was the work of the May Movement.
Revolutionary action was no longer addressed to those
excluded from the social system but to those at its
very heart, those most closely bound to the structures of
growth and change and most directly confronted with
the domination of the massive politico-economic structures.

Among this group, the students are the most ready
for action—not as a professional class but as a group
close enough to the centers of decision-making and at
the same time far enough removed from them to sense
and broadcast loudly the disorganized tension and contradictions of the entire society. While the working
masses are largely integrated into the social and cultural order and the farmers are either entering the
market economy or are being more and more relegated
to a state of underdevelopment, the students and intellectuals, who cannot by themselves constitute a force
of social and political opposition, escaped the grip of the
dominant society through intellectual criticism and physical violence. They anticipated and prepared future social struggles. They also sought a difficult alliance with

the groups that bear the heaviest social constraints—farmers, laborers, ethnic minorities.

The worldwide unity of the student movement is not due to a common political orientation in Japan, Brazil, Poland, and the United States, for example, but arises from the symptoms of post-war confusion. It is not a programmatic unity but a unity of attitudes and methods. Universal and powerful institutionalization and reinforcement of structures made the conflict wild, disorganized, and non-negotiable, a force aimed at the dismemberment of institutions, political criticism, scandal, and cultural utopia. This general unity must not, nevertheless, conceal the differences that are due to the varied nature of established power in different countries. In Latin America, the end of populism and the strengthening of dualism—the opposition between a sector increasingly devoid of resources and urban centers of growth largely dominated by foreign interests—provoked the students to speak of national independence and development for the benefit of all the people. The intelligentsia fights against economic domination and the destruction of the national collectivity.

In the more industrialized countries, on the other hand, the new fact, as we have already said, is that power is no longer an instrument of economic exploitation for the benefit of a minority but rather a structure of management, control, and manipulation of all social life. Whether it takes the form of authoritarian State control of education, propaganda, and investments, or whether it is a nebulous unity of big businesses more or less closely bound to each other, it exerts a growing influence over what was before the domain of private life, over local and professional organizations and even over class heritage. In this situation, the students do not intervene as an avant-garde intelligentsia but because their activity and professional situation confront them directly with the dominating and manipulating action of those in power. Education and research are such important determinants of growth that they must be planned by those in power and, hence, be subject to political decisions. In Czechoslovakia, the students' desire for intellectual liberty quite naturally joined the anti-bureaucratic efforts of the economists led by Ota Sik. In the United States, the conflicts began with the denunciation of the direct or indirect aid given by some universities to the Vietnam War. In France, the problem of student selection posed political choices. Like teachers and researchers, students are no longer the spokesmen for a people reduced to silence by wretchedness and oppression; they are workers directly concerned with the economic and social choices imposed in one form or another by politico-economic power.

Among the industrialized nations, the French situation was the least favorable to the formation of a student movement that would be the forerunner and revealer of new conflicts: because it had long been entangled in the liquidation of its colonial empire; because, as a semi-industrial country, it possessed a labor movement that remained partly revolutionary, fanning the flames of past conflicts without enkindling new ones; and finally political and cultural criticism was actively led by "left-wing intellectuals" whose protests expressed opposition but did not achieve political power. Why then did the Paris movement, a latecomer, shake up French society more profoundly than the Berkeley or Berlin movements shook up the United States or Germany?

Its importance was not due to its original orientations, which most often resembled those of other student movements, but to the condition of French society. In the East, political repression is too strong; in the West, the universities are too independent for their crises to affect the State. France, both liberal and rigid, centralized and disorganized, modernist and archaic, grandiose and mean, exacerbated tensions within a university world that was in rapid expansion and absolute crisis.

These observations, made a hundred times, not only explain the extent of the crisis; they also explain the formation, in France more than elsewhere, of a new class struggle and especially the partial and limited, but real, alliance between students and other groups close to them because of their social situation: researchers, professional experts, technicians. The struggle had a broader and more clearly defined front in France than elsewhere. The student revolt that faced the State in the East and the culture in the West faced the whole of society in France.

The principal cause of this is assuredly the role of the State in French society: not the legendary Napoleonic State which is more often evoked than precisely analysed, but the Gaullist State which insured unity between the old and new ruling classes, the bourgeoisie and the technocracy. Thanks to it, the student revolt combined rejection of the exhausted old liberal university with the struggle against the new centers of economic power. While its influence on French society was profound, the Gaullist State is the very opposite of a national and popular State. It mobilized no sentiment in its own favor, neither for the construction of the nation (something long since accomplished) nor for the voluntary transformation of society. It was driven by the idea of national *grandeur,* which has no meaning except on the international scene and has almost no effect on the attitudes of Frenchmen toward the workings of their own society. It brought about social and political changes for which it took the principal responsibility and at the same time it made them meaningless for those who lived through them. It was too liberal to use totalitarian propaganda or repression; it was too authoritarian to allow decisions and conflicts in any particular sector of national activity to be worked out independently. Therefore, the May Movement unloosed not only a profound crisis within the State but it also presented grievances against the State in the name of society, the people, and the meaning of change.

In Germany, the student movement was closed in on itself and was creative of more ideas. In France, it transformed the situation of society. Against the State, it succeeded in uniting political opposition and cultural revolt within a social movement. In a country that is practically outside the great international rivalries, imperialism or foreign domination could not mobilize collective action. But in a country where the State dominates economic life and the functioning of society, the cultural revolt became a struggle against power. The result was that the conflict, slower to appear in France than elsewhere, took on greater importance there.

Social Conflicts and the University

What enflamed some and scandalized others for those few weeks in May and June was the realization that anything could happen, given the profound disruption of a society that had thought itself peaceful, rich, and set on a course of modernization that seemed to relegate to the past the great conflicts and visions that had accompanied a century of industrialization. Society revealed its opposite side. The ease and suddenness with which the crisis burst forth, the university was occupied, the strike movement was spread, and the political regime was shaken up aroused either hopes or fears. It rearoused passion in a purportedly rational world. But there is a real danger that this situation will not be analyzed accurately. The event is both so extraordinary and so important that there is a tendency to explain it either by very particular reasons—the sclerosis of the university system or the blindness of the government— or by the overly general reasons—generation gap or a crisis of civilization. Both cases ignore equally the essential consideration that historically situates and explains this social, political, and cultural crisis: the revelation of the conflicts and forces at work in a type of society still too new to be conscious of its own nature and problems. A new class struggle between the dominate politico-economic structures and the people who must go through great change lent the May Movement importance. It is not the central moment of one crisis, but the beginning of many new conflicts that will be as fundamental and as enduring, as the worker movement was in the period of capitalist industrialization.

As at the birth of every major social movement, the most specific demands and the most utopian visions were juxtaposed or mixed, without being joined in the kind of political action and organization. This can only come about gradually, through long struggles as political relationships are disentangled from older problems and rearranged to cope with new problems and new conflicts. University reform and the recognition of union negotiation, if they are singled out, are only elements of a more general social change that, in many other countries, was accomplished without such a storm. On the other hand, the cultural revolt proclaimed by what Edgar Morin called the Student Commune, advocated a drive for immediate gains to the tension and constraints that are imposed by a longer term investment that allows growth.* In isolation, this revolt had no lasting political importance.

The importance of the May Movement lies in neither

* Claude Lefort, Edgar Morin and Jean-Marc Coudray, *La Brèche* (Paris: Fayard, 1968).

of these alternatives, nor in the reforms that it will probably make possible, nor in the cultural revolt that gave it its passionate character, but in the social rupture that it created at the heart of a society dominated by the utopianism of the ruling class. In the name of rational modernization and of technical progress that is supposed to bring social progress about naturally—a larger pie makes the problem of how it is cut secondary —this ruling class identified itself with the future. It did not speak in the name of special interests and made no political choices. It wanted only what was rational and did only what was reasonable. Certainly, obstacles to progress and resistance to change must be eliminated but more information, clearer thinking, and greater decisiveness would be enough to take care of that.

Now French society knows once again that its decisions are political choices, even when they rest on the best technical studies and when they take account of the demands of economic coherence. Behind the ideology of rationality, the power of special interests has been laid bare; not so much those of speculators or even private capital as of the massive structures that control production and consumption. Social conflict reappeared. Those who reduce all social activity to adaptation, to necessary, rational change were opposed by those who demand a democratic power capable of regulating the massive structures that both ensure economic growth and manipulate society.

The movement simply revealed this conflict rather than solved the crises or contradictions and could not be considered "constructive." Those who, in their search for its virtues, marvel over the movement's positive results should be reminded first off of this. Isn't an entirely new university system going to emerge from the May–June debates? Aren't reforms that were long judged impossible now going to be easy? Yes, certainly, but this is a weak justification that can be answered easily by saying that the prize was not worth the game. Other European countries have raised salaries in a less brutal manner and the reform of the faculties of letters or even of the whole university system did not merit a general social crisis. If the May Movement is to be judged on the basis of its modernizing effects, it must be condemned because the means were incommensurate with the limited and uncertain results.

Must we then say just the opposite? If there was a revolutionary movement, it was because France was already in a revolutionary situation, and that only betrayal or the decadence of the political structures had kept society from moving into a new socialism, equally distant from both capitalist society and Soviet bureaucracy? This isn't true either. The regime was certainly shaken but, even if it had succumbed, the social revolution would not have triumphed. If a government directed by either the Communist or non-Communist left had been formed, the measures that it would have taken would have been very different from the inspiration of the movement.

We have experienced an impossible revolution, a revolutionary movement without revolution. We must not confuse revolutionary self-expression in an extra-territorialized Sorbonne with political preparation for a real social revolution. Revolutionary consciousness cannot take the place of revolution. The more it was expressed, the less it nourished the forces that are committed to a new social conflict, and the more it revealed the crisis and disorganization of the university system in which it was rooted.

Therefore, it seems to me that the importance of the May Movement is best represented by the March 22 Movement, which kept its distance both from university reform and from the rhetoric of the Sorbonne and the

Odéon. Its strength lay in confrontation and combat
rather than in proclamation and reform. While its passionate and naïve activity attracted some students who
were simply rebellious and had broken with a life-
condition they found absurd and limiting, this activity
alone had deep political significance. It helped create a
new consciousness and new class action by joining students with other groups of workers. It accomplished this
by clashing with the unions and those political organizations that were the leaders of past social struggles but
today are reduced to institutionalizing old conflicts—not
that this is such a negligible task.

It is no longer possible to accept the image of our
industrial society as one enormous organization concen-
trating on its own growth and discarding a new class of
poor or unfit individuals around its edges. The May
Movement made clear what certain industrial conflicts of
a new type had already indicated: the struggle is not at
the periphery but at the center of this programmed
society. It also demonstrated that revolutionary action
in France cannot be reduced to support for the Vietnam
struggle or the Che Guevara-type guerillas through
proclamations, meetings, or violent gestures. Solidarity
among revolutionaries has meaning only if each individual contributes in some practical way to the social
struggle. This is what happened in France during May.
The rebellion turned back toward French society and the
other advanced industrial societies. It spoke to these
societies, not that the nonintegrated elements which
protest from the outskirts are important but that the
producers themselves oppose the power system to which
they are subjected.

This movement is important because it transcends any
particular institution. Those who judge the movement
only from the point of view of the university system can
only find it frantic, excessive, costly, and ineffective. In

the same way, general strikes always appeared costly and excessive to those who wished to see the labor movement only as an instrument of liberalization to promote participation within firms. Like the worker movement, the May Movement indicted an entire system of social power above and beyond a national political system. For that reason, the movement was internationalist and expressed solidarity with all who struggle against techno-bureaucratic power, whether they are part of capitalism or are degraded within the worker parties.

What differentiates this student revolutionary movement in the industrial countries from those in the developing and colonialized countries is that this is the first time that education in the economically advanced countries has become a factor of production and decisive growth, not merely the transmission of a cultural heritage. No one dreams of saying that now the students are the dominated class or even that they alone are the militant avant-garde of the oppressed. But students are more than the spokesmen for unaware or inarticulate groups. They are the representatives of all those who suffer more from social integration and cultural manipulation directed by the economic structures than from economic exploitation and material misery.

Because the movement was revolutionary force rather than the instrument of an actual revolution, its role as spokesman and advocate of a new class struggle is inseparable from its other aspects; conflict behavior was constantly accompanied by crisis behavior. Since rejection of the present society was not transformed into an organized struggle to form a new society, the revolt confused itself with revolution. Begun in rebellion and ending by rejecting society, the students' spring was marked by the increasing, then decreasing hope to affect the cultural crisis in some meaningful way. Without the first rebellion, revolutionary intent would have always remained enclosed in the "little groups"; by June, revolutionary intentions were diluted into reform of university institutions. The May Movement was not launched by a "new working class" or by the students in the most modern and best organized sections of the university. It was born in the crumbling faculties of letters in reaction to pointlessness and crisis. If this reaction did not give the movement its complete meaning, at least it gave it the initial strength to break with a system that fulfilled no real function and was, to that very degree, determined to perpetuate itself and to reject all debate over its purpose and means. The Week of the Barricades was the central moment of the events of May, the moment of maximum possible action; it was much more than a rebellion, much less than a revolution, and certainly not an insurrection. For a few days, words were joined to action and individual spontaneity became part of a collective struggle. After that, revolutionary intent wore itself out in the illusion of creating a worker revolution, which, however, led the movement to make its greatest progress, for it called forth the social groups outside the university which constitute, with the students, the new opposition. The cultural revolt became absorbed in self-expression, and university reorganization transformed the possibility of revolution into institutional reform.

Here, as we draw our conclusions, we rediscover the propositions presented at the beginning of this book, but each of the themes we sought to isolate has been substantiated with concrete images. We see clearly that within the movement there were three types of attitudes and preoccupations and almost three different types of individuals.

On one side were those committed to the precipitation of social and political conflicts. In common they held

that university and student issues were secondary considerations. Some aimed directly at the downfall of
capitalist society; others wished more immediately for
the fall of Gaullism. There were many major differences
among them, as marked as those that separated the
Week of the Barricades from the week of May 27–
June 1; or those that separated Daniel Cohn-Bendit
and Jacques Sauvageot. But whether the accent is put
on the social movement or on political action, it was
always a question of revealing and exploding the contradictions of society.

On the other extreme, the university and professional
rebellion remained close to the situation in which it was
formed and the crisis that it expressed, but from which
it wished to free itself. Whether it took the form of
university reformism, a struggle against governmental
control of television, or a rejection of traditional professional organizations, it was a matter of affirming
absolute, undefined, force against constraints and repression. It was Man and the People against barriers
and control.

Between the two were the utopians whose central
theme was self-direction. While the first group involved
itself in conflicts and the second affirmed itself against
society, these wished to take possession of the social
organization and to discover a way to fuse their individual spontaneity with collective life. Because, as I
have said, the function of utopianism was to create unity
beyond the opposition between the social conflict and
the cultural crisis, the utopians affirmed the movement
most vigorously and defined its objectives, while the first
group worked out its action and the second group gave
it its climate. The May Movement was utopian communism. On the Night of the Barricades or the evening
of May 13 on the Champ de Mars, social combat, cultural

revolt, and self-directive utopia were mixed, not fused, associated in the strength of a movement that was much more than a defensive solidarity against the police.

Now, after the May uprising, will each of these trends follow a different course, while a few individuals nostalgic for the spring strive to revive the lost unity of the movement? We cannot predict the future and we must answer the question by asking another. Under what conditions will the class conflict enkindled in May be able to develop and the movement that carried it be able to pursue its efforts? The conditions of such a future are the opposite of those that gave the movement its strength in May. The movement will develop to the degree that the social conflict frees itself from the rebellion which was a by-product of the university and cultural crisis.

Hope for an immediate revolution has disappeared. The movement born in the university returned to it. It can remain there either in terms of codirection of the university or of rejection of any institutionalization of the revolt. In the first case, the movement as such would disappear; in the second, action having no other objective than to bring out rebellion could lead to a new crisis, more limited in its dimensions but more paralyzing for the university, which the rejection of a weak minority of students could lead into chaos. However, in the university itself, it can also regain the meaning of its political action. This supposes first of all that the crisis must be overcome, that a new organization will be set up, and also that student action will steer clear of the problems of the internal workings of the departments and the university as a whole.

The autonomy and codirection introduced into the university will mark both the end of a crisis and the beginning of new struggles. The old style of direction, in which the ministry and the faculty councils managed to mutually impede each other from acting while neither had the capacity to make decisions, no longer exists. The representative bodies must allow practical problems to be treated so that the risks of fragmentation can be overcome. Today, these bodies represent the structure that can include the most diverse tendencies. Therefore, it is essential that they be organized as soon as possible.

From that point on there will be no agreement. Those who aim at student participation in working out the common good and those who wish to develop political contestation within the university will part company. But it is possible that they will oppose each other within a new institutional framework. This seems to be exemplified by the Paris Faculty of Law where the majority among the students, the former strike committee, carries on political action directly opposed to the government at the same time that it participates in the organization of codirection.

Two opposing tendencies appear quite clearly above and beyond the multiplicity of local situations. On one side, there is the will or need to take up again the direct action of May, to reject institutional reforms, to reoccupy the university premises. At Nanterre and the Ecole des Beaux Arts, some limited efforts have shown the strength of this tendency. Certain groups of students at the Sorbonne, among whom the influence of the F.E.R. seems strong, published communiques that announced the resumption of counterinstitutional action. But so far only at the Faculty of Medicine have serious incidents taken place. The calling in of private policemen, which was, to say the least, very alien to university custom, provoked, along with the reactionary response of many professors at the faculty, a clash which was surprising almost solely because it had no further serious consequences.

Opposite to this tendency, whose chances in the im-

mediate future seem directly proportionate to how much
resistance the faculties put up to the governmental
reforms, the U.N.E.F. and many of the most politicized
members of the movement play the game of reform,
allow the government to dismantle the bastilles of university resistance and provide the students with the
bases of future contestation within the representative
assemblies. No one can foresee which of the two partners, the government or the student opposition, will
draw the greater benefit from the reforms introduced
by the former but which are the direct result of the
action of the latter. This, rather than the fits and starts
of rebellion, will spell out the future of the movement
—at least its immediate future.

Political liberties within the university was rightly
considered at the beginning of the summer as the problem that would determine the future. For it cannot just
be a matter of organizing debates over ideas; this has
always been possible. It is a matter of deciding whether
scientific and pedagogical activity on the one hand and
political activity on the other can manage to coexist
without violent rupture, even in constant interaction. No
regulation or agreement can govern a problem that is
so new and so difficult. For a long time, "productive"
activity will try to exclude or dampen political life
and, on the other side, the temptation will return to
politicize all university activity.

Industrial firms have not been able to resolve a
similar problem and union activity was only firmly established when it reduced itself to collective bargaining.
Nevertheless, the university is condemned by its present
role to live with this problem. In a society dominated by
massive organizations, the university is both an element
of the production and growth system and a counteror-
ganization. Its laboratories and research centers, whether
or not tied to applied programs, are an increasingly

important element of the structure of development. The power of tomorrow's "masters" will make that of yesterday's mandarins appear pale. At the same time, the university is a place of education, where men affirm their personalities and resist being manipulated by the centers of power. Scientific knowledge supports this resistance with all its critical strength.

When power was in the hands of the monarch or the oligarchs, the writer, the journalist, and the cartoonist could defend public liberties against personal domination. In the face of the power structures of techno-bureaucracy, only a powerful organization that is anti-technocratic in its ends and functioning can fulfill this role. From now on, the university will live within the necessary conflict between these two functions. This conflict can exhaust it, break it, lead to the separation of teaching from research, of politics from knowledge, but can also give it, if it bears up, an importance in society that it has never before possessed.

I do not believe that the May Movement will be reabsorbed in the exercise of codirection. Neither do I believe that it can perpetuate itself under the form of an increasingly undefined and politically impotent cultural revolt. It will undertake, I think, a double role in the university: criticism and contestation directed not only against certain orientations of the university itself but against the social and political order; and secondly, opening the university world and the student movement itself to the workers mobilized for the same objectives in the social and political struggle.

Perhaps there will not be continuity in time between the May uprising and the acts that will mark the beginning of this new phase of the movement. The explosion was too sudden and too violent not to have disorganized those who set it off. In the confused period that is beginning, when attempts at reform will move side by side with cries of rejection, outbursts of violence, and attempts at reaction and repression, what was the May Movement will seek to discover the meaning of what took place through it and new battles will be prepared that will probably take different forms from the first ones.

The cry of the May demonstrators, "This is only the beginning, we will continue the combat," does not signify that the revolt of the spring will not be pacified and that the social order will not be reestablished. It is rather the discovery that, beyond the crisis, the revolt, and the barricades, a new period of social history is beginning. The old problems will be gradually reabsorbed, negotiated, and institutionalized. For a period, perhaps ten years, and during the Gaullist internal peace, the rise of a new, more technical, more calculating, more prosperous and mobile society made many believe that the subsidence of these older problems marked the end of great social disruptions. Since May, we know that new problems and new conflicts are being formed. They erupted wildly without theory, party, or policy. Now, long, theoretical, and practical work must be undertaken in the light of the events of May. It must transcend utopianism and imaginary power; it must develop a social movement and foster its conflicts with the powers that rule society.

My goal in this book was not to describe an historical event as its participants lived it, but to note the birth of these new social struggles; to grasp not simply the content of this particular consciousness, but the meaning of what happened.

Index

Action: of May Movement, 51, 53,
61–2, 66–9, 77, 137, 143–4, 151,
153, 159f., 242–59, 275
as new tactic, 13f., 137–8, 151,
174
Africa, 44f., 344
agrégation, 93, 106, 256f., 293, 309
Algerian War, 41, 176f., 228*n*, 240,
248, 262, 284
Alienation, 19, 36*n*, 55, 60, 77, 141,
190, 202, 224, 250
student, 16, 104f., 107, 140, 272–
3, 274–5
Amiens Conference, 114, 117–18,
167, 264
Anarchist groups, 155, 232, 290–1
Anti-Gaullism, 193, 210, 217, 227–
8, 234–5, 239f., 250, 301
Antisociety, 9, 14, 32, 48, 51, 53,
62, 65, 66–7, 69, 72, 74, 190,
242–80
Aragon, Louis, 75, 252
Asia, 289, 318, 344f., 347

assistant, 93, 101, 102–4, 105f., 128,
132f., 146f., 290, 299–300, 301,
309
Association pour l'Expansion de la
Recherche Scientifique, 114–
18, 129, 167, 222, 264, 332
Authoritarianism, 49ff., 97, 222
industrial, 66, 67*n*, 209, 215, 265–
6
opposed, 9, 253–67
university, 97, 118–19, 148, 256–
7, 266
Automobile industry, 50, 58, 69,
71f., 184, 190, 199, 205, 214–
17, 219, 234, 249

Barjonet, André, 72, 209, 228, 235,
240
Barricades: Nights of the, 71, 121,
159, 162ff., 171f., 173–8, 180,
182, 186ff., 192f., 213, 215, 231f.,
234, 243, 252, 357

Barricades (continued)
  Week of, 12f., 26, 60, 72, 159–
    92, 255, 256, 282, 357
Berkeley. See California
Berlin, University of, 28, 90–1, 143,
    147–8, 348
Bourdieu, Pierre, 88f., 91
Bourgeoisie, 26–7, 46, 62, 71, 88–97,
    119, 123, 222, 225, 256–7, 295,
    323, 334, 337, 349
Budapest uprising, 77, 345
Bureaucracy, 6–9, 39f., 49f., 66, 83–
    6, 91, 100, 102–4, 112, 116, 131,
    139f., 178, 249, 273

Caen Conference, 114–18, 129, 167,
    222, 332
California, University of, 9, 12, 17,
    28, 79, 147, 149, 271, 348
CAL's (Comités d'Action Lycéens),
    253, 255, 258–9
Capitalism, 6ff., 12–14, 16, 19, 59f.,
    63, 78, 112, 179, 199
C.F.D.T. (Confédération Française
    et Démocratique du Travail),
    66, 67n, 72, 198, 203–4, 209–
    10, 218f., 233
C.G.T. (Confédération Générale du
    Travail), 7–8, 18–19, 66n, 67n,
    72, 149, 187, 191, 196f., 199,
    203f., 209f., 213ff., 217ff., 230f.,
    233, 234–5
Charléty Stadium, 58, 189, 217, 229,
    231, 234, 240
Chinese revolution, 289, 318, 344f.
Class, social. See Social class
Class conflicts, 10, 45f., 52–4, 55f.,
    71, 77, 195, 206
  May Movement as, 64–5, 67–8,
    81, 178, 221–6, 267
Class consciousness, 36–7, 206, 224ff.
Class struggle, 10, 28, 40–1, 45ff.,
    52–4, 55f., 58–9, 61–2, 65, 68f.,
    73, 75, 178, 215, 238, 326, 349,
    351
Classics, 92, 94, 132
C.N.R.S. (Centre National de la
    Recherche Scientifique), 85ff.,

C.N.R.S. (continued)
    106, 124, 133, 211, 282, 297,
    312–13
Cohn-Bendit, Daniel, 13, 64, 74, 78,
    137, 139–40, 141–6, 166, 171,
    174f., 182, 188, 195, 228, 231ff.,
    240, 246ff., 252, 269, 357
Cold War, 41–2, 236, 345
Collège de France, 85ff.
Colonial system, 44, 78, 111, 247,
    279
Columbia University, 53, 79, 255n
Commissariat for the Plan, 86, 111,
    113
Committees, action, 248–50, 251ff.,
    255–6, 258–9, 265, 315f., 320
Communism. See Utopianism
Communist Party: French (P.C.F.),
    18–19, 41, 61–8, 71, 82, 111, 113,
    129, 142–4, 149f., 164, 173, 182,
    194f., 196n, 217ff., 228–31, 249,
    258, 290, 301, 320, 343, 345, 353
  present attitude/role of, 197, 217,
    219, 230–7, 238ff.
  teachers, 202–3
  Italian, 148, 199
Conservatism, 41, 48, 50f., 86, 92–4,
    106, 193–5, 203, 277, 299, 323,
    342
Consumption, mass, 33, 44, 50, 59,
    79–80, 111, 141, 220, 272, 275
Corporations, 30, 39, 46, 55, 112,
    205–6, 215–16
Courses, 100–2, 104, 110, 132
C.R.S. (Compagnies Républicaines
    de Securité), 163–4, 173, 175f.,
    183, 187–8, 219, 234, 269
Cultural revolt, 10f., 32–3, 35f., 41,
    43–4, 51, 53, 55–7, 59–61, 66,
    68, 77f., 122, 137–41, 150, 153,
    159, 242–53, 265–80, 351
  in lycées, 253–59
  in public information, 259–67
  social/political struggle vs., 53,
    56, 58, 61–2, 71, 141, 176, 182,
    270, 275
Culture, 94, 137–41, 251–2, 266–7,
    273–6
  technocracy vs., 88–97, 153

Czechoslovakia, 77, 219, 318, 345, 347f.

Dadaism, 48, 52, 274
Decision-making: industrial, 66, 95, 221, 223, 277
  in May Movement, 291
  political, 159f., 166–9
  university. *See* Universities, French
Degrees, 37–8, 83, 85, 93, 102–4, 106, 109, 118–19, 130–2, 255
Demonstrations, 58, 69n, 71, 129, 149, 159ff., 165, 171–3, 186, 190, 229, 233, 240
Despotism, 49, 59
Domination: technocratic, opposed, 11, 33–5, 43–4, 46, 54, 59–60, 61, 71, 77f., 117, 190, 221–4, 226, 265, 315, 345

Economic system, 42, 48ff., 112–13, 179, 197, 202, 220, 278
Economics, faculties of, 85–7, 102, 105, 302–3, 306
Education, 13, 31, 41f., 59f., 76, 78–9, 85, 89, 92, 95, 331, 348
Elite, 43, 108, 178, 277, 336
  schooling of, 15f., 31, 37, 90, 99f., 102, 113, 255
Employers, 49f., 58, 86n, 90
Employment, 90, 95, 105, 110, 114, 132, 180, 212, 220–1
"enragés," 54, 71, 75, 135, 144f., 154, 164, 167, 232f., 271, 285, 323
Exams, 37, 83, 89, 91, 93, 105, 110, 119, 126, 136, 153, 255n, 257, 293–4
Experts, 6, 8, 38ff., 96, 107, 178, 218–24
Exploitation, 44, 55, 71, 190, 202, 205

Factory occupations, 72, 176, 180, 182, 208–13, 214ff., 238
Faculties of letters, 109–10, 115, 119f., 132f., 148, 160, 203, 212, 294, 297, 302f., 337, 356
  Nanterre, 122–3, 128f., 151

Faculties of letters (*continued*)
  Paris, 49, 161, 232, 288, 290, 306–7, 315
  provincial, 299, 307f.
Faculty, faculties, 15–16, 25n, 65, 67, 70, 83–90, 93, 104, 113
  occupied, 284–90, 305
  Paris, 67, 104, 165, 339–41
  provincial, 104, 307–8
Family, 88, 94, 97, 108, 255, 257, 273
Fascism, 111n
Faure, Edgar, 170, 292, 323, 339, 342
February Revolution, 50
Fédération pour Proposer un Gouvernement de Front Populaire, 143, 191, 194, 217, 228f., 231, 236, 240
F.E.N. (Fédération de l'Education Nationale), 233, 249
F.E.R. (Fédération des Etudiants Révolutionnaires), 157, 166, 173, 182f., 359
F.O., 204, 209, 214
Fouchet Plan, 37, 75, 118–19, 130, 133, 153, 157, 164, 294
Freedom, 46n, 50, 54, 59, 70, 99–100, 138–41, 149, 254, 260–7, 333, 337–9
French Revolution, 46n, 239, 253n, 268, 274

Gauche Prolétarienne, 342f.
Gaulle, Charles de, 17–18, 19, 50, 53, 61, 71, 154, 165, 167, 170, 173, 179, 185, 191, 193, 198, 215, 222f., 227ff., 249, 252, 269, 322, 349, 357, 362
Geismar, Alain, 64, 72, 170f., 181, 183, 187f., 195, 203, 231, 234, 240, 249, 320, 342
General strike, 12, 58, 176ff., 180, 182, 184f., 190, 193, 212, 227, 233, 243, 248, 319
Germany, 28, 34, 52, 57, 80, 90–1, 121, 132, 137, 143f., 147ff., 197, 246f., 263, 271, 346, 348, 350

Government, French: archaic/over-
centralized, 11, 14, 19, 48f., 52–
3, 61–2, 111–13, 251
as authoritarian, 49f., 254, 260–7
crisis of, 185, 189, 266–7. *See also*
Social crisis
after crisis, 323, 339–41, 360
elections, 18f., 236, 319
referendum, 191, 229
historically, 28, 46, 90f., 105,
169f., 188, 196, 198, 222, 226,
228n, 240, 253, 335
initial reaction of, to May Movement, 49–54, 61–2, 71, 139–40,
149ff., 158ff., 164, 166–73, 176f.,
181, 183–4, 232, 271
international/domestic priorities
of, 41–2, 49f., 111–13, 169–70,
173, 227, 254, 349
labor relations and, 58, 86, 189,
196, 198, 227
and May Movement, 11, 16–21,
48, 55f., 79, 110–14, 150, 273
negotiating efforts of, with May
Movement, 58, 189, 191, 229,
243
relationship of, to universities,
14–17, 49–50, 90–1, 94, 110–19,
153–4, 169–73, 256–7
role of, 14, 52–3, 112–13, 179, 252,
266–7
ruling class and, 94f., 113
Governments, 10, 12–14, 19, 34f.,
43–4, 45–6
Graffiti, 36, 137, 146, 249f., 269
Grandes Ecoles, 15f., 85–8, 90, 92,
102, 104, 113, 125–6, 133, 222,
249, 255n, 282, 303, 359
Grappin, Pierre, 128–30, 134, 136–7,
139, 144f., 151, 166, 269, 299
Great Britain, 67, 92, 108, 132, 225,
256, 261, 291
Grenelle agreements, 58, 72, 209,
215, 217, 234
Groups, opposition, 6, 8ff., 13, 35,
39f., 45, 50, 54
in May Movement, 65, 71, 105–6,
151, 155, 156–8, 162, 174–6,

Groups, in May Movement (continued)
182–3, 232, 248–50, 282, 284–5,
290–1, 343. *See also by name*
movements as, 9–14, 47, 54
primary, 118f., 273
Guevara, Che, 13, 232, 354

Harvard University, 99, 255n

Individual, 60, 118
Industries, 66, 67n, 72, 79, 95, 215,
221, 223, 277
and May Movement, 199, 202,
204–17, 227, 260–7, 305
Information, public, 13–14, 50, 59f.,
94, 254, 260–7, 333
Integration, social, 33ff., 41, 48, 51,
60, 112–13, 118, 143
Intellectuals, 15f., 42, 51, 73–6, 151,
251f., 301, 334
Italy, 34, 52, 108, 147ff., 197, 199,
247

J.C.R. (Jeunesse Communiste Révolutionnaire), 65, 82, 182f.,
188, 232, 240, 255

Korean War, 196, 345

Labor. *See* Unions, Work
Langlois, Henri, 254
Language, of May Movement, 65,
130, 137, 139, 162, 164f., 174,
227, 233, 238f., 242ff., 250–1,
269–71, 362
Latin America, 35, 44f., 73f., 100,
132, 247, 326, 344ff., 347
Law, faculties of, 85–6, 94f., 102,
184, 284–5, 302–3, 306, 321,
343, 359
Leaders: labor, 7–8, 58, 72, 193–5,
197, 199, 213, 216, 219, 231, 330
student, 64, 72, 141–6, 152, 170–1,
182–3, 210, 230f., 248
Lectures, 76, 97, 104, 118–19, 128,
293
Lefort, Claude, 317, 351n
Left, French, 18, 58, 114, 194, 203,
228, 231, 301

Left (continued)
  parties, 194, 229, 235
  student groups, 134, 142f., 153, 170, 239, 258, 343
Lenin, Vladimir I., 231, 238
Liberalism, 9, 13–14, 267, 278
  university, 14, 73, 98–9, 100, 107, 177, 299, 310, 334–8, 349. See also Nanterre
Liberty, 4–9, 141, 219, 338–9, 360
licence, 37–8, 83, 85, 130–1
Life, private, 32–3, 127, 140–1, 244–6, 251, 265, 273
"Little groups," 69, 71, 75, 120, 131, 135, 142, 144, 156, 159, 162, 164, 232, 248, 356
lycées, 65, 75, 93, 212, 254–9

Maîtres-assistants, 93, 103, 106, 132, 147, 290, 299
maîtrise, 37f., 131, 313
Management, 102, 140
  industrial, 199–202, 204, 207–13, 220–1, 223, 227, 312, 330
  university. See Universities, French
Managers, 46, 96, 107, 117, 123, 201
Manipulation, opposed, 13–14, 33ff., 41, 60, 95, 140, 224, 250, 275
Maoist groups, 49, 137, 232, 248
Maoist Marxist-Leninists. See U.J.C.M.L.
March 22 Movement, 56f., 60, 71–2, 75, 92, 121, 135, 137, 143, 147, 155, 157, 162, 178, 182, 188, 196, 232, 234, 240, 243, 248f., 316, 353
Marches, mass, 143f., 163ff., 173, 187, 191, 213, 217, 228, 233, 301, 357
Marcuse, Herbert, 5, 12, 17, 334, 346
Marxism, 13, 47, 138, 141, 182, 342. See also groups by name
Matignon agreements, 217–18, 227
May Movement: action as method of, 77, 159, 242–59, 275

May Movement (continued)
  aims of, 51, 174, 191–2, 195, 221, 230, 275f., 289, 292–3, 338, 356–7
  as anti-Gaullist, 193, 210, 227–9, 250
  approaches to, 76–8
  attitudes of, 32, 48, 57, 62, 76–8, 116f., 130–7, 191, 221, 320
  cause (s) of, 10, 48–50, 53, 56f., 62, 71, 78, 98, 117–19, 120–1, 141, 178, 180, 267, 274–5, 346, 349–50
  police repression as, 160–5, 181–2, 193
  as crisis of change, 55, 57–8, 69, 77f.
  excesses of, 269–71, 317–18, 324
  failure of, 62, 77f., 229–30, 239–40, 267–8, 275, 281–4, 316
  final phase of, 272, 314–22, 359
  formed. See Nanterre
  future of, 55, 63–4, 70, 77–81, 143, 303–4, 317, 324–5, 358, 361
  and insurrection, 64, 158f., 163–5, 174, 176, 181, 188, 191, 194, 239
  internationalism of, 79–81, 246–7, 355
  meaning of, 62–4, 65–7, 77–81, 117, 119, 178–80, 185–6, 191–2, 222, 237–41, 265–7, 272, 275, 278–80, 315, 330–9, 350, 353–4
  as revolutionary, not revolution, 64–70, 73, 122, 159, 164, 174, 176, 180, 182, 194–5, 237–41, 268, 270–2, 346, 353–6
  structure of, 248–50
  student movement center of, 76–7, 156–8
  success of, 62, 79
  unity of, 58–9, 62, 71, 77f., 159–60, 162, 178–9, 182–3, 185
  on university level, 37–8, 51, 57–8, 62, 71, 73, 75–6, 78–9, 96, 114, 281–90, 292–3, 305–7, 315–22, 324–5, 327, 330–2, 341–3, 359

May Movement (*continued*)
  what happened to, 54, 77,
    267–9, 275, 341–3
Medicine, faculties of, 37f., 85, 88,
    94, 116, 309–12, 323, 339
Mendès–France, Pierre, 210, 239
Middle class, 46, 90, 93, 97, 104,
    107, 150, 153, 221f., 271
Militants, student, 13f., 17f., 75,
    82, 128, 160–3, 191, 234, 239,
    246–50, 276, 302, 321
  Nanterre, 69, 128f., 133–4, 136–46,
    147, 150, 152f., 163, 168, 232,
    244–6, 287, 289, 342–3
Ministry of National Education, 17,
    50, 85, 112–19, 123f., 131f., 134,
    151, 166–7, 168, 170, 172, 181,
    189, 211, 289, 298f., 320, 322,
    340f.
Moderates, 53–4, 131, 146, 173
Modernization, 43–4, 47f., 51,
    66–7, 272
  university,
    after crisis, 323–5, 337
    and May Movement, 65ff.,
      116–17, 303
    pre-'68, 112–19, 127–8
  See also Nanterre, Reformism
Movements, social, 44
  civil rights (U.S.), 12f., 61,
    148–9
  revolutionary, 52f., 190, 225–6
  when formed, 60, 185–6, 237–8

Nanterre: after crisis, 305f., 314,
    317–18, 342–3, 359
  cultural revolt at, 36, 137–41,
    150, 153
  faculty, 36, 48–9, 83–4, 100–1,
    122–3, 125–6, 127–8, 131ff.,
    136–7, 144f., 146–7, 148f.,
    151, 154–5, 171, 298–9
  groups at, 36, 131ff., 142, 144,
    155, 249, 342–3
  growth of, 125, 153
  inability of, to cope, 128, 130–5,
    139, 143–4, 149, 152, 160f.,
    167, 169

Nanterre (*continued*)
  issue (s) of conflict at, 75, 124,
    126, 130–1, 133–7, 141–4, 153,
    168
    blacklist as, 136, 153, 269
    dormitory regulations as, 137–
      41
    police/arrests as, 136–7, 143,
      152f., 166
    Vietnam War as, 137, 141–2,
      144
  as liberal, 9, 15, 121, 127f., 129–
    30, 131, 134, 146, 155
  management of, 25n, 83–4, 126–7,
    134, 139, 149
  May Movement formed at, 48–9,
    75, 78, 120–2, 134–5, 141–6,
    149, 150–8, 182, 243, 247,
    269, 271, 282–3, 285
  modernizing efforts at, 15, 100–1,
    127–8, 232, 305f.
  November '67 strike at, 50, 75,
    130–5, 147, 156
  occupied, 287f., 290f., 298–9,
    301–2
  physical situation of, 122–6, 127,
    244
Napoleon I, 50, 90, 93n., 222, 256
Nationalism, 25, 34, 45, 77f., 279,
    345
Newspapers, 13–14, 59, 65, 74–5,
    249–50, 319, 333

Occident groups, 147, 160–1
Organizations: in May Movement,
    193–5. *See also by name*
  opposed, 39, 95, 151, 220, 253–4
O.R.T.F. (Office de Radiodiffusion
    Télévision Française), 28, 40,
    50, 72, 254–5, 260–3, 266, 276

Passeron, Jean-Claude, 88n, 91
P.C.F. *See* Communist Party,
    French
Poland, 77, 80, 132, 347
Police repression, 9f., 13f., 49, 63,
    66, 71, 82, 121, 136–7, 138, 143,
    146, 151, 152f., 154, 166, 343,
    359

Police repression (*continued*)
  brutality of, 177, 187–8, 342
  at factories, 213, 215, 234, 342
  at Sorbonne, 160–3, 164–5, 167f.,
    171ff., 176f., 182–3, 187–8,
    190–1, 193, 219, 234, 243,
    269, 321
  as trigger of crisis, 158, 160–3,
    165, 167, 181–3, 190–1, 193
Political struggle: May Movement
  as, 53, 55f., 58, 61–2, 71, 77, 122,
    141, 150–1, 153, 176f., 182, 275
  May Movement as not, 66–9, 194,
    224–30, 239, 258
  May Movement as utopian, not
    political, 63, 67f.
Politics, 12f., 113–19, 191, 198, 252
  parties in, 13, 17–18, 198. *See also*
    by name
  universities and, 70, 99–100, 137,
    140, 290, 324f., 336–9
Pompidou, Georges, 15, 50, 167–71,
  173, 243
Populism, 9ff., 41–7, 48, 55, 58, 68,
  74, 344, 347
Posters, 146, 165, 242ff., 249f., 269
Poujade, Pierre, 111*n*, 200
Production, mass, 6–7, 11, 44, 50,
  59, 79–80, 111, 220, 272
  opposed, 33–4, 39, 54, 274–5
  students as, 124, 126, 153
  university and, 324f., 332
Professional schools, 107, 119, 282,
  293, 312f.
Professional training, 97, 100–4,
  107, 110, 292–3, 323, 331–2
Professionals, 6ff., 38ff., 79, 95, 218–
  24, 253–4, 260, 263, 349
P.S.U. (Parti Socialiste Unifié),
  129, 229–30, 237, 248–9, 255
Public opinion, 79, 163, 172, 175,
  180, 188, 234, 349, 265, 285,
  323, 343

Radicalism, 8, 13–14, 18, 25, 48
Radio-Luxembourg, 170f., 175,
  260*n*
Reformism: labor, 66, 72, 205,
  216–17

Reformism (*continued*)
  radicalism vs., 8, 18, 25, 48
  revolution vs., 48, 65f., 69, 75,
    116–17, 129–30, 134, 167–8,
    185, 216–17, 258, 324, 331–2
  technocracy and, 6, 9f., 69–70,
    96, 114, 119
  university, 48, 55, 97
    after crisis, 302–14, 323–30,
      339–41, 360
    of May Movement, 51, 65–6, 67,
      69–71, 79, 114, 116–19, 284,
      292–7, 324, 327
    pre-'68, 15–16, 85, 90, 96, 112,
      113–19, 127–8, 130–1, 134,
      167–8, 203, 232, 291–2,
      309–12, 323
Repression, 9f., 13, 55, 271, 348
  all forms of, opposed, 141, 245,
    250, 265–7
  anti-union, 215
  of May Movement. *See* Police
Research, 37–8, 79, 85–6, 92, 95, 99,
  113, 115, 117f., 211, 312, 348.
  See also Teaching
Revolution (s) : 67–8, 154, 225–6,
  270, 353
  student movements and, 9, 11, 16,
    20, 52, 61f., 64–81, 147–55, 190
  See also May Movement,
    Reformism
Roche, Rector, 161, 165f., 172
Ruling class, 31–2, 43, 46f., 49, 62,
  77, 91f., 94ff., 100, 107, 113,
  218–26, 267, 279, 323, 334f., 349
Russian Revolution, 9, 52, 73, 247

Sartre, Jean-Paul, 15, 74–5
Sauvageot, Jacques, 64, 72, 170, 183,
  187, 247, 249, 328, 357
Schools, French, 25*n*, 76, 79
  Great-Schools, 15, 85–8, 90, 282
  secondary, 132f., 254–9, 282
Science, 75, 100, 117, 245, 337–8
  research, 85–6, 92, 99, 113, 115,
    118
Science, faculties of, 37, 83, 85, 87–8,
  109, 113–19, 166, 168, 171, 291,
  298, 301–2, 308, 310, 315, 340

S.D.S. (German), 121, 137, 144, 247
Séguy, Georges, 195, 217, 231
Situationists, 36, 139, 150, 157
S.N.E.Sup. (Syndicat National de
    l'Enseignement Supérieur), 71,
    106, 162, 170, 181, 183, 188,
    203, 249, 261, 283, 320
Social change (adaptation, social
    transformation), 35, 44, 48, 51,
    53, 54–5, 58–9, 60f., 66f., 84–7,
    94, 97, 100–7, 110–13, 273–4,
    276–80
Social class, 46, 56, 195
    education and, 88–97, 108–9, 221,
        256, 293, 295, 318, 323
Social conflicts, 328, 344–62
    areas of new, 6–14, 19, 32–5, 39,
        42–4, 58–60, 69, 79, 220–1,
        265–6, 275–6, 324, 336, 352
    dealing with, 13–14, 20, 131, 225,
        267, 325
Social crisis: May Movement as, 19,
        48–50, 51, 52–6, 58–9, 61–2, 111,
        162–3, 166–73, 176f., 185, 266–
        76, 350, 353
    not political crisis, 224–30
Social order, 58–9, 96, 132, 140, 154,
        176f., 189–90, 223, 252–3, 259,
        265, 273, 324, 337, 346
Social sciences, 51, 86f., 95f., 127,
        131–3, 167–8, 263f., 282, 303
Social struggle, at center of May
        Movement, 53, 56, 58, 61–2, 67,
        69, 78, 79–80, 192, 194, 240–1,
        278–80
Socialism, 34, 345
    early, 9, 25f., 45, 73, 151
    French, 18, 61, 164, 202, 207, 228
    utopian, 26, 63
Socialist countries, 81, 108, 222, 227
Socialization, 42, 59, 97, 303
Societies: post-industrial, 6–7, 9–
        14, 32, 58–60, 63, 111–13, 267
    theories of, 5–6, 8, 267, 273–6, 346
    transitions in, 44, 53ff., 66, 110
Society: French, 32, 41f., 110–13,
        179–80, 222, 267, 273–6, 348–9,
        352
    organization of, 66

Sociology departments, 131–4, 136,
        139–40, 142, 145–7, 168, 263,
        306, 336
Sorbonne, 63, 82, 102f., 123, 125ff.,
        151, 232, 240
    after crisis, 305–6, 314, 317, 321,
        339–40, 359
    approach of students at, 65, 69,
        249, 353
    arrests/police at, 16–17, 121, 161,
        163, 165–6, 167f., 243, 321
    cultural revolt at, 36, 72, 74, 159,
        242–4, 252, 268f.
    May 1968, 16–17, 71, 121, 144,
        147, 159–65, 211, 282–3, 290
    occupied, 36, 58, 71, 78, 163, 176,
        180, 188, 215, 242–6, 252, 268f.,
        287f., 291, 299, 301
Spain, 76, 222, 247
Specialization, 101, 104–5, 107,
        206, 294
Spontaneity, students', 36, 48, 51,
        62, 67, 69, 143, 155, 162, 164,
        174, 248, 250, 317f.
Suppression, 13–14, 50, 260–7
Stalin, Joseph, 233, 236, 252
Strasbourg, 36n, 57, 157, 288–9, 307
Strikes: earlier, 196, 208, 214, 345
    May–June '68, 39–40, 50, 58, 69,
        71f., 178, 184, 189f., 199f., 207–
        16, 234, 254–5, 260–7, 276
    November '67, Nanterre, 50, 75,
        130–5, 147, 156
    See also General strike
Student (s), French: alliance of, 38,
        144–6
    attitudes of,
        about society, 43–4, 46, 71, 73,
            140–1
        about themselves, 71, 74, 140,
            244–6
        about universities, 57, 61, 102,
            104f., 107, 130f.
    attitudes towards, 44, 89, 124,
        126, 153, 232, 324
    Catholic, 133
    first-year, 105, 126
    as future workers, 76, 90, 95,
        100–2, 104–5, 212, 220f.

Student (s) (*continued*)
  increased number of. *See*
    Universities, French
  inherited culture of, 94, 273–6
  militant. *See* Militants
  social class of, 36f., 39–41, 46, 56,
    88–9, 108f., 113, 221, 346, 355
  -teacher relationship. *See*
    Teacher
Student movements: American, 9–
    10, 12f., 53, 60–1, 79f., 348
  as class struggle, 10, 40–1, 45ff.,
    326
  as cultural revolt, 10f., 32–3, 35f.,
    43–4
  international, 9–11, 57, 73–4, 76,
    80, 132, 147–9, 247, 271, 326,
    347, 350
  as populist uprising, 10f., 41–7
  as revolutionary, 9, 11, 16, 20,
    64–81
  societal issues of, 9–10, 11f., 13–
    14, 19, 32–4, 43–4, 61
  university issues of, 11, 16, 43–4,
    46, 61
Student-worker alliance. *See*
  Worker-student alliance

Tautin, Gilles, 213, 215, 234
Taylor, Frederick W., 29, 225
Teacher (s) , 25*n*, 48–9, 73, 88ff.,
    100, 106, 121, 126, 148, 285,
    290, 322–3
  alliance of, with students, 133,
    146–7, 166, 168, 174, 181, 237,
    258, 287f., 300–4, 315, 342
  becoming, 38*n*, 86f., 93f., 101–4,
    106, 130–1
  degrees of. *See* Degrees
  hostility of, towards students,
    104, 118–19, 129–30, 132ff.,
    136–7, 146–7, 151, 155, 287,
    297–9, 315, 342
  mediating efforts of, 168, 171–2
  reforms of, after crisis, 306ff.,
    315, 340–1
  retreat of, during crisis, 297–304
  rigidity of, 102–3, 105f., 151,
    245–6

Teacher (s) (*continued*)
  -student relationship, 97, 104,
    118–19, 127–8, 257, 331
  unions, 83, 86, 106, 197, 202–3,
    301
Teaching, 51, 85, 97, 114, 293–4
  research vs., 16, 37–8, 85–8, 101,
    105, 118–19, 133, 148
Teaching methods, 97, 100–1,
    256–7, 293–5. *See also*
    Lectures
Technicians, 35, 37, 40, 46, 49, 79,
    95f., 107, 178, 200f., 206, 209,
    211, 218, 237, 253, 264, 312,
    326, 349
Technocracy: May Movement op-
    posed to, 32–4, 38, 54, 56, 62,
    74, 95, 178, 221–2, 265–7, 272–3,
    275, 278, 332, 349, 355
  as new enemy, 32–4, 153, 178f.,
    194, 221–4, 250, 273f., 278–80,
    315, 349
Technocrats, 9f., 30, 31–2, 44, 58–60,
    66, 73, 272
  professionals vs., 218–24
  universities and, 73, 90, 96, 107,
    114–19, 221, 323
Terrorists, 324
Theater, street, 36*n*, 252–3
Third World, 25, 45. 77f., 227, 324,
    336, 345
Totalitarianism, 59f.
Trotskyites, 65, 133, 155, 182, 232,
    248

U.E.C., 144, 232
U.E.R., 339–40
U.J.C.M.L., 144, 160, 178, 203, 213,
    218–19, 232, 234, 290
Underemployment, 207, 212
U.N.E.F. (Union Nationale des
    Etudiants de France) , 70, 79,
    109, 120, 151, 156f., 162, 170,
    183, 189, 210, 248f., 283f., 360
Unemployment, 22, 25, 28, 35, 38,
    46, 179, 190, 212
Union of Soviet Socialist Republics,
    9, 31, 45, 52, 73, 77, 80, 99, 108,

Union of Soviet Socialist Republics
(*continued*)
    132, 219, 222, 247, 292, 318,
    344f., 347
Unions, trade: as anti-Gaullist,
    217f., 227–9
    early, 18f., 200
    renewal of, 199–203, 218, 223
    role of, in May Movement, 18–19,
        39–40, 49, 58, 66, 72, 130–7,
        142f., 193–5, 197–9, 204,
        208ff., 213–19, 230–7, 288,
        301, 312, 320, 354
    role of, in recent years, 143,
        196–9, 255, 345
    See also by name, Strikes,
        Workers' movement
United States, 30, 108
    civil rights movement in, 12f., 61,
        148–9
    influence of, 18–20, 35, 41, 147,
        149, 227, 345
    university situation in, 12f., 14–
        15, 17f., 31, 53, 61, 79, 99, 101,
        132, 141, 147–9, 255n, 259, 271,
        347f.
Universities: crisis in, 98, 100f.
    freedom and, 70, 99–100, 337–9
    function of, 98ff., 117, 334–9
    liberal, 14, 73, 98–100, 107, 177,
        299, 310, 334–8, 349
    types of, 76, 79, 92, 98–100, 117,
        175, 326, 348
    See also by country, by name
Universities, French, 35–6, 48–9,
    66f., 116f., 319
    archaic/overcentralized, 11, 51,
        57, 62, 83–4, 87, 94, 112, 115–
        17, 134, 139, 333
    areas of conflict in, 37–8, 43–4,
        48, 51, 55, 57, 75f., 97, 100–5,
        107, 110, 114, 118–19, 127–8,
        130–1, 133f., 167, 291–4, 323,
        331–2, 339, 348
    as bureaucratic, 102–4, 112, 139
    construction in, 50, 122–6, 168
    as crisis/conflict situation, 11, 14,
        46, 48–51, 98, 101–7, 116–22,

Universities, French, as crisis/con-
flict situation (*continued*)
    134, 149, 151–5, 160–3, 165–9,
    171–3, 185, 242–6, 270–1, 325
    culture/technology in, 87–8, 92,
        97, 100–5, 107, 110, 293, 323,
        337–9
    decentralized, 339–41
    decision-making in, 51, 83, 112–
        16, 131, 134, 139, 148f., 161,
        165–73, 285, 296
    entrance selection in, 75f., 167,
        291–2, 348
    freedom and, 96–7, 107, 149, 296,
        328–9, 334–9, 360
    future of, 327–30
    government control of, 14–17, 48–
        50, 90–1, 95–8, 110–16, 171–3,
        288–9, 296
    group alliances in, 38, 102–5
    historically, 90–1
    increase of students at, 42f., 46,
        94, 102, 104, 108–9, 123, 125,
        153, 257, 291
    inflexibility of, 84–7, 94, 102–7,
        109–113, 115, 120, 149
    isolation of, 95, 98, 106, 295
    occupied, 242–6, 284–90
    organized/managed, 25n, 51, 94,
        112–17, 296, 312, 325
    as political, 14, 16–17, 70, 110–13,
        324f.
    political activity in, 290–1, 324f.,
        336–9
    problems of, 83, 92, 109–10
    pre-'68, 82–8, 120, 291–3
    reorganized, after crisis, 79, 283f.,
        322–30, 339–43
    in retreat, 91, 98–107
    role of, 84, 96–8, 106–7, 110, 117,
        331–9
    new, 94–5, 100–5, 107, 110, 114,
        117, 221, 292–3, 323ff., 331–2,
        337–9
    ruling class and, 32, 43, 62, 91f.,
        94ff., 221, 323, 334f.
    social classes and, 90–7, 107, 221,
        293, 295, 318, 323

as traditional, 41, 62, 84, 87, 93–4, 102–4, 109–10, 127f., 130, 167, 337–8
Utopianism, 9, 19, 47, 53, 55, 98, 239, 269–70, 271f., 275, 279, 281, 330
Communist, 25, 56–65, 238, 357

Vietnam committees, 57, 137, 143, 233, 255
Vietnam War, 9–13, 18, 34, 61, 82, 137, 141–2, 144, 148–9, 173, 264, 271, 274, 348, 354
Vincennes, 340, 342–3
Violence, 12f., 19, 53, 61, 65, 68, 70, 121, 153, 215, 274
at Nanterre, 129, 136–7, 143, 153, 342–3

Work, 6–7, 29, 49, 55, 59, 71, 118, 202, 215, 295, 330
Workers, 6f., 35, 224, 346
conservative, 8, 38–40, 64–5
early, 8, 28, 36–8, 140, 200f.
foreign, in France, 216, 246–7, 342
marginal, 202, 213, 295

Workers (continued)
militant, 199, 204, 206, 214f., 218–19, 253, 257
skilled, 8, 37, 39–40, 193, 200, 204ff., 218
young, 8f., 37, 72, 207, 211ff., 227
Workers' movement, nineteenth century, 9, 28, 36–7, 40–1, 45, 56, 63f., 67–8, 70, 73, 77f., 117, 155, 162, 194, 201, 221, 247, 275, 279, 303, 324, 330, 336f., 351
Worker-student alliance, 8f., 14, 27, 38–40, 42–3, 46, 56, 58, 65f., 70–81, 142, 149, 155, 157f., 164, 173–5, 178f., 182, 184ff., 190, 207–15, 227, 234, 238, 248, 295, 342, 354
categories of workers in, 193, 200–2, 206–13, 218–24, 237, 260–7, 349
Working class, 18, 39–41, 58, 69f., 72–3, 88f., 113, 182, 193f., 213–14, 248
evolution of, 195–203, 220

Yugoslavia, 247, 345